An Outline History of Music
of Music

SIXTH EDITION

An Outline History of Music

Milo Wold
Edmund Cykler

wcb
Wm. C. Brown Publishers
Dubuque, Iowa

Consulting Editor
Fred Westphal
California State University, Sacramento

Library of Congress Catalog Card Number: 84–71829

ISBN 0–697–03534–4

Printed in the United States of America
10 9 8 7 6 5 4 3

Contents

Preface

The sixth edition of *An Outline History of Music* marks the twenty-second year since the first publication of this book. The authors conceived the work as a brief historical overview of the development of Western European music. Numerous narrative histories have provided the student and reading public with detailed accounts of western musical development. Most of these works are long scholarly narratives containing much technical information as well as interpretive discussions. We believed that there was a need for a ready reference of a concise nature to furnish the lay reader with an introduction to the history of western music, and to provide the student of music with a readily and immediately available outline to music history.

In subsequent editions the authors were mainly concerned with minor changes, some at the suggestions of users, and with expanding some of the material, especially in the twentieth century. Musical examples to illustrate compositional devices were added. Reference material, both in the bibliography and for specific recordings, particularly of pre-classical compositions, were updated.

As the authors in this sixth edition considered the problems of twentieth century music since the Second World War, they were faced with the problem of either making a separate chapter, or incorporating recent trends into the existing chapter of the twentieth century. It became increasingly apparent that the outline format would not accommodate the variety of experiments and compositional trends that have occurred since the Fifties. The authors, therefore, decided to add, where appropriate, an additional section to the outline under the heading, "Some Recent Developments," where important diversions from earlier twentieth century musical practices and styles are considered. Unfortunately, we do not have the luxury of the perspective of time to evaluate the comparative importance or the lasting qualities of these recent developments.

Because of the importance of popular music in present day society, the authors have included a short chapter on "the peoples' music" in the twentieth century.

A chronology of important historical events, composers and artists has been included in this latest edition to serve as a frame of reference. Because performers in recent years have become increasingly important as an influence in compositional style, the more prominent have been included under the section of "Practice and Performance."

Appreciation for the numerous suggestions for change from the many users who have been kind enough to make their expertise available to the authors is gratefully extended.

Introduction

An Outline History of Music has been planned and organized to be used in a variety of ways. (1) It can be used as a basic text in music history with collateral readings in the many authoritative studies in the specialized periods and styles in the history of music that are readily available to the student. In this manner the text will serve as a practical core from which the student can expand his studies to include the vast amount of source material that has been edited and published in recent years. (2) It is designed to be used as an outline and review for any standard text on the subject. The student can utilize its plan and material to focus attention on the most important developments and still have the benefit of the complete discussion usually found in such texts. (3) The present volume will prove valuable to the student who wishes to embark on a study of the literature and history of music on his own without the guidance of an instructor. Its information on scores, recordings and collateral readings can be a guide to unlimited reading and to a selected list of musical examples that will serve as a basis for the understanding of musical styles.

The authors are of the strong opinion that the primary source material of music history is the music itself. Consequently the present volume is designed as a guide to musical examples that explain and illustrate the historical development of music. Obviously it would be impossible to include actual scores of all the music necessary for such a study in a single volume. Therefore, it has been indicated where both the music and the recordings are to be found in each case. In the earlier periods especially, anthologies that are accompanied by recordings are listed. This makes it possible to use actual music as source material with a minimum of library facilities. Great care has been taken to use only music and records that are currently in print, and recordings of anthologies that give strong evidence of continuation have been the basis of much of the selection rather than outstanding performance. The student is urged to study the music, listen to the recordings and, whenever possible, to perform selected examples as a part of the classroom experience. Examples need not be confined to those listed. Other music that the instructor might suggest or the student might seek out will serve to broaden the student's acquaintance with forms and styles.

The authors have avoided the temptation to divide music history in a series of short, specialized periods of time. On the contrary, only the rather large, but generally accepted, designation of periods of history (Gothic, Renaissance, Baroque, etc.) are specified. While the music of every composer is different from that of his contemporaries in specific details and the earliest music in a style differs from the later music in the same style, it is the opinion of the authors that a general adherence to a basic stylistic pattern is rather consistent over a long period of time. For example, the principal characteristics, patronage, function, performing practice and musical style in the Renaissance are fairly uniform for a period of about 200 years. Moreover, in spite of the widely publicized *isms* of twentieth century music, there is still a constancy of style in modern music that has already lasted over eighty years.

The present volume subjects each major period of music history to analysis by means of an outline of important movements that influence the patronage and function of music, musical devices, forms, composers. No claim is made to exhaustiveness of the categories or of the items in each category. Only those facts that seem pertinent to a basic understanding of the development of music have been included. No doubt teachers and others who use this outline will wish to supplement it with additional material. The following is a brief survey of the plan of each chapter.

I. Sociocultural Influences on Music

Under this heading any important trends and movements in such areas as religion, economics, government, social and cultural life that seem to have a bearing on the patronage, types and style of music are set forth. Because such influences are usually subjective and vague in nature, only generalizations as to their relationships can be suggested.

II. Function of Music

Because composers usually write with a purpose in mind and because the various cultural conditions call for different types of music, the functions of music in a historical period are significant. Moreover, the economic conditions under which a composer lives are partially determined by the demand for, and support of, music with a specific function. Needless to say, function has a great deal to do with the style and expressiveness of music.

III. Characteristics of Style

Each basic element of music is examined from the point of view of its general stylistic qualities and also any special devices or techniques that are prominent in the music itself. The subdivisions of the basic elements are:

1. *Formal organization*
2. *Melody*
3. *Rhythm*
4. *Harmony*
5. *Texture*
6. *Media and tone color*

IV. Practice and Performance

Each important device or practice that enables performers to realize the composer's purpose is defined and explained. Such techniques as notation, dynamics, instrumentation, are included under this heading.

V. Vocal Compositions

Each important vocal form is defined and the general characteristics of its musical substance is commented upon. In addition, specific examples which are representative of the form are suggested, together with available scores and recordings. In the case of more important forms, more than one example is given. The instructor, or student, may substitute or use additional examples as further illustrations. It is realized that no one form can be fully represented by one or two examples.

VI. Instrumental Compositions

The same procedure is applied to instrumental forms. In those periods of music history where instrumental forms predominate, this item in the outline will appear before the vocal forms.

VII. Important Composers

Composers are listed as being of major importance not only because of the permanency and quality of their works but also because of their innovations and influence. These composers are listed in the chronological order of their dates of birth, together with brief biographies. Important works and suggested examples with scores and recordings are also given. From the Classic period on, specific scores and recordings are omitted, due to the fact that there are numerous editions and recordings from which to choose.

VIII. Other Composers

Composers of lesser importance are listed in the chronological order of their dates of birth and according to countries. The authors are aware that the classification of composers into the foregoing two lists is an arbitrary one, and that it is often only an opinion that places one in the list of major composers and another in the list of minor composers.

IX. Important Writers on Music

Writers on music often give an illuminating account of the musical scene in which they live. They are also important sources for the practices and interpretations of a musical style. With few exceptions, only those writers whose works serve these purposes have been included. Information as to title, place and date of publication of the important writings is given. In addition, a brief statement regarding the contents of the writings is made where pertinent.

X. Manuscript Sources

In the earlier periods especially, the only sources of the music itself are the collections of manuscripts, usually preserved in monasteries or universities, which are of great value to the scholar. This item is dropped from the outlline after the Renaissance because from then on widespread publication of music made authoritative editions accessible. It is realized that for scholarly research it is still necessary to examine original manuscripts whenever possible, even of present-day composers.

Supplementary Readings

Collateral readings from current major texts on music history, as well as specialized studies in the various periods, are listed together with specific page numbers at the end of each chapter. The following are the abbreviations used for these readings:

Austin	Austin, William W. *Music in the 20th Century*. New York: W. W. Norton, 1966.
Borroff	Borroff, Edith. *Music in Europe and the United States*. Englewood Cliffs: Prentice-Hall, 1971.
Bukofzer	Bukofzer, Manfred F. *Music in the Baroque Era*. New York: W. W. Norton, 1947.
Cannon-Johnson-Waite	Cannon, Beekman C.; Johnson, Alvin H.; Waite, William C. *The Art of Music*. New York: Crowell, 1960.
Crocker	Crocker, Richard L. *A History of Musical Style*. New York: McGraw-Hill, 1966.
Einstein	Einstein, Alfred. *Music in the Romantic Era*. New York: W. W. Norton, 1947.
Grout	Grout, Donald Jay. *A History of Western Music*. New York: W. W. Norton, 3rd. ed., 1980.
Hansen	Hansen, Peter. *Introduction to Twentieth Century Music*. New York: Allyn & Bacon, 4th ed., 1978.
Lang	Lang, Paul Henry. *Music in Western Civilization*. New York: W. W. Norton, 1941.
Machlis	Machlis, Joseph. *Introduction to Contemporary Music*. New York: W. W. Norton, 1961.
Oxford	*New Oxford History of Music*. London: Oxford, 1954.
Reese-MA	Reese, Gustave. *Music in the Middle Ages*. New York: W. W. Norton, 1940.
Reese-R	Reese, Gustave. *Music in the Renaissance*. New York: W. W. Norton, Rev. ed., 1959.

Schirmer	*Schirmer History of Music,* Rosenstiel, Léonie, general editor, New York: Schirmer Books, 1982
Sachs-RMA	Sachs, Curt. *Rise of Music in the Ancient World, East and West.* New York: W. W. Norton, 1943.
Wold-Cykler	Wold, Milo; Cykler, Edmund. *An Introduction to Music and Art in the Western World.* Dubuque: Wm. C. Brown Company Publishers, 7th ed., 1983.

Basic References, Anthologies of Scores and Recordings

Only basic reference works and anthologies are included in the following list. Comprehensive bibliographies will be found in every standard music history and other scholarly studies.

Basic References

Apel, Willi, ed. *Harvard Dictionary of Music.* Cambridge: Harvard University Press, 1969.

Baker's Biographical Dictionary of Musicians. 6th ed. Revised by N. Slonimsky. New York: G. Schirmer, 1978. Dates and spellings in the present volume are according to *Baker's Dictionary.*

Die Musik in Geschichte und Gegenwart. Kassel: Bärenreiter, 1945.

New Grove's Dictionary of Music and Musicians. 20 vols. London: Macmillan, 1980. This edition of Grove's is by far the most comprehensive in the English language. It contains extended articles on every facet of music as well as complete biographical sketches.

New Oxford History of Music. 10 vols. (8 to date). London: Oxford, 1954–1975. The volumes are: I. Ancient and Oriental Music (1957); II. Early Medieval Music up to 1300. (Rev. 1965); III. Ars Nova and the Renaissance, 1300–1540. (1960); IV. The Age of Humanism, 1540–1630. (1968); V. Opera and Church Music, 1630–1750. (1975); VI. The Growth of Instrumental Music, 1630–1750. (Not yet pub.); VII. The Age of Enlightenment, 1745–1790. (1973); VIII. The Age of Beethoven, 1790–1830, (1983). IX. Romanticism, 1830–1890. (Not yet pub.) and X. The Modern Age, 1890–1960. (1974).

Thompson, Oscar, *International Cyclopedia of Music and Musicians,* 10th ed. Bohle and Bouce, eds. New York: W. W. Dodd, 1975.

Scores and Recordings

AMA   Burkhardt, Charles. *Anthology for Musical Analysis.* 2nd ed. New York: Holt, Rinehart and Winston, 1972.

EM   Gleason, Harold. *Examples of Music before 1400.* New York: Appleton Century Crofts, 1946.

GMB   Schering, Arnold. *Geschichte der Musik in Beispielen.* Leipzig: Breitkopf and Härtel, 1931.

HAM   Davison, Archibald and Apel, Willi. *Historical Anthology of Music.* 2 vols. Cambridge: Harvard University Press, 1946. (Examples nos. 9 through 41 in vol. 1, are recorded under the Orpheus label. Examples 42 through 181 are recorded under the Pleiades label.)

   Note: Readers are advised that it is apparent that the Orpheus label (Musical Heritage Society Recordings) is supplanting the Pleiades label for the complete recordings of the *Historical Anthology of Music.*

HMS   *History of Music in Sound.* 10 vols. London: Oxford, 1953. Recorded by RCA. (This anthology contains only partial scores, but the recordings are complete.)

MM   Parrish, Carl and Ohl, John F. *Masterpieces of Music before 1750.* New York: W. W. Norton, 1951. Recorded by the Haydn Society.

NS   Kamien, Roger. *Norton Scores.* Expanded Edition (2 vols.). New York: W. W. Norton, 1970.

OM   Starr, William J. and Devine, George F. *Omnibus,* parts 1 and 2. Englewood Cliffs: Prentice-Hall, Inc., 1964.

SS   Lerner, Edward R. *Study Scores of Musical Style.* New York: McGraw-Hill Book Company, 1968.

TEM   Parrish, Carl *Treasury of Early Music.* New York: W. W. Norton, 1958. Recorded by the Haydn Society. (Available in paperback form.)

Additional Anthologies

Cohen, Albert and Whilte, John D. *Anthology of Music for Analysis.* New York: Appleton Century Crofts, 1965.

Fellerer Karl Gustav, ed. *Anthology of Music.* 47 vol. Cologne: Arno Volk, 1959.

Hardy, Gordon and Fish, Arnold. *Music Literature.* 2 vol. New York: Dodd, Mead and Company, 1966.

Hoppin, Richard H. *Anthology of Medieval Music.* New York: W. W. Norton, 1978.

Lang, Paul Henry. *Concerto 1800–1900.* New York: W. W. Norton, 1969.

Lang, Paul Henry. *Symphony 1800–1900.* New York: W. W. Norton, 1969.

Wennerstrom, Mary H. *Anthology of Twentieth Century Music.* New York: Appleton Century Crofts, 1969.

Norton Critical Scores. New York: W. W. Norton. Each volume contains an authoritative study-size score of a major musical work and a comprehensive body of materials for the study of the work.

Norton Anthology of Western Music. Two volumes edited by Claude V. Palisca have been published by W. W. Norton to accompany the Third Edition of Donald Grout's *A History of Western Music.* The scores found in these two volumes are discussed briefly in the Grout text. A partial recording of the Norton Anthology of Western Music is also available.

Recordings of a number of examples of early music are to be found in the *Archive Productions* of the Deutsche Grammaphon Gesellschaft, as well as under *Heritage, Folkways* and *Nonesuch* labels.

All recordings are designated according to the *Schwann Record Catalogs,* both domestic and foreign. The only exceptions to this are records published by Music Heritage (M.H.), such as those under the Orpheus label, which can only be found in the complete catalog of the Musical Heritage Society.

Further References

Reference for more detailed and independent study will be given under this heading. Because of their great numbers, biographical studies will not be listed except in those instances where a work is of major significance. The student can easily seek out biographies of those composers in whom he is most interested.

An Outline History of Music

Chinese Musicians: a wall painting from the caves of Tung-chuan in the province of Kan-su from the time of the Tang dynasty (618–907). Pictured from top to bottom are Chinese glockenspiel, zither, pan-pipes, oboe, guitar, flutes, cymbals, and drums. While no notation or instruments of this period remain today, the picture reveals a high degree of instrumental development. (Bärenreiter-Bildarchiv)

1

Chronology
of Ancient Sources of Western Music

B.C.

c. 1122 Chou Dynasty
(c. 1122–c. 255)

c. 1010 David, King of the
Jews
(c. 1010–c. 974)

c. 974 Solomon
(c. 974–c. 937)

c. 604 Loatse (c. 604–c. 531)

c. 582 Pythagoras
(c. 582–c. 500)

c. 563 Buddha (c. 563–c. 483)

c. 551 Confucious
(c. 551–479)

525 Aeschylus (525–456)

496 Sophocles (496–416)

490 Persian Wars
Phidias (490–432)

470 Socrates (470–390)

427 Plato (427–347)

404 Athens at war with
Sparta

390 Praxiteles (390–330)

384 Aristotle (384–322)

360 Lysippus
(c. 360–c. 316)

336 Alexander the Great
(336–323)

206 Han Dynasty (206–221
A.D.)

106 Marcus Tullius Cicero
(106–43)

100 Julius Caesar (100–44)

70 Publius Virgil (70–19)

4 Birth of Christ

A.D.

274 Constantine I—The
Great (c 274–337)

313 Edict of Milan

325 First Council of
Nicaea

570 Mohammed
(c. 570–632)

618 T'ang Dynasty
(618–905)

1

Ancient Sources
of Western Music

I. SOCIOCULTURAL INFLUENCES ON MUSIC

The knowledge of the music of the cultures that preceded the present Western European culture is at best very sketchy and piecemeal. The perishable nature of music limits all real knowledge of it to those systems which had devised some adequate method of notation. At no time previous to the Romanesque has a system of notation existed that enables scholars to reconstruct more than a mere handful of melodic fragments with any degree of certainty. Music among primitive as well as civilized peoples existed in practice principally as a form of free improvisation.

The best sources of study of music's pre-western history, and these can be only partially adequate, are:

1. The musical practices of primitive groups such as the various African, North and South American Indian, and Oceanic tribes. Through a study of the music of such primitive groups, scholars are able to reconstruct in part, at least, the music of early historical civilizations.

2. The musical practices of ancient civilized peoples whose cultural institutions are in some measure still in existence today, such as the Chinese, Indian, Siamese, Japanese and other Oriental groups.

3. The reconstruction of musical systems by the study of pictorial descriptions of instruments, fragments of notation, writings about music, and some few examples of ancient instruments still intact. Such material has been used particularly in the study of music of the Mediterranean area, the Egyptian, Hebrew, and Greek.

During the past fifty years and especially since the middle of the twentieth century there has been a tremendous surge of interest in the musical expressions of folk and nonwestern cultures. Indeed, the influence of systems of music which were scarcely known before 1950 on the popular as well as the esoteric musical expression of Europe and America has really been felt for the first time. Performances of native groups from Asia, Africa, and those countries where folk music has been able to maintain itself in face of the wide spread dissemination of the western tradition have acquainted the general public as well as the creative musician with rhythms, melodic systems, and instrumental and vocal colors which have long remained unknown to the world of art music.

It is difficult to determine the historical development of this nonwestern music. Over the centuries, and still in the present, the great body of musical expression has been orally transmitted from generation to generation. It is undoubtedly true that ritualistic music may be of very ancient origin. Much that is heard today has been influenced by European tradition within the past century or two, especially in the twentieth century with the universal use of radio, recordings, motion picture, and television.

It is doubtful that any culture previous to our own western European culture used music as a purely independent art form. Music as an expressive medium is, however, as old as man himself. Evidence of its use is to be found among all peoples, primitive and civilized, though the extent of its use varied from culture to culture. Since music lacked any abstract artistic independence, it was associated primarily with overt emotional expression. Like the pictorial and plastic expressions of cave paintings, rock carvings, sculptures, ceramics, design and painting, music was closely associated with the rites of the community as well as with the emotional expressions of the individual. Most references to music, whether in written or pictorial form, lead us to believe that its practice was particularly dependent on the strength and attitudes of the dominant religious organization and practices of each culture. This does not exclude, however, a wide spread use of music for secular purposes. The attitude of the dominant religion determined not only whether music was to be used, banned, or merely tolerated, but also the kind of music that was permissible, its manner of presentation, the instruments to be used and many other factors dealing with practice and performance.

For example, it is quite definitely established that the ancient Hebrews used instruments in the Temple service where professional musicians were in charge of musical performance. Chant was used to read the scriptural passages of the Old Testament. There are indications that antiphonal singing as well as sung responses by the congregations were commonly used. These practices as well as hymn singing were unquestionably of great influence on the early Christians in the use of music in their religious service where chant played the dominant musical role for over a thousand years.

Seasonal and geographic considerations were often determining factors in musical practice. Among the Chinese, for instance, the use of certain instruments was dictated by their close relationship to these considerations rather than by aesthetic factors.

Occupational choices and habits are vitally affected by geographic location, and occupations in turn have been very influential on the folk as well as cultural music of all peoples. Other economic factors; wealth, natural resources usable for sound media, skill of construction, have also wielded their influence in determining musical development.

Such influences are to be found on the music of all early cultures, and some remnants of these socio-cultural forces still determine the use of music in the Western World. Some religious sects today forbid the use of certain music and certain instruments. The Greek Orthodox church allows no instruments whatsoever in its services. The Roman Catholic church generally forbids all instruments except the organ, and at one time allowed only male voices in the sung liturgy. Some of the early Protestant sects were very intolerant of most music in the church service.

The Greeks ascribed certain ethical values to their music, depending on the tonal relationships within the scales or modes on which the melodies were built. Melodies built in one mode were considered effeminate and damaging to the morals of the youth, while melodies in another mode might be stimulating to warlike action. Plato in his *New-Republic* and the *Laws* assigns a vital role to the type of music that could be used in education.

In India the melodic patterns called *ragas*, that act as basic elements for improvisation, are divided into those that are appropriate for certain periods of the day. Ragas designed for use in the morning must not be used in the afternoon, and vice

Picture on a Greek urn of a man playing the lyra, a simple form of a harp-like string instruments of the very early Greeks. The amphora or Greek wine jar served as a medium for painting among the ancient Greeks, and remains of these artifacts record many aspects of Greek life, among them musical instruments and performance. The Lyra had a sound box usually made of a tortoise shell and the strings were struck with a plectrum which is depicted here in the right hand of the performer. (The Metropolitan Museum of Art, Rogers Fund, 1922)

versa. In Oriental cultures magical powers are attributed to scale patterns, pitch levels, and intervals themselves. These powers are interpreted in accordance with the religious, economic, and political institutions of the various cultures.

II. FUNCTION OF MUSIC

The more primitive the society the more closely tied to ritual was the musical expression. Monotonous incantations and instrumental rhythms accompanied religious rites and festivals to achieve a kind of magic hypnosis. In highly civilized societies too, the use of music was mainly for religious ritualistic purposes, but other uses of music are also to be found.

An outgrowth of the combination of music and religious ritual was the musical drama and the incidental use of music in spoken drama. The musical dramas of the Chinese represent a highly developed relationship of music and dramatic presentation. In Greece there was a definite use of music in the performance of the great dramatic works of the classic Greek theater. Unfortunately there is little or no knowledge of what the music was like or precisely how it was used.

From the paintings, reliefs, and the writings of ancient peoples it also is obvious that forms of secular music existed. Folk dances and songs, as well as a highly organized kind of secular music, were used for festive occasions. Songs of love and work are found among all peoples, past and present.

III. CHARACTERISTICS OF STYLE

In general it can be said that factors other than aesthetic ones dictated not only the melodic and rhythmic character of the music of early cultures but were influential in shaping the formal structure and giving preference to instrumental and vocal qualities. The overwhelming difference to be found in music of the early Eastern cultures, primitive peoples and that of our western European tradition, is the tendency for the Eastern musicians to express themselves in an unending, repetitive and rhapsodical manner while the Western composers have shaped their media into concise and formal structures. The Eastern music's repetitive quality is a result of the dictates of magic and religious considerations in the desire for hypnotic expression.

    1. *Formal organization.* Generally speaking, the music was based upon melodic or rhythmic patterns which constituted a point of departure for the performer, and upon which he improvised rather freely. The formal organization was one of repetition and rhapsodic variation.

    2. *Melody.* Melody was one of the two dominant elements of music. Although often based on traditional fragments or patterns, the art of the singer consisted of spinning out variations that used arabesque-like decorations characteristic of all non-western music. Trills, turns, rapid, and florid scale passages were the main features of the melodic line.

Melody took on an almost unending character in the music of the nonwestern peoples. This character is the most distinguishing one between the melodic expression of Western music and that of other cultures, particularly that of the Orient.

All pre-western melodic invention was based on the recognition of the octave as a closed system. As far as can be determined most pre-western societies seem to have constructed their melodic patterns on a selection of five tones within the octave, a basic system of melodic construction known as pentatonic. The music of the present day Oriental cultures, Chinese, Japanese, Siamese, Indonesian, is built on a five tone division of the octave closely resembling the relationships represented by the first, second, third, fifth, and sixth tones of the modern major scale. There are no intervals corresponding to the half steps found between the third and fourth and the seventh and eighth tones in the modern major scale. However, many Oriental systems divided this basic pentatonic scale into very small intervals representing one-fourth, one-eighth, and even one-sixteenth of a modern whole step. Writings of the Greeks indicate a vast knowledge of musical theory. They had available, through scientific discovery, the actual twelve tones of the octave which constitute the modern chromatic scale. Their melodies were based on a system of tetrachords which, when placed side by side, resulted in an octave scale of seven tones similar to those in the modern major scale. Since each of the seven tones might be used as the basic tone, a series of seven different modal scales was theoretically possible for the construction of a melody. These were the scales or modes to which the Greeks ascribed ethical values.

3. *Rhythm.*   The second important element of nonwestern music was rhythm. In many respects rhythmic patterns among primitive as well as civilized groups achieved a complexity that western civilization did not cultivate until the present century. Rhythm is generally quantitative—long and short beats, rather than qualitative—strong and weak beats. Irregular rhythmic patterns of seven, ten and fourteen, for example, are not uncommon, especially in India.

    Rhythmic patterns were often used by African tribes to convey specific meanings. Among some African groups the development and cultivation of rhythmic expression resulted in extremely complicated patterns. Polyrhythmic expression is also frequent in the music of the Javanese and Balinese.

4. *Harmony.*   Harmony in the modern sense of the term was nonexistent. However, the use of drone bass and ostinato accompanying patterns was probably more widely spread than heretofore realized. This type of heterophony is particularly true of the music of the southeastern Asiatic societies such as Java and Bali.

5. *Texture.*   Texture was achieved through multiple playing and singing of the same basic melodic line by various voices and instruments. Accounts and pictures of large groups numbering into the hundreds of instrumentalists and singers would indicate that there was appreciation for tonal texture achieved through the heterophonic duplication of the same melodic patterns at the unison or octave, or even at other intervals, by various media.

6. *Media and Tone Color*

    a) Since music and word were so closely connected in early musical performance, it is obvious that the voice was by far the most important medium of expression.

    b) Instruments consisting of wind, string, and percussion families were widely used to accompany the voice, generally at the unison or octave. The development of the percussion instruments was very advanced with all types of material used. Percussion instruments were made of wood, metal, stone and even of vegetable fibre such as gourds. They were divided into groups which were accurately pitched according to scale divisions and those which were merely used for sound effects with no pitch accuracy. Division of the octave system into smaller intervals than the half step of our western system was exploited in many of the tuned instruments.

c) Both bowed and plucked string instruments were used. The bowed strings were very simple one-stringed instruments, but the plucked strings reached a high state of perfection second only to the percussion instruments. Much skill was evidenced in both their construction and performance.

d) The least developed of the pre-western instruments were the wind instruments corresponding to our present brasses and woodwind types. The brasses never advanced beyond the simple natural form and were made of various materials, metal, bone and wood, the primitive mouthpieces being part of the horns themselves. Woodwind instruments were only fitted with open holes, if indeed such were even used. There was a great variety of both flute and reed type instruments, however, ranging from simply made folk instruments to those elaborately constructed.

IV. PRACTICE AND PERFORMANCE

Lacking a fixed notation, all practices were a matter of tradition within the culture. The selection of instruments, voices, dynamics and tempi was undoubtedly the result of traditional usage. References to musical performance indicate that certain instruments, for example, were used only for certain occasions due to the association of their timbre with moral and ethical values.

Judging from practices now in use in cultures other than those of western Europe, it is probable that the voice also was used in a different fashion from the European tradition. Various tonal qualities were cultivated by such practices as tightening of the throat passage, falsetto, guttural grunts. Among most nonwestern peoples, especially the east Asians, the use of the voice suggests that it is desirable to make singing as different from speech as possible. The eastern singer's vocal production makes use of a tightened throat and vocal chords whereas the western singing tradition desires to produce a kind of refined and beautified speech.

Again from the evidence of other contemporary cultures it is probable that a strikingly high perfection of performance skill was achieved in the use of percussion instruments. This is especially evident in the present day performance of African, Indian, and western Oriental peoples.

V. VOCAL COMPOSITIONS

It is impossible to speak about vocal forms beyond the fact that vocal music, both spiritual and secular, was employed. The improvisational character precluded most set formal structure, and lack of notated examples gives us no basis for reconstruction of formal designs if any existed.

VI. INSTRUMENTAL COMPOSITIONS

As in vocal music there were no set forms. Instrumental music like vocal music was improvisational in character. Purely instrumental music unrelated to song or dance was found in some instances. The orchestral groups of percussion instruments used in Java and Bali are notable instances. Instrumental music was usually descriptive and illustrative of poetic or pictorial ideas. The flute and zither music of China and Japan are examples.

VII. COMPOSERS

There are no records of any composers or their works. Accounts of performers such as David in the Old Testament are the only records which would give any indication of composers as such, since every performer was in fact a composer.

While there are no specific composers to whom compositions can be attributed, examples of ancient music do exist. Volume 1 of *The History of Music in Sound* gives fifty-two short examples of the music of pre-western cultures from the early music of China to that of Greece and Islam.

> Ex: 52 works of nonwestern cultures
> HMS, vol. 1, pp. 13–38
> Rec. RCA LM—6057

Examples of recorded nonwestern music can also be found in the UNESCO collections of *Music in the Orient and Africa* issued under the labels of Bärenreiter-Musicaphon and Phillips. (See Schwann Foreign Catalog.) Numerous further examples can be found under the Folkways label.

VIII. IMPORTANT WRITERS ON MUSIC

Early writers dealt either with music in a mathematical-theoretical way or in a philosophical-ethical manner. Among the former the most important are those who based their theories on the work of Pythagoras, the early Greek mathematician and speculator of the harmony of the spheres. Among the latter the most extensive writings are those of the Greek philosophers, although references to music can be found in the works of many ancient writers, Chinese, Indian, Hebrew and others.

1. *Pythagoras* (c. 582 B.C.—c. 500 B.C.) was a Greek philosopher and mathematician to whom is ascribed the discovery of musical ratios of which only the octave and fifth were considered pure consonances. There is no record of any of Pythagoras' writings and his theories are known only as they were developed by his followers.

2. *Plato* (427 B.C.—347 B.C.) was the great Greek philosopher whose concern with music was almost entirely that of ethical values. Passages in the *Timaeus* and the *Republic* state his concepts of music and its place in society.

3. *Aristotle* (384 B.C.—322 B.C.), a pupil of Plato, also was concerned with the ethical values of music as evidenced in several of his writings, notably in the *Politics.*

4. *Aristoxenus* (354 B.C.—?) was the most important of the Greek writers on music. Two works, *Harmonic Elements* and *Elements of Rhythmics,* have come down to us, the first complete; the second in fragmentary form. An English edition of these two works by H. S. Macran was published in 1902.

5. *Cleonides* (first half of the second century A.D.) was a Greek writer. *Harmonic Introduction* was an early source of information for the Renaissance musicians on classic Greek music, having been published in Venice in 1497.

6. *Aristedes Quintillianus* (flourished c. 200 A.D.) was a Greek theorist whose treatise, *De Musica Libri VII,* provides a basic source for knowledge of the music of ancient Greece. A German translation by Schafke was published in 1937.

7. *Athenaeus* (flourished c. 200 A.D.) was a Greek writer who lived in Rome. While he was not a musician his descriptions of musical performance in his books, *Sophists at Dinner,* are a valuable source in giving an insight into the regard for and place of music in Roman life.

Excerpts from most of the foregoing are to be found in Strunk, *Source Readings in Music History.*

IX. MANUSCRIPT SOURCES

Again the lack of notation and the fact that music was not an independent art form precludes any large manuscript collections of early music. What few examples of Greek music there are have been deciphered from inscriptions on stone. Music of the Orient was handed down orally until recent centuries when it was recorded in writing.

Supplementary Readings

Borroff	pp. 3–16
Cannon-Johnson-Waite	pp. 5–25
Grout	pp. 1–34
Lang	pp. 1–36
Oxford, v. 1	pp. 1–464
Sachs, RMA	pp. 57–290
Wold-Cykler	ch. 3

Further References

Brandel, Rose. *The Music of Central Africa*. The Hague: M. Nijhoff, 1961.

Idelsohn, Abraham. *Jewish Music in its Historical Development*. New York: H. H. Holt, 1929.

Kunst, Jaap. *Ethno-Musicology*. The Hague: M. Nijhoff, 1959.

Malm, Wm. P. *Music Cultures of the Pacific, The Near East, and Asia*. Englewood Cliffs, N.J.: Prentice-Hall, 1967.

May, Elizabeth, ed. *Music of Many Cultures—An Introduction* (20 Essays, 3 Recordings). Berkeley: University of California Press, 1980.

McPhee, Colin. *Music in Bali*. New Haven, Conn.: Yale University Press, 1966.

Merriam, Alan P. *The Anthropology of Music*. Evanston, Ill.: Northwestern University Press, 1964.

Nettl, Bruno. *Music in Primitive Culture*. Cambridge: Harvard University Press, 1956.

Prajnanananda, Swami. *A Historical Study of Indian Music*. Calcutta: Anandadhara Prakashan, 1965.

Winnington-Ingram, R. P. *Mode in Ancient Greek Music*. Cambridge: Cambridge University Press, 1936.

King David playing the rotta; an eighth century miniature from the Canterbury Psalterium. The rotta was a medieval instrument referred to in very early sources. It was most probably a psaltery on which the strings, like the those of the harp, were plucked by the fingers. Other medieval instruments are pictured: four zinks or cornetti and two small straight flutes or recorders. The clapping dancers at the bottom of the picture suggest that the music being played is secular in nature. (Bärenreiter-Bildarchiv)

2
Chronology
of the Early Middle Ages

354	St. Augustine (354–430)	955	Guido of Arezzo (955–1050)
481	Boethius (c. 480–584)		
540	Pope Gregory (c. 540–604)	1073	Winchester Troper
	Gregorian Chant	1079	Abelard (1079–1142)
650	Rise of Monasteries	1100	St. Martial Organum
742	Charlemagne (742–814)	1150	Troubadours
787	Second Council of Nicaea		School of Notre Dame
912	Otto the Great (912–1073)		

2
Romanesque – Early Middle Ages
500-1100

I. SOCIOCULTURAL INFLUENCES ON MUSIC

The term Romanesque is generally used to describe the medieval style of art that was influenced by the Roman Empire. While the term is more accurately used to designate architecture, it is also commonly used to refer to that period of music that was dominated by monophony. While the monophonic chant continued its development beyond 1100, it lost its importance as a style after the introduction of harmony and the development of polyphony in the Gothic period. Sacred monophony is generally referred to as plainsong, or chant.

It must be noted that our knowledge of Romanesque music in general is based upon rather meager evidence. While we have examples of early sacred music which have been preserved by the Catholic Church, its interpretation is open to question. This is due to the fact that there was an inadequate system of notation, particularly in relation to time values. We have even fewer authentic examples of secular monophony because of the lack of a systematic preservation of tradition.

Under the patronage of early Catholicism, music was organized according to the specification of the church service and in keeping with a simple ascetic faith.

The many monastic orders that flourished during this period were mainly responsible for the development and organization of sacred music. In keeping with liturgical practice, this music was always set to an ecclesiastical Latin text.

The medieval denial of physical matter was partly responsible for the apparent lack of instrumental music in the Church.

Another reason was that the Church fathers could sanction only music with a religious text.

In general, the music of the early Church took its forms and liturgical order from the Byzantine church and the Jewish service, but modern scholarship is in doubt as to the exact details of such connections.

Feudalism gave rise to a society with a well-developed social consciousness. Consequently, a large body of secular music and poetry in the vernacular was derived from its entertainments and its desire for self-expression outside the confines of the Church.

II. FUNCTION OF MUSIC

The function of sacred plainsong was to express a simple faith in God in keeping with the other-worldly spirit of early Christianity. This function was achieved by the musical setting of portions of all rituals of the Church, of which the most important was the Mass. Other rituals that also used music were the so-called Divine Offices or canonical hours, such as Matins, Lauds, and Vespers.

The liturgy of the Catholic Mass called for the musical setting of eleven texts; the remaining texts were spoken. The musical settings were divided into two parts. One part, the *Ordinary*, consisting of the Kyrie, Gloria, Credo, Sanctus, Agnus Dei (Benedictus), and its Ite missa est, used an invariable text. The other part, the *Proper*, used a variable text from service to service in accordance with the church calendar. It consisted of the Introit, Gradual, Alleluia, Offertory, and Communion.

In addition to the Mass and the Divine Offices, plainsong was used extensively in musical settings of hymns, psalms, and some nonliturgical texts inserted between words of liturgical texts. These latter were called *tropes.* (see p. 26).

Secular music, in addition to music for dancing, served as a chronicle of news events and as a vehicle for the expression of the folk traditions.

Portal of St. Trophime (c-1105) Arles, France. The use of sculpture as a part of the architectural design emphasizes not only the lack of natural and humanistic qualities, but the distortions to which the human form was subjected in order to deny the worldly nature of mankind. There is little or no plastic form and elements of the bodies are greatly out of proportion. The restriction of music to simple melodic line with a definite avoidance of secular tonality or stressed rhythm is a striking parallel to the sculpture of the time.

III. CHARACTERISTICS OF STYLE

1. *Formal Organization*

    a) The organization and forms of sacred plainsong were
       determined by the Latin text of the particular portion of the liturgy.

    b) In a few instances, mainly the trope and sequence, the organization was based on melodic

Example 1. Chart of Modes

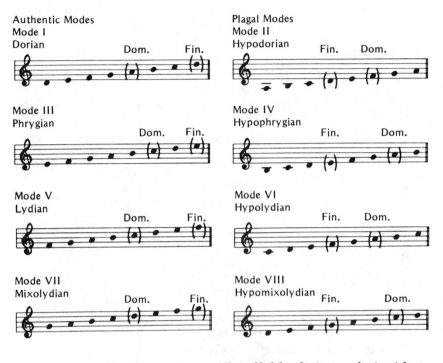

configuration, with syllables being only incidental.

   c) The forms of secular monophony were also determined by the text, but these texts were most
often poetic in form and consequently the music
reveals such patterns as verse with refrain or repeated melodic phrases.

2. *Melody*

   a) Sacred melody (plainsong) is monophonic, without accompaniment.

   b) Plainsong melody has a narrow range that rarely
exceeds the interval of a fifth

   c) The church modes differ from one another by the
order of the steps and half steps within the octave. Four modes: I, III, V, and VII are known as
the authentic modes. The order of steps and half
steps in these modes corresponds to the diatonic
octave scales based on D(Mode I), E(Mode III)
F(Mode V), and G(Mode VII). (see example 1.)

Each of these modes, however, could begin on any pitch. The church modes did not represent a fixed pitch. Each authentic mode had a corresponding plagal mode. Each pair of modes, I and II, III and IV, V and VI, VII and VIII, had the same final or principal tone. The over-riding difference between an authentic mode and its corresponding plagal partner was the range or ambitus. The authentic mode had a range within the octave of its final. The plagal mode had a range within the octave of the fourth below its final to a fifth above. The secondary principal tone in each mode was called the dominant.

d) Some plainsong chants, especially those used in the psalm settings, made use of a reciting tone. This is a tone upon which most of the syllables of the chant are executed and is usually the dominant of the mode.

e) There are three types of plainsong melody: (1) syllabic, in which each note is set against a syllable of the text; (2) neumatic, in which a small group of notes are sung to one syllable; and (3) florid, or melismatic, in which extended groups of notes are set to one syllable.

f) Melody in secular monophony often uses a wider range of notes than plainsong.

g) Secular monophony is not restricted by the church modes and often approaches tonality.

h) Secular monophony is also usually cast in regular phrases, while plainsong is more irregular.

3. *Rhythm*

a) Plainsong rhythm was determined by the poetic flow of the prose and the quantitative quality of ecclesiastical Latin. The long and short syllabic structure of Latin regulated the rhythm. As a consequence, rhythmic patterns of stressed and nonstressed accent are absent in sacred monophony.

b) Because secular monophony used the vernacular in which there is a more qualitative accent, its rhythm is most often metric and shows more symmetric organization than plainsong.

4. *Harmony*

a) There was no systematic harmonic development during the Romanesque. However, both sacred and secular monophony were accompanied on occasion by instruments and consequently some harmonic practices, such as drone bass and ostinato figures, were probably present.

b) As early as the ninth century a practice of singing in parallel fourths and fifths began and was called *organum*. Several types developed that were variously named. They all had the common characteristic of using a pre-existing chant (the *vox principalis*) to which was added one or more melodic lines. Parallel organum added a second voice (*vox organalis*) a fifth or fourth below the vox principalis (ex. 2).

Example 2. *Sit gloriosa* (Parallel organum)

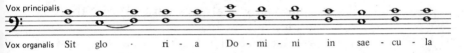

Free organum employed contrary and oblique motion in the vox organalis (ex. 3).

Example 3. *Cunctipotens genitor* (Free organum)

A later type, melismatic organum, used elaborate decorative note groups in the vox organalis against the very slow moving values of the vox principalis (ex. 4).

Example 4. *Cunctipotens genitor* (Melismatic organum)

All organum styles emphasized the use of the basic perfect intervals of the unison, fourth and fifth at cadential points.

5. *Texture*

   a) Since sacred plainsong was monophonic, there was no texture in the sense of a combination of lines or tonal coloring of later music. However, the austere line of plainsong sung by the priest, or the chant sung in unison or organum by a choir, created a mystic simplicity of linear sound that complemented the stark simplicity of the Romanesque cathedral itself.

   b) Secular monophony, because of its wider range, more definite rhymic patterns, and frequent use of instruments, together with its vernacular text reveals a fuller texture that expresses human feelings and emotions.

6. *Media and tone color*

   a) Sacred plainsong is always vocal. While there is some evidence that instruments were occasionally used as accompaniment, as a rule instruments were prohibited in the Romanesque church.

   b) Secular monophony was mainly vocal, but was often accompanied by instruments, especially when used as dance music.

   c) Instruments used in secular music were the stringed instruments, both plucked and bowed, and a variety of wind and percussion instruments.

IV. PRACTICE AND PERFORMANCE

There were five important types of sacred plainsong, or chants as they were called when in collections. Each of these collections formed the basis of musical practice in the particular area of its origin. (1) Byzantine chant is the earliest collection and came as the result of the establishment of the Eastern church by Constantine. It is still used in the Greek Orthodox church. (2) The Ambrosian chant is a collection organized by

Ambrose, Bishop of Milan during the fourth century. (3) Gallic chant was used in France until about 800. (4) Mozarabic chant was prominent in Spain and first appeared about 900. (5) Gregorian chant is still the most often used, and is so named because it was collected and organized under the leadership of Pope Gregory (c. 540–604). Its continued wide use is due to the fact that it was the collection used in Rome. When Rome became the center of Catholicism the Gregorian chant spread throughout the whole Catholic world.

Ex: *Byzantine Music*
        HMS, vol. 2, p. 2
        Rec. RCA, LM-6015

Ex: Ambrosian psalmellus for Quadragesima: *Redde mihi*
        TEM, p. 3
        Rec. HSE-9100

Ex: Ambrosian chant: Verse *Eructavit*
        HAM, p. 11
        Rec. OR-349

Ex: Gallican *Improperia* for Good Friday: *Popule meus*
        TEM, p. 8
        Rec. HSE-9100

Ex: Mozarabic Antiphon for Easter: *Gaudete populi*
        TEM, p. 12
        Rec. HSE-9100

Ex: Gregorian hymn for Whitsunday: *Veni Creator Spiritus*
        TEM, p. 16
        Rec. HSE-9100

Ex: Gregorian chant: Gradual: *Haec dies*
        HAM, p. 12
        Rec. OR-349

The musical setting of psalms provided the most important body of plainsong literature for both the Mass and the Office hours. There are three types of psalm settings, defined according to the practice of performance:

1. Responsorial—a soloist sings the verse and is answered by a choir.

2. Antiphonal—the choir is divided into two groups, singing alternately.

3. Direct psalmody—the psalm is sung by a soloist or single choir with no refrain.

It is probable that sacred plainsong was sung with a nasal quality of voice, without vibrato and with the use of the falsetto voice. Only male singers were permitted to participate in the liturgy.

Chants of the Mass and Office hours were sung by the clergy, but the congregation joined in the hymns and some processional chants.

A device to aid in sight-singing, called the hexachord system, was perfected by Guido d' Arezzo in the eleventh century. The six tones of the hexachord were designated by six syllables in order, from the lowest to the highest—ut, re, mi, fa, sol, la—corresponding to the first syllables of successive lines of a hymn to St. John the Baptist (ex. 5). A system of mutation was devised that enabled the singer to sing melodies that lay outside the range of a single hexachord.

Example 5

UT que-ant la - xis RE-so -na -re fi -bris MI - ra ge- sto-rum FA-mu-li tu-o - rum,

SOL - ve po-lu -ti LA -bi- i re - a-tum San - cte Jo - an - nes

The practice of singing in parallel fifths and fourths, called organum, was probably improvised. While it is generally associated with sacred music, there is evidence that it was also practiced in secular music as well. In its simplest form a second voice, *vox organalis*, sang a melody at the interval of a fifth or fourth below the principal voice, *vox principalis* (see example 2). Later developments brought the practice of contrary motion and the use of nonperfect intervals (see examples 3 and 4). By the end of the eleventh century, organum was so well established that it was referred to in theoretical treatises. Rules were established for avoiding the tritone, the augmented fourth, for arriving at unison cadences, and for identifying those parts of the liturgical chant that were permitted to be used in this manner. The practice of organum led directly to the development of polyphonic forms in the Gothic.

V. VOCAL COMPOSITIONS

A. Single Movement Forms and Structural Devices.

With few exceptions, the musical form and organization of specific plainsong chants were based solely on the form of the text. Any suggestion of A-B-A or similar formula was the result of textual considerations. There were some traditions that placed specific texts in certain of the Church modes and naturally those chants set to the same texts show a degree of similarity. However, there are few distinguishable forms as such. For example, there is nothing about the formal organization of an Introit to distinguish it from a Sanctus, other than the difference in text. The Monophonic Mass is not a true musical form but is a collection of appropriate chant settings of the Ordinary and Proper of the Mass.

Ex: First Mass for Christmas
     Liber Usualis
     Rec. DGG, ARC-198153

   1. *Antiphon.*   A short sentence of scripture, or other verse, sung both before and after the psalm in syllabic style. The formal effect was that of a refrain to the psalm.

Ex: *Laus Deo Patri* and *Psalm 113, Laudate pueri*
     MM, p. 3
     Rec. HS-9038

Ex: *Psalm 146* with Antiphon
     HAM, p. 11
     Rec. OR-349

   2. *Alleluia.*   The alleluia is added at the end of sections of many chants. It consists of a refrain on the word *alleluia* and is then followed by a verse or section with the refrain repeated. The final vowel, the *jubilus,* of the word *alleluia* provides a strong basis for musical form.

Ex: *Vidimus stellam*
     MM, p. 6
     Rec. HS-9038
Ex: Alleluia: *Angelus Domini*
     HAM, p. 12
     Rec. OR-349

3. *Trope.*   A trope is music with a text inserted between phrases of the liturgical text. The words provided a commentary on the liturgy. The trope is one of the first forms to provide opportunity for creative expression on purely musical terms. Because tropes had a tendency towards secularism, they were abolished by the Council of Trent. The following *Agnus Dei* is in organum.

Ex: *Agnus Dei*
MM, p. 18
Rec. HS-9038

Ex: Polyphonic trope; *Kyrie Jhesu dulcissime,* Fronciaco
TEM, p. 66
Rec. HSE-9101

Ex: Kyrie-Trope: *Omnipotens*
HAM, p. 13
Rec. OR-349

4. *Sequence.*   The sequence evolved from the practice of troping, and consisted of added poetic words to the final melisma of the alleluia, replacing the verse that followed the alleluia. The texts that provided the musical incentive were usually long and in a free style with repeated sections. Such formulas as A BB CC DD E were common and represented independent compositions. Like the trope, the sequence inclined toward secularism. Only five were eventually retained in the body of Church music.

Ex: Sequence: *Victimae Paschali*
MM, p. 8
Rec. HS-9038

Ex: Sequence: *Rex caeli, Domine*
MM, p. 16
Rec. HS-9038

Ex: Sequence: *Alleliua: Dominus in Sina,* with Sequence: *Christus hunc diem,* Balbulus
HAM, p. 13
Rec. OR-349

5. *Conductus.*   The monophonic conductus was probably first sung while a participant in the Mass or liturgical drama was "conducted" from one

place to another in the Church. The text was non-liturgical and metric. The melody was always freely composed, not taken from a chant collection. While this form first appeared in the Church, it soon became a secular form and the title was applied to almost any Latin song of a serious nature.

Ex: Conductus: *Song of the Ass*
Christo psallat
Beata viscera
Sol oritur
HAM, p. 14
Rec. OR-349

Secular monophony of the period to 1100 has not been preserved as well as that of sacred music. No doubt this was partly due to the fact that no adequate notation had been devised, and that there was no institution whose duty it was to maintain the traditions, as was the case in sacred music.

It is known that secular monophony flourished during the Romanesque through the songs of the Goliards, Jongleurs, and Minstrels. Some of the most important of these songs were those of the Goliards who were wandering ecclesiastical students. The most noted collection of Goliard poems is the *Carmina Burana*, made famous in modern times by Carl Orff. Only one of the Goliard songs has been deciphered into modern notation *O Admirable Veneris*, dating from the tenth century. Its melody also appears as *O Roma Nobilis*. It is metric and in strophic form with a refrain.

Ex: *O Admirabile Veneris*
HMS, vol. 2, p. 25
Rec. RCA LM-6015

The Jongleurs and Minstrels were itinerant performers and entertained with song, dance, tricks, or juggling. While they cannot be considered either poets or composers, they sang verses in the vernacular. One of the early types of Jongleur song was *Chanson de Geste*, a narrative song telling of heroic deeds. The most famous of these is the *Song of Roland* which became a national epic of France. Unfortunately no authentic music has survived. It is probable that the Jongleurs and Minstrels helped to spread the folk song tradition that ultimately made its way into art music.

VI. INSTRUMENTAL COMPOSITIONS

While instrumental music was generally banned in the Church, it is known that organs existed in the churches as early as 800. We do not know, however, how they were used, or what music was played.

It is evident from manuscripts and pictorial representations that instruments were used in secular music both as accompaniment to song and independently as dance music. As is the case with all Romanesque secular music, we have no information about specific forms, as none of the music has survived in decipherable notation.

VII. COMPOSERS

Because of the improvisatory nature of early music, almost every performer was a composer. This was especially true in secular music and no doubt the same procedure was responsible for the origin of most of the chants that later became traditional. It is known, however, that the following were composers of some stature and influence during the Romanesque.

1. *Notker Balbulus* (c. 840–912) was one of the earliest identified composers and was especially known for his sequences.

Ex: Sequence; *Sancti Spiritu avidit nobis gratia*
HMS, vol. 2, p. 21
Rec. RCA, LM-6015-2

2. Rodulphe of St. Trond (d. 1136), composer of plainsong melodies.
3. *Wipo of Burgundy* (d. 1048).

Ex: Sequence: *Victimae paschali laudes*
HAM, p. 13
Rec. OR-349

4. *Hermannus Contractus* (1013–1054), also known as Herman the Cripple, was a theorist as well as a composer. His *Alma Redemptoris Mater* achieved a great popularity and became the basis for numerous works in both monophony and polyphony.

Ex: *Alma redemptoris mater*
      HAM, p. 70
      Rec. Plei-251

> 5. *Abelard* (1079–1142) is known to have made a collection of hymns that were used by the monks and nuns. One of these nuns was the famous Heloise.

VIII. IMPORTANT WRITERS ON MUSIC

Most of the early theoretical writings on music were not derived from the current musical practices of the times. They were, in effect, either interpretations of the music theory of the ancients and the subsequent concept of music as a science or attempts to link music and religion by means of allegorical writings.

> 1. *Boethius* (c. 480–524) was one of the earliest theorists. He was also a philosopher and mathematician. His chief work was *De Institutione Musica,* in which he related the music of his time to the theories of the Greek philosophers.
>
> 2. *Cassiodorus* (c. 485–c. 580) was a historian, philosopher, statesman, and the founder of a monastery. His important work was *Institutiones musicae,* written between 550 and 562.
>
> 3. *Isidore of Seville* (d. 636) was a Spanish scholar. His *Etymologiarum sive originum libri xx* is an encyclopedia of the arts with an account of liturgical music.
>
> 4. *Odo of Cluny* (d. 942) was a theorist of the tenth century. The *Dialogus de Musica* contains an account of modes and medieval notation. He was the first to use letters to indicate pitches.
>
> 5. *Guido d'Arezzo* (c. 990–1050), a Benedictine monk, was the most important writer of his time concerned with the actual practices of music. He dealt with the problems of notation and especially with the technique of singing. His numerous writings have been an important source for modern scholars on the musical practices of medieval times.

6. *Musica enchiriadis* (c. 900) a treatise noteworthy for its
description of early organum, the authorship of
which has never been established. For a long time it
was thought to have been written by Hucbald
(c. 840–930) but recent scholarship has denied his authorship. *Musica enchiriadis* covers the whole range of
musical knowledge. Most of its material was bor-
rowed from the ancients, including the concept of
music as mathematics and the acceptance of Pythagorean theory of numbers and the division of the
scale according to intervallic ratios.

The writings of the foregoing theorists are not readily
available in English. Important excerpts from each can be found
in Strunk, *Source Readings in Music History.*

Boethius	p. 79
Cassiodorus	p. 87
Isidore	p. 93
Odo	p. 103
Guido	p. 117
Musica enchiriadis	p. 126

IX. MANUSCRIPT SOURCES

There is only one important collection of original manuscripts prior to 1100. This is called the *Winchester Troper,* a liturgical book containing tropes and organum.

The great literature of plainsong melody has been in the
process of being collected, edited and published by the Bene-
dictines of Solesmes since 1889. To date sixteen volumes have
been published in the *Paleographie Musicale.*

Supplementary Readings

Borroff	pp. 17– 80
Cannon-Johnson-Waite	pp. 26– 72
Crocker	pp. 1– 68
Grout	pp. 34– 64
Harman-Meller	pp. 1– 39
Lang	pp. 37–121
Oxford, Vol. II	pp. 58–219
Reese-MA	pp. 57–272
Schirmer	ch. 1– 4
Wold-Cykler	ch. 5

Further References

Apel, Willi. *Gregorian Chant*. Bloomington: University of Indiana Press, 1958.

Fortescue, A. *The Ceremonies of the Roman Rite Described*. London: Burns and Oates, 1930.

Hoppin, Richard H. *Medieval Music*. Ch. I-VII. New York: W. W. Norton, 1978.

Hoppin, Richard H. *Anthology of Medieval Music*. New York: W. W. Norton, 1978.

Seay, Albert. *Music in the Medieval World*. Englewood Cliffs: Prentice-Hall, 2nd ed., 1975.

Young, Karl. *Drama of the Medieval Church*. Oxford: Clarendon Press, 1933.

Cathedral of Amiens, France (c-1225). An excellent example of the great thrust of Gothic architecture. The pointed arches which frame the massive entrance doors and cover the niches of the sculptured figures above the doorways, the greatly elongated openings of the belfry towers, and the pointed decorated spires adorning the facade and the top-most roof all give a breathless feeling of heavenly lift to this massive building. The beginnings of part singing in the form of organum parallels the interweaving of sculptural and architectural elements evidenced in this cathedral. (Courtesy Metropolitan Museum of Art)

3

Chronology of the Gothic — Late Middle Ages

(Ars Antiqua — Ars Nova)

1100   Crusades (1100–1300)
1170   Perotin (c. 1170)
1175   Leonin (c. 1175)
1182   St. Francis of Assisi
       (1182–1226)
1200   Trouveres and
       Minnesingers (c. 1200)
       Organum
       Ars Antiqua
1225   St. Thomas Acquinas
       (1225–1274)
1230   Adam de la Hale
       (c. 1230–1288)
1250   Franco of Cologne
       (1250–1280)

1265   Dante Aligheri
       (1265–1321)
       Ars Nova
1300   Guillaume Machaut
       (1300–1377)
1304   Francesco Petrarch
       (1304–1374)
1304   Papacy in Avignon
1313   Giovanni Boccacio
       (1313–1375)
1340   Geoffrey Chaucer
       (1340–1400)
1348   The Black Death

3

Gothic — Late Middle Ages
(Ars Antiqua — Ars Nova)

I. SOCIOCULTURAL INFLUENCES ON MUSIC

The period from 1100 to about 1430 has been designated as Gothic mainly to describe a type of architecture that is characterized by the pointed arch, ribbed vaulting, and flying buttresses. The term was introduced by seventeenth century writers who looked upon this style as unclassical and vulgar, associating it with the medieval Goths of northern Europe. In its present connotation the term merely identifies the artistic style of this period without derogatory implications.

The rise and development of polyphonic forms, the merging of secular and sacred musical styles, were the major musical contributions of the Gothic. In fact, many of the forms, as well as musical practices, that have come down to modern times were Gothic in their origin. We have a fairly adequate knowledge of Gothic music, due to the fact that a system of notation was devised during this period that makes it possible for modern scholars to re-create much of the music with authority and accuracy. Both rhythmic and pitch notation made polyphonic music possible. The development of Gothic music was accelerated by a number of varied sociocultural movements that took place between 1100 and 1430.

Scholasticism was a medieval philosophy that systematized every area of intellectual and religious experience according to rigid rules of medieval logic. Its effect on religious music was twofold. First, it regulated the theory and practice of music according to canons of acceptable practice in the Church. For example, triple rhythm was held to be more perfect than duple rhythm and perfect intervals were ruled necessary on all strong

beats while dissonant intervals were generally avoided whenever possible. Second, scholasticism also controlled and codi-
fied the emotional content of sacred music. Church officials
frowned upon ornate melodies because they felt such melodies
obscured the meaning of the texts. Any move to make music
more emotionally expressive was to be avoided because it appealed to the senses and not to the soul. Expressive qualities
were finally to appear in sacred music, but only after a long
period of development. Although scholasticism had little direct effect on secular music, there was an indirect influence inasmuch as church composers who rebelled against strict control
found freedom in the secular style.

Western man was becoming more and more independent
economically, intellectually, and artistically. He was becoming
skeptical of the authority of the Church to order and control
all of the activities of life. Communication with the East, the
result of the Crusades (eleventh to the thirteenth centuries)
opened new channels of trade, brought new wealth, new ideas,
and new incentives for living. New social customs and cultural
practices were eventually integrated into western civilization.
As a consequence, a favorable climate for artistic development
existed during the Gothic in contrast to the rather severe asceticism of earlier times. Entertainment outside the Church became widely cultivated and even religious music was infused
with this new humanism.

The rise of towns stimulated centers of learning in newly
established universities. This was especially true in England,
The Netherlands, and France. Music became an integral part of
education, first as a science and eventually as an art. The real
leaders and innovators of Gothic music either were at the universities or associated with the courts where music was given
great importance. It is interesting to note that beginning with
the Gothic period musical leadership came from northern Europe instead of Italy where musical activity had been centered
up to this time.

The Gothic period also saw the beginning of the struggle
between Church and State which, in effect, was a struggle between asceticism and humanism. In music it took the form of
a conflict between the sacred and the secular, a conflict in which
each reached new heights of musical expressiveness.

II. FUNCTION OF MUSIC

Gothic sacred music served the same function for religion as Romanesque music. The same liturgical texts were set to music as previously, but in polyphony instead of monophony. An important addition to sacred music was the motet, a form that was later to become one of the most important vocal polyphonic forms. The Gothic spirit precipitated a great program of church building, an activity that in turn led to an increased demand for church musicians. This led to the establishment of a number of schools such as St. Martial and Notre Dame where sacred music was especially cultivated.

Music also took on increased importance in the social fabric of the Gothic. The rise in the social status of secular music, as is evidenced by the nobility of the Troubadours and Trouvères, shows the wide interest in secular song in the vernacular. The establishment of courts and the growing power of non-church institutions encouraged strong centers of secular culture in many medieval cities. This was the age of chivalry and the time when courtly love became the subject of lyric love songs. For the first time in music history, individual composers achieved recognition for their creative efforts. Moreover, the most significant developments in music have been traced to many of these secular composers.

III. CHARACTERISTICS OF STYLE

Although both sacred plainsong and secular monophony continued in the Gothic, the growth and refinement of the polyphonic style was the major concern of Gothic composers. This concern for devices of polyphony marked the beginning of the emancipation of music from its dependence on plainsong and pre-existing materials, a process that was to continue through the Renaissance.

In the twelfth century the composers of the School of Notre Dame, Ars Antiqua, mainly Leonin and Perotin, were among the first to develop the basic devices of polyphony (counterpoint). The fourteenth century saw the development of Ars Nova in both France and Italy in which the element of rhythm and harmony were expanded by the acceptance of duple rhythm divisions and the use of thirds and sixths which were then treated as dissonances.

1. *Formal Organization*

   a) All vocal music was organized according to the text, but poetic and syllabic considerations were frequently submerged in favor of rhythmic and harmonic structure.

   b) Composers of sacred polyphony were able to organize sections of text into complete units by means of short repeated rhythmic patterns called rhythmic modes. In the fourteenth century longer sections were combined on the basis of the isorhythmic principle, a repetition of longer and more complicated rhythmic patterns.

   c) Organum continued to be used as an organizational principle. Much use, however, was made of contrary motion and elaborate melismatic settings.

   d) Both monophonic and polyphonic secular forms, like the rondeau, virelai, and ballad were known as *forms fixe*. They were organized on the basis of two musical phrases combined in repeated patterns such as Ab Ab Ab. A number of secular forms also contain a two-line refrain both at the beginning and at the end of each stanza. Those forms which used more than one stanza (strophe) of text to the same musical setting are referred to as strophic.

   e) Secular polyphony made extensive use of canonic imitation as a means of formal organization. The most obvious example of this is the rondellus.

   f) All characteristics of vocal forms were also present in instrumental music.

2. *Melody*

   a) All Gothic melody was vocal in style with a limited range. Melodies from the secular literature and the fourteenth century sacred forms sometimes use more than an octave range.

b) Sacred melody in polyphonic forms, other than plainsong, usually consisted of short phrases in repeated metric patterns. Secular melody both monophonic and polyphonic was often cast in longer phrases and was more lyric in character.

c) There was no attempt to express the meaning of the text in sacred melody, but secular melody often captured the mood of the text.

d) All Gothic melodies, both monophonic and polyphonic, were modal. In the Ars Nova, however, secular songs had a tendency toward intervals that suggested tonality.

e) A common melodic practice of many Ars Nova composers was to move from the leading tone to the sixth tone before proceeding to the tonic. This has been referred to as the Landini cadence, but it is known that the composer Landini did not initiate the practice (ex. 6).

Example 6.

3. *Rhythm.* The problem of rhythm held the attention of all Gothic composers who were concerned with extending the expressiveness of music. To emancipate musical form from the rhythm of text and to gain some agreement of accent between the voices of polyphonic forms, it was necessary to invent some sort of rhythmic system that was independent of poetic rhythm.

a) Composers devised a system by which rhythmic cohesion could be brought to a melody by means of repeated notational patterns called rhythmic modes, a rigidly repeated rhythmic sequence. These patterns were usually separated by a rest before repetition. There were six rhythmic modes,

Example 7. Rhythmic Modes

each identified by number (ex. 7). It was not un-common for each line of a melody in a poly-phonic form to have its own separate rhythmic mode. In the late Gothic (Ars Nova) these modes were extended to longer patterns which formed the basis of isorhythmic compositions. While the principle of rhythmic modes involved a series of exact repetitions, the practice was to introduce a degree of flexibility by varying the patterns.

b) Rhythmic patterns in triple meter were used ex-tensively in sacred music, while secular forms had the privilege of using either triple or duple meter.

c) Subdivision of beats of many kinds appeared in the fourteenth century (Ars Nova) to give the rhythmic flow more freedom and subtlety.

d) Alternate interruption, between the voices, of the rhythmic flow by means of pauses called "hock-ets" was introduced in early polyphony.

4. *Harmony*

a) All Gothic harmony was the result of polyphonic texture. Because there was no systematic chordal structure, there often were sharp and unresolved dissonances between voices. This was partly due to the fact that, in the early Ars Nova, each of the upper voices was related to the lowest voice and not to one another.

b) Because melodies were composed in modes, harmony was also modal, although secular polyphony on occasion tended toward major and minor tonality.

c) The harmonic vocabulary was largely limited to the use of perfect fourths, fifths, and octaves. All other intervals were considered dissonant and were the result of voice leading. In the Ars Nova, thirds and sixths were considered imperfect consonances and were utilized, first in secular forms and then in sacred music.

d) Chromaticisms were generally avoided as expressive devices. Chromatic alterations were introduced in cadences (ex. 8). Chromatics were used to avoid the intervals of the augmented fourth (or diminished fifth) above the root of a chord. Such an interval was called a tritone.

Example 8

e) The practice of *musica ficta*, or false music, enabled performers to introduce flats or sharps into the modes in order to avoid certain intervals, to modify the church modes, or to make intervallic adjustments for the sake of beauty.

5. *Texture*

   a) A polyphonic texture prevailed in almost all Gothic music after 1300. Prior to this secular music was monophonic, while religious music used primitive polyphony in the form of organum in addition to the traditional plainsong.

   b) Three voice polyphony was the most common, but four voices were in frequent use by the end of the fourteenth century.

   c) In three voice polyphony the lower voice contained the cantus firmus and the two upper voices usually moved more rapidly and were often ornamented. In four voice polyphony the tenor contained the cantus firmus and the lowest part was the contratenor. It had the same range as the tenor and frequently crossed the tenor line.

   d) There was no distinction between the texture of sacred and secular polyphony.

   e) There was frequent crossing of voices but the different voices retained their melodic independence.

   f) There was an openness about the sound of early polyphony. This was due to the extensive use of the intervals of the fourth, fifth and octave which lack the harmonic direction of dissonant intervals.

6. *Media and Tone Color*

   a) Vocal performance was still the most important in both sacred and secular music.

   b) Instruments of all kinds, both winds and strings, were sometimes substituted for the cantus firmus in polyphonic forms. No doubt instruments also doubled vocal parts, especially in secular polyphony.

   c) Secular monophony was usually accompanied by instruments. The lute, viol, and harp were the most commonly used for this purpose.

   d) Combinations of instruments were also used for dances and out-of-doors music, but because this

Crucifixion of St. Andrew
This page of a Flemish-Rhenish Antiphonary (circa 1230–40) illustrates the art of illumination practiced in the manuscripts of the
Gothic period. The elaborate "U" depicting the martyrdom of St. Andrew serves as the first letter of the word *Unus* (one) which begins
the text of this antiphon. The notation and the four line staff of the
late Gothic era became the official notational style of the Gregorian
Chant for the Roman Catholic Church. The translation of the Latin
text is: "One of the two who followed the Lord was Andrew, the
brother of Simon Peter, alleluja, e u o u a e. Walking by the sea of
Galilee, Jesus saw Peter and his brother Andrew and said to them,
'Follow me and I will make you fishers of men.' " (St. Louis Art Museum)

kind of music was either improvised or played from memory, we have few actual examples.

e) See Appendix A for description of instruments.

IV. PRACTICE AND PERFORMANCE

The most vital innovation in the practice of Gothic music was the development of a system of notation. After the emergence of a system of lines and spaces in the eleventh century, pitch designation was fairly accurate. The next pressing need was for the notation of duration and stress. By the thirteenth century a kind of notation called mensural (measured) had been developed by Franco of Cologne. This system, with many variations, was to remain in use until c. 1600.

The values of the 14th century mensural system and its modern equivalents can be illustrated by the following example. Black notes used in the 13th and 14th centuries were changed to white notes in the 15th. (ex. 9)

Example 9

Black notes	White notes	Modern equivalents
Maxima	Maxima	Double whole note
Longa	Longa	Whole note
Breve	Breve	Half note
Semi-breve	Semi-breve	Quarter note
Minim	Minim	Eighth note

Unlike modern notation which assumes a division into two of the next smaller degree, mensuration divided the notes into either two or three of the next smaller degree. The divisions of the longa, breve, and semi-breve were named as follows:

Modus perfectum	Modus imperfectum
1 longa= 3 breves	1 longa=2 breves
Tempus perfectum	Tempus imperfectum
1 breve=3 semi-breves	1 breve=2 semi-breves
Prolation major	Prolation minor
1 semi-breve=3 minims	1 semi-breve=2 minims

The division of the longa, breve, and semi-breve into two or three smaller units was indicated by the use of symbols of mensuration as follows:

1. A complete circle indicated *tempus perfectum*, the division of the breve into three semi-breves.

2. A broken circle indicated *tempus imperfectum*, the division of the breve into two semi-breves.

3. The use of a period within the circle indicated *prolation major*, the division of the semi-breve into three minims.

4. The absence of the period indicated *prolation minor*, the division of the semi-breve into two minims.

Schematically this system looked as follows (ex. 10), and corresponds to the indicated modern notation.

Example 10

Tempus perfectum   Prolation major

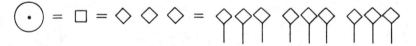

which corresponds to the modern notation of 9/8

Tempus imperfectum   Prolation major

which corresponds to the modern notation of 6/8

Tempus perfectum   Prolation minor

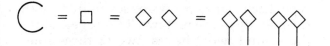

which corresponds to the modern notation of 3/4

$\mathbf{\flat}. = \mathbf{\flat}\ \mathbf{\flat}\ \mathbf{\flat} = \mathbf{\Pi}\ \mathbf{\Pi}\ \mathbf{\Pi}$

Tempus imperfectum   Prolation minor

$C = \Box = \Diamond\Diamond = $ ♀♀ ♀♀

which corresponds to the modern notat on of 2/4

$\mathbf{\flat} = \mathbf{\flat}\ \mathbf{\flat} = \mathbf{\Pi}\ \mathbf{\Pi}$

V. VOCAL COMPOSITIONS

A. Single Movement Forms and Structural Devices.

1. *Secular monophony.*   There are a great many forms
of secular monophony in the music of the Troubadours, Trouvères and Minnesingers such as the
Viralai, Rondeau, and ballade. The Troubadours
were poet-musicians of Southern France and
wrote in Provencal French. They were often
gentlemen of high birth and wealth who could
afford to hire performers to sing their songs.
Trouvères who lived in northern France were the
counterpart of the Troubadours. The songs of
both the Troubadours and Trouvères were mainly
of an amorous character, including love songs to

the Virgin Mary. The Minnesingers were German poet-musicians who were inspired by the Troubadours and Trouvères. However, their songs were usually more narrative and often of a devotional nature. Individual songs were poetic types designated according to subject matter. As far as musical form and organization is concerned there are only four types, each derived from a well-known strophic form that was already in existence: (1) the hymn type; (2) the litany type; (3) the rondel-type; (4) the sequence type.

a) *Canso.*   The canso is an example of the hymn type. Each stanza has six or seven lines with the melody of the first two lines repeated for the second two. The last two or three lines use a different melody. For example, AB AB CD. The German version found in the literature of the Minnesingers is called a *bar.*

Ex: *Be m'an perdut,* Bernart de Ventadorn
TEM, p. 27
Rec. HSE-9100

Ex: *Reis glorios,* Guiraut de Bornelh
HAM, p. 15
Rec. OR-349

Ex: *Nu al'rest,* Walther von der Vogelweide
HAM, p. 18
Rec. OR-350

b) *Rotrouenge.*   The Rotrouenge, an example of the litany type, is a form in which the same melody is used for all the lines of the poem except for the last two. The pattern would be AA AA BB.

Ex: *Pour mon coeur*
HAM, p. 17
Rec. OR-349

c) *Virelai.*   The virelai is a rondel-type form with a refrain and stanza principle. The general musical pattern is: AB CC AB AB. The verse pattern is: AB CD EF AB. The cantiga and lauda also used this pattern.

Ex: *C'est la fin*
  HAM, p. 17
  Rec. OR-349
Ex: *Or la truix*
  MM, p. 11
  Rec. HS-9038
Ex: Cantiga: *Gran dereit'*, Alfonso El Sabio
  TEM, p. 33
  Rec. HSE-9100
Ex: Lauda: *Ogne homo*
  TEM, p. 37
  Rec. HSE-9100

d) *Lai.* The lai is derived from the sequence with one melody to every two lines of poetry. The lai text is usually addressed to the Virgin Mary and is cast in irregular stanzas of from six to sixteen or more lines. The musical form consists of AA BB CC DD. In Germany it was called *leich.* This form was commonly used by the Trouvères and Minnesingers.

Ex: *Ey ich sach in dem trone*
  HMS, vol. 2, p. 32; OM, p. 14
  Rec. RCA, LM-6015–2
Ex: *Espris d'ire* Guillaume le Vinier
  HAM, p. 17
  Rec. OR-350

2. *Notre Dame Organum.* In the thirteenth century a type of polyphony called Notre Dame Organum was developed. It can be considered a form because the principle of organum was restricted to those portions of the chant which were normally sung by a solo voice. Other sections were sung in plainsong. In the organum the tenor sang the plainsong melody in long pedal tones while the upper voices, or voice, sang rhapsodic melodies above it, usually in a metric manner.

Ex: *Hec dies,* attributed to Leoninus
  HAM, p. 27
  Rec. OR-351
Ex: *Alleluya (Nativitas),* Perotin
  MM, p. 22
  Rec. HS-9038

3. *Clausula.*   A polyphonic form which used a melismatic section of a chant as a cantus firmus was called clausula. It was often only a section of an organum. The upper voices move in a quick but measured rhythm against the tenor which moves in even length notes. Because the melisma used only a few syllables, or at the most two or three words, there was no meaningful text to the clausula. All parts vocalized on the vowel sounds of the tenor line.

Ex: *Viderunt omes,* Leonin
      TEM, p. 41
      Rec. HSE-9100
Ex: *Domino,* School of Notre Dame
      HAM, p. 25
      Rec. OR-351
Ex: *Clausula for "Hec Dies"*
      HAM, p. 30
      Rec. OR-351

4. *Polyphonic conductus.*   The conductus is a two, three, or four voice form in which the lowest voice is a freely invented melody on a Latin text. An important feature is the syllabic and rhythmic unity between the voices, giving the effect of chords.

Ex: *De castitatis thalamo*
      MM, p. 31
      Rec. HS-9038
Ex: *Hac in anni janua*
      HAM, p. 41
      Rec. OR-351

5. The motet was the most important vocal form in the thirteenth and fourteenth centuries in both secular and sacred practice. In the earlier motet the lowest voice, the tenor (cantus firmus), is a melody selected from religious (plainsong) or secular sources, in a slow moving rhythmic mode. The two upper voices, the *duplum* (motetus) and the *triplum* respectively, move more quickly each with its own text. At times even the language of each text was different. Due to the fact that the tenor notes were an elongation of the original

cantus firmus, its text was unimportant and it was a common practice to play the tenor line on an instrument. Note that the title of the following examples include the text of each part—tenor, duplum (motetus) and triplum.

Ex: *En Non Diu! Quant voi; Eius in Oriente*
     MM, p. 27
     Rec. HS-9038
Ex: *Ave gloriosa mater-Ave Virgo-Domino*
     TEM, p. 46
     Rec. HSE-9100
Ex: *Aucun-Lonc tans—Annuntiantes,* Petrus de Cruce
     HAM, p. 36
     Rec. OR-351

6. *Isorhythmic motet.* The isorhythmic motet was developed in the fourteenth century and had much the same characteristics as the earlier motet already described. The basic difference was that the rhythmic modes were extended. Isorhythm consists of a rhythmic pattern called *talea* which was repeated a number of times to form the rhythm of an entire melody called *color.* The melody was usually repeated, but its repetition did not always coincide with the beginning of a talea (ex. 11). This led to a much more complex and interesting rhythmic structure. While the isorhythmic principle was first applied to the tenor, in later works it was often present in all voices.

Ex: *O Maria-Virgo-Davidica*
     HMS vol. 2, p. 53
     Rec. RCA, LM-6015-1
Ex: *S'il estoit nulz,* Machaut
     HAM, p. 46
     Rec. OR-437

7. *Rota.* The rota is a medieval round, or canon, in which each singer returns from the end of the melody to the beginning. The phrases of the melody are so composed that each one makes functional harmony with the others. All voices end on a cadence at the finish of any phrase. The rota

Example 11. Tenor from Three-part Isorhythmic Motet

S'il estoit nulz

Machaut

was usually a secular form. In the following example the rota is accompanied by an ostinato bass line in canonic style.

Ex: *Sumer Is Icumen In*
     HAM, p. 44, OM. p. 17
     Rec. OR-437

8. *Ballata.*   The ballata is an Italian secular form that was derived from the virelai. It was written for two or three voices. The ballata has a chain of six line stanzas with a two line refrain before and after each stanza. It has two melodies, one for the refrain and one for each of the two first pairs of lines from each stanza. The third pair of stanza lines use the refrain melody. The pattern is A b b a A.

Ex: *Chi piu le vuol sapers,* Francesco Landini
     MM, p. 40
     Rec. HS-9038
Ex: *Notes pour moi,* Anthonello de Caserta
     TEM, p. 83
     Rec. HSE-9101
Ex: *Io son un pellegrin,* Giovanni da Florentia (Firenze)
     HAM, p. 54
     Rec. OR-437

9. *Caccia.*   The caccia is a hunting song that appeared in the fourteenth century. It often has three voices with the two upper voices moving in strict canonic imitation when three voices were used. The lower part is independent and was probably performed on an instrument. The example in the French version of the form is called *chace.*

Ex: *Si je chante main*
     HMS, vol. 3, p. 13
     Rec. RCA, LM-6016-1
Ex: *Con brachi assai,* Giovanni da Firenze (Florentia)
     TEM, p. 76
     Rec. HSE-9101
Ex: *Tosto che l'alba,* Ghirandello da Firenze
     HAM, p. 55
     Rec. OR-437

10. *Madrigal.*   The fourteenth century madrigal is a lyric poem of two or three-lined stanzas ending with a couplet called a ritornello. The entire text is set for two or three voices. The same music is used for each stanza while the ritornello is set to different music. The upper voice usually contains coloraturas. Instruments could double or substitute for the lower voice parts.

Ex: *Nel mezzo a sei paon,* Giovanni da Cascia
      HMS, vol. 3, p. 19
      Rec. RCA LM-6016–1
Ex: *Non al suo amante,* Jacopo da Bologna
      HAM, p. 52
      Rec. OR-437

B. **Composite Forms**
   1. *Polyphonic mass.*   The polyphonic setting of the sung portions of the Mass is the only music of the Gothic that can be compared to a composite, or multiple form. While the Mass was not a musical form in itself, late Gothic composers began the practice of setting the liturgical texts of the Ordinary of the Mass with some semblance of unity among the various sections. This unity is achieved by means of motives common to each section: by similarity of moods and by similarity of imitative devices.

Ex: Messe de *Nostre Dame,* Machaut
      Kalmus Edition
      Rec. DG, ARC-2533054
Ex: *Agnus Dei,* Machaut
      MM, p. 38, NS, p. 3
      Rec. HS-9038
Ex: *Agnus Dei from* the Mass of Tournai
      TEM, p. 62
      Rec. HSE-9101
Ex: *Et in terra pax,* Johannes Ciconia
      HAM, p. 59
      Rec. OR-438

VI. INSTRUMENTAL COMPOSITIONS

A. Single Movement Forms and Structural Devices.

1. *Dance forms.* Notated instrumental forms were very slow to develop. Most dances during the Gothic were still improvised as they had been earlier. Many medieval dances were cast in pairs—dance and afterdance. There was usually a slow moving section in duple time followed by a faster movement in triple time. Sometimes the section in triple time used the same melody as the first part. Because of the improvisatory nature of these dances, very few have come to us in notation.

Ex: *Four Dances*
HMS, vol. 2, p. 43
Rec. RCA LM-6015-1

Ex: *Lamento di Tristan, with Rotta-Saltarello, Italian Dances*
HAM, p. 63
Rec. OR-438

2. *Conducti, motets,* and even polyphonic sections of the Mass were sometimes played instead of sung. It was a common practice to perform almost all the vocal music on instruments. It must be remembered that many vocal forms were dance melodies.

Ex: *Instrumental Motet, In seculum longum*
TEM p. 54
Rec. HSE-9100

Ex: *Organ paraphase of a Kyrie*
TEM p. 72
Rec. HSE-9101

3. *Estampie.* The dance form most commonly notated in the thirteenth and fourteenth century was the estampie. It is similar to the vocal sequence and consists of a number of sections called *punta* which were repeated. Its form is AA BB CC.

Ex: *Estampie*
MM, p. 33
Rec. HS-9038

Ex: *English Dance*
HAM, p. 43
Rec. OR-351

VII. IMPORTANT COMPOSERS

1. *Leonin* (twelfth century) was the first of the great masters of the Notre Dame School. He is noted for his style of organum. He made extensive use of the syllabic technique, but also foreshadowed the motet principle by lengthening the notes of the plainsong solo as a cantus firmus with a freely moving voice above it. He wrote a cycle of two-part liturgical settings for the church calendar known as the *Magnus Liber Organi*, (The Great Book of Organum).

Ex: *Viderunt omnes*
TEM, p. 41
Rec. HSE-9100

2. *Perotin* (twelfth century) was the successor to Leonin at Notre Dame. He developed organum from the Leonin style by instilling a greater rhythmic accuracy, and making additions and modifications to the *Magnus Liber Organi* attributed to Leonin. His tenor was cast in a series of rhythmic motives that were the predecessors of the rhythmic modes. He expanded two-voice organum to three-voice and four-voice. In addition, his music shows evidence of canonic imitation. His most famous work is *Sederunt Principes*, a quadruple organum.

Ex: *Sederunt principes.*
Universal, ed.
Rec. Van., HM-1

3. *Adam de la Hale* (c. 1240–1287) is one of the best known trouvères. He was both a poet and a composer. Many examples of both his monodic as well as polyphonic compositions survive. Besides many rondeaux and virelais, his musical play *Le jeu de Robin et de Marion* written for the entertainment of the Aragonese court at Naples is still performed.

Ex: *Le jeu de Robin et de Marion*
Em, p. 16
Rec. Turn., 34439

4. *Guillaume de Machaut* (c. 1300–1377), leader of the *Ars Nova*, was the most important composer of the fourteenth century. Born in France, Machaut was more than just a musician. He was a theologian, holding many important ecclesiastical posts, including that of Canon of Rheims. He was also secretary to King John of Bohemia. Among Machaut's musical innovations was the development of a more lyric style of melody and a more suave harmonic texture using thirds and sixths to soften the dissonance of earlier organum. He was the first to compose a complete polyphonic setting of the Ordinary of the Mass with some degree of unity between sections. He wrote in all the forms of his time, both sacred and secular. Among the secular forms, he excelled in the ballade form, bringing to it an ingenuity of imitation, a sonorous harmony and an expressive melody that foreshadowed the Renaissance style.

Ex: *Ten Secular Works*
Guillaume de Machaut, Musikalische Werke
Breitkopf and Hartel, vol. 1 and 3
Rec. DGG, ARC-2533054
Ex: Ballade: *Je puis trop bien*
HAM, p. 48
Rec. Or-437

5. *Francesco Landini* (1325–1397) had the distinction of being the most famous Italian *Ars Nova* composer of the fourteenth century. Blinded in his youth, he managed to become a virtuoso performer on a number of instruments, but was best known as an organist. His skill as a performer and as a composer won him legendary fame in the annals of Italian music. Landini's compositions number over 150 works that have been preserved and include every form of secular music, although the greater portion are two-part and three-part ballatas. His melodies are very expressive and the resulting harmonies are exceedingly smooth and fluid.

Ex: Madrigal: *Amar Si Le Alti Tue Gentil Costumi.*
      HMS, vol. 3, p. 21
      Rec. RCA, LM-6016-1
Ex: Madrigal: *Sy dolce non sono*
      HAM, p. 57
      Rec. OR-437

VIII. OTHER COMPOSERS

A. France
1. *Franco of Cologne* (active 1250–1280)
2. *Pierre de la Croix* (active 1270–1300)
3. *Philippe de Vitry* (1291–1361)

B. Italy
1. *Giovanni da Cascia* (Giovanni da Firenze) (fourteenth century)

IX. IMPORTANT WRITERS ON MUSIC

The Gothic writers still considered music the servant of the Church and their philosophy is mainly a repetition of the earlier authors. However, the major portions of their writings are concerned with practical problems of music, mainly those of rhythm and notation. An especially important subject was the interpretation of rhythmic notation.

The conflict between the more conservative style of the early medieval with that of the fourteenth century "new art" was made articulate by Gothic writers. This controversy is made especially clear in the writings of Jacques de Liege and Jean de Muris. The former was an ardent foe of the new style and a champion of the more traditional manner.

1. *Franco of Cologne* (active 1250–1280) was a medieval theorist and a practical musician. A number of medieval writings were attributed to Franco, but only one work has been definitely authenticated as genuine, *Ars Cantus Mensurabilis.* Franco made a great contribution to notation and in its earlier stages it was called "Franconian." In other areas of musical knowledge his writing is based on the earlier theorists.

2. *Marchetto da Padua* (fourteenth century) was an Italian who wrote an account of the musical practices in Italy. He was also the author of a theoretical treatise, *Pomerium*, which was a justification of duple time in music.

3. *Jacques de Liege* (Jacob of Liege) (c. 1270–c. 1330) was a Belgian and the author of *Speculum Musicae*, written about 1325, which was an attack on the modern musical practices and more particularly an attack on the writings of Jean de Muris. In addition to its controversial nature, the *Speculum* is a compendium of all medieval knowledge about music.

4. *Jean de Muris* (c. 1290–c. 1351) was a writer on music, astronomy and mathematics. He was the author of *Musica Speculativa* and the important treatise, *Ars Novae Musicae*. He championed the cause of the "new style" and also dealt with the interpretation of rhythmic notation.

5. Philippe de Vitry (1291–1361) was the first writer to theorize on the "new art." His treatise, *Ars Nova*, in which he describes the new way of measuring time, gave the name to this period first in France and then in Italy. De Vitry was also known as a composer.

The writings of the foregoing Gothic theorists and historians are not readily available in English. Important excerpts from each can be found in Strunk, *Source Readings in Music History*.

X. MANUSCRIPT SOURCES

There are a large number of collections of manuscripts from the twelfth to the fourteenth centuries. However, the following are generally recognized as the most important:

1. *St. Martial MSS* of the twelfth century is a collection of early organum.

2. Two important collections of motets from the thirteenth century are the *Codex Montpellier* and the *Codex Bamberg*.

3. Fourteenth century Italian secular music is adequately represented by the *Codex Squarcialupi*. It contains works by Francesco Landini and other Italian composers. Forms included are madrigals, ballatas and caccias.

Supplementary Readings

Borroff	pp. 69–143
Cannon-Johnson-Waite	pp. 73–141
Crocker	pp. 81–146
Grout	pp. 64–144
Lang	pp. 122–167
Oxford vol. 2	pp. 220–404
vol. 3	pp. 1–133
Reese-MA	pp. 272–424
Schirmer	ch. 5– 8
Wold-Cykler	ch. 6

Further References

Apel, Willi. *The Notation of Polyphonic Music.* Cambridge: Medieval Academy of America, 1949.

Apel, Willi. *French Secular Music of the Late Fourteenth Century.* Cambridge: Medieval Academy of America, 1950.

Hoppin, Richard H. *Medieval Music.* Ch. VIII-XX. New York: W. W. Norton, 1978.

Hoppin, Richard H. *Anthology of Medieval Music.* New York: W. W. Norton, 1978.

Parrish, Carl. *The Notation of Medieval Music.* New York: W. W. Norton, 1957.

Seay, Albert. *Music in the Medieval World.* Englewood Cliffs: Prentice-Hall, 2nd ed., 1975.

(fol. 142 b)   Die geschicklheit in der musiken und was in seinen ingenien und durch
in erfunden und gepessert worden ist.
(Cod. 3033.)

Sixteenth century woodcut from Der Weisskuniq, depicting a large number
of Renaissance instruments. The number of instruments and the
conditions of performance indicates the great rise in instrumental
performance and the secular nature of court music in this period.
(The Metropolitan Museum of Art, Harris Brisbane Dick Fund)

4
Chronology
of the Renaissance

1400 Guillaume Dufay
(c. 1400–1474)
1420 Johannes Ockeghem
(c. 1420–1496)
1430 Rule of the Medici
family (1430–1495)
1435 Andrea del Verrochio
(1435–1510)
1440 Sandro Botticelli
(1440–1510)
Meistersingers in
Germany (c. 1440)
1444 Donato Bramante
(1444–1514)
1449 Lorenzo de Medici
(1449–1492)
1450 Josquin des Pres
(1450–1521)
Heinrich Isaac
(1450–1517)
1452 Leonardo da Vinci
(1452–1519)
Jacob Obrecht
(1452–1505)
1454 Gutenberg (1398–1468)
invented printing from
moveable type.
1469 Niccoló Machiavelli
(1469–1527)
1471 Albrecht Dürer
(1471–1528)

1473 Nicolaus Copernicus
(1473–1564)
1475 Michelangelo
Buonarroti (1475–1564)
1478 Giorgio Giorgione
(1478–1511)
1480 Mathis Grünewald
(1480–1528)
1483 Raphael Sanzio
(1483–1520)
Martin Luther
(1483–1546)
1490 Adrian Willaert
(c. 1490–1562)
1492 First voyage of
Columbus
1496 Johann Walter
(1496–1570)
1497 Da Gama voyage to
India
1498 Execution of
Savonarola
Ottaviano dei Petrucci
granted a license to
print music
1503 Julius II as Pope
1520 Andrea Gabrieli
(1520–1586)
1525 Giovanni Perluigi
Palestrina (1525–1594)

1532 Orlando di Lasso
      (1532–1590)
1534 Church of England
      separates from the
      Papacy
1540 Founding of the Jesuit
      Society
1543 William Byrd
      (1543–1623)
1545 Council of Trent
1548 El Greco (1548–1614)
1553 Luca Marenzio
      (1553–1599)
1557 Giovanni Gabrieli
      (c. 1557–1612)
1560 Don Carlo Gesualdo
      (1560–1613)
1564 William Shakespeare
      (1564–1616)

4
Renaissance
1400–1600

I. SOCIOCULTURAL INFLUENCES ON MUSIC

In its narrowest sense the term Renaissance means a rebirth of interest in the ideals and forms of classic antiquity as applied to the artistic and cultural life of Italy during the fifteenth and sixteenth centuries. In its wider sense, however, the Renaissance implies a general renewal or rebirth of interest in the dignity and inherent value of man, a trend already indicated in the Gothic period. This attitude is reflected in all the political, religious, and social institutions of the period as well as in the several arts, and is most adequately expressed in the philosophy of humanism. Music partook of the movement only in the broader sense, and found its greatest expression in the works of the Burgundian and Netherland composers until the final half of the sixteenth century. At that time the Italians, educated in the style of the period by the long influx of northern composers, blossomed into a dominating school. With the contributions of these greater schools of composition the Renaissance witnessed the birth of music as an art.

Institutions arising out of humanism and phenomena manifesting its spirit which often exercised a direct influence on music were:

The Roman Catholic Church retained its important position as leading patron of musical production throughout the world even though there was a growing tendency toward secularization. The abolition of tropes and sequences (except for four), as well as the secular canti firmi for the composition of motets and masses by the Council of Trent (1545–1563) was evidence of its deep concern in counteracting the increasing secularization of religious music as well as the influence of Protestantism. The Council's, determination to stem the great wave

of secularization almost resulted in the banning of all polyphonic settings of liturgical music and a return to the exclusive
use of the traditional plainsong.

The Protestant Reformation exercised a greater influence upon
the historical course of religious music specifically, and European music generally, than any other movement initiated in
the Renaissance.

Both the Huguenot and the English Reformations gave rise
to musical expressions appropriate to these movements. It was,
however, the positive inclusion of music by Luther as a vital
and important part of the religious ceremony in the form of
congregational chorale singing that sowed the seeds of a musical renaissance in the German speaking lands. It was this
movement that ultimately led to the supremacy of German and
Austrian music from the middle of the seventeenth to the end
of the nineteenth century.

The rise of wealthy and powerful aristocratic patrons in the
ruling courts of Burgundy in the fifteenth century, the Holy
Roman Empire of Charles the Fifth and Philip the Second, and
the princely courts such as those of Florence, Mantua, and Venice were powerful influences on music. Usually these aristocratic rulers were as influential in religious as in secular affairs,
since they maintained important chapels within the courts and
patronized composers for their religious as well as secular compositions.

The invention of printing in the fifteenth century led to devices for printing music, and the first successful music printing
from moveable type took place at the beginning of the sixteenth century. Ottaviano Petrucci (1466–1539), an Italian, was
the first to print an edition of part music, *The Harmonice Odhe-
caton*, in 1501. Pierre Attaignant, a Frenchman, published the
first collection of French chansons with moveable type in Paris
in 1528. Thomas Tallis (1505–1585) and William Byrd (1542–
1623) published the first English collection of motets in 1575.
By the end of the sixteenth century large numbers of printed
musical works were available, particularly editions of considerable magnitude in the area of secular music such as madrigals, airs, chansons. While the aristocracy and wealthy upper
middle class were the principal purchasers of such works, the
multiplicity of printed copies tended to spread the musical literature of important composers over a wider area than was
heretofore possible through limited manuscript examples.

II. FUNCTION OF MUSIC

The primary purpose of Renaissance sacred music was liturgical. It served both the traditional Roman Catholic service and the newly founded Protestant church, particularly the Lutheran sect. The Roman Catholic church had the more highly organized musical service. The greater body of religious music will therefore be found in Catholicism during this period.

Secular music provided a highly cultivated group of amateur performers among the aristocracy and upper middle class with appropriate music for singing and playing. The cultivated lady and gentleman of the Renaissance were capable performers in either singing or playing, if not in both.

During the last half of the sixteenth century, instrumental music was employed to provide a select society with entertainment performed by professional and skilled amateur players. These performances took place in the salons of the nobility and the homes of wealthy burghers.

Dances were written by serious composers in response to the demand for formal court functions.

Popular songs and dances of folk-like character supplied the great mass of people with music that was appropriate to festivals and other social occasions, both religious and secular.

III. CHARACTERISTICS OF STYLE

All music of the Renaissance was based on polyphonic practices. Consequently there was a unity of style in both secular and religious music. This unity applied to vocal and instrumental compositions as well. It may be said that the Renaissance represents the last period of musical history in which there is such unity of style in all forms and in all media.

    1. *Formal organization.* Except in the case of small poetic and dance forms of a secular nature, Renaissance music shows a unity of formal organization.

        a) The technique of employing a cantus firmus derived primarily from plainsong literature or from folk song sources gave rise to works which were basically polyphonic elaborations of a pre-existing melodic idea. The cantus firmus was generally placed in the tenor voice which in the early Renaissance was the lowest pitched voice.

b) The imitative use of melodic material became an increasingly important organizational device. In order to give variety to such practice, various forms of imitation were used, such as:

(1) *Canonic imitation.* By this device all voices use the same melodic material, but each voice begins at a different time. Canonic imitations vary from strict to free imitation of the original melodic ideas, and can be constructed so that the pitches of each voice are at the same or at different intervals (ex. 12).

Example 12. Canon in Three Voices at the Unison

Illumina oculos meos   Palestrina

(2) *Imitation by inversion.* This is one of changing the direction of the original melodic intervals so that the ascending interval in the original melody becomes a descending one in the inverted version and vice versa. In the following example voice two is in canonic

imitation of voice one at the unison. Voices three and four are in canonic imitation of voices one and two but inverted (ex. 13).

xample 13. Canon in Inversion   Scheidt

(3) *Imitation by retrogression.* In this case the original melodic idea is repeated note for note in the reverse order. This device is also called *crab* or *cancrizans imitation.* It can also be used in combination with imitation by inversion (ex. 14).

In the following example the scheme of imitation is as follows:

Voice 1: A to B, D to C.
Voice 2: C to D, B to A.
Voice 3: E to F, F to E.

Ma fin est mon commencement

Example 14. Imitation by Retrogression   Guillaume de Machaut

(4) *Imitation by augmentation.* Here the original melodic idea voice one, is repeated in voice two, but in notes of twice the time value of the original (ex. 15).

(5) *Imitation by diminution.* The original melodic idea voice one, appears in voice two in note values one-half the time value of the original (ex. 16).

Example 15. Imitation by Augmentation

Example 16. Imitation by Diminution

c) The technique of using pre-existing material even went so far as to employ complete short form polyphonic works in larger works. (See parody Mass under Vocal Compositions in this chapter.)

d) Formal organization was episodic (see Glossary) in the case of most of the strictly polyphonic works, both secular and religious. Compositions consisted of a number of sections, each treating its thematic material individually and exhaustively. In the highly developed polyphonic forms such as the motet and Mass there was rarely any repetition of a previously used musical section or text. Each section constituted the complete treatment of a line of text.

e) Secular poetic song forms were often character-ized by a formal organization which used a prin-cipal refrain in contrast to other musical phrases.

f) With the exception of the Mass, all works were in single rather than multiple movements.

g) Dance forms were based on folk idioms and gen-erally consisted of an application of the principle of repetition and contrast.

2. *Melody*

a) Melody is the determining factor in Renaissance music. Consequently, all musical expression is the result of melodic treatment. Harmony and rhythm cannot be analyzed apart from melodic structure.

b) Melodies are modal in structure.

c) Melody is distinctly vocal in style and limited to a range which rarely exceeds the octave. Wide skips are avoided, and most melodic movement is diatonic or restricted to the tones of the scale being used. Chromaticism, the use of other than the seven natural tones of the modal scale (flatted or sharped tones) is rare in the early works of the Renaissance but frequently found in the secular music of the late Renaissance. (See musica ficta page 77).

d) Melodic form is determined by textual rather than musical considerations.

3. *Rhythm*

a) Rhythm is free from strict metrical phrasing. However, many rhythmic clichés are used, in-cluding syncopation.

b) The restrictive isorhythmic devices of the Gothic period disappear in the fifteenth century al-though there are some examples of this method of rhythmic organization to be found among the early Renaissance composers.

c) Rhythmic phrases are generally long, free from metrical accent, and often overlap between the voices (ex. 17).

Example 17. *Zwischen perg und tieffemtal*   Heinrich Isaac

d) Rhythms are often complex as a result of the problems of polyphonic writing and the metric intricacies of the texts (ex. 19).

e) Composers in the Renaissance delighted in writing musical puzzles based upon the use of a variety of clefs and mensural signatures, leaving the performer to find the key to their solution. Puzzles varied from rather simple to very intricate ones, often with additional instructions for their solution (ex. 18). Ex. 18 is the original notation of a puzzle canon by Des Prez. Ex. 19 is the modern realization of Ex. 18.

Example 18. *Agnus Dei*   Josquin Des Pres

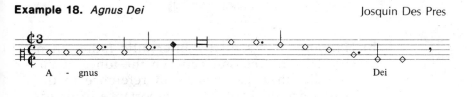

A - gnus   Dei

EXample 19

Josquin Des Pre

4. *Harmony*

    a) Harmony is a result of simultaneous sounding of more or less independent lines of melody, and not a result of functional harmonic patterns. The composer has no preconceived notion of the chordal background which functions within a tonal system, and therefore does not feel compelled to use certain tones for each of the melodic parts at any one place. Such a predetermined function of harmony slowly makes its appearance at final cadences, however, and begins to point the way to the dominance of harmonic considerations over melodic voice leading. Example 20 is an authentic cadence, one of a large variety such as the plagal, Landini, Lydian, and Phrygian cadences.

Example 20

    b) Harmony is essentially intervallic rather than chordal. The relation between the tones of the melodic lines, particularly in reference to the cantus firmus, is of prime importance in determining the melodic progression and the treatment of dissonance. These relationships are intervallic rather than chordal.

c) Harmony is a consequence rather than a determinant in musical structure. Since rules and conventions governing voice leading are determined by treatment of intervals between voices, that which strikes the ear as harmonic progression is a result of voice relationships rather than the basis for harmonic construction.

5. *Texture*

a) The texture of Renaissance music is predominately polyphonic. Even in the late Renaissance where a tendency toward homophonic treatment is found in secular songs, the accompanying voices are treated more or less as independent melodies rather than as mere chordal accompaniments.

b) In the sixteenth century there are works in which harmonic texture is used as a contrast to the predominating polyphonic texture. These passages are designated as being in *familiar style* (ex. 21), suggesting that this might have been a practice generally used in folk or popular music.

Example 21. Familiar Style   Josquin Des Pres

c) Due to the independence of voice leading, there is much overlapping of rhythmic, melodic, and harmonic cadences.

6. *Media and tone color*

a) The human voice, both in solo and ensemble, was the generally accepted medium of performance for all Renaissance music. Voice ranges, cantus or superius (soprano), altus, tenor, and bassus became the framework for all vocal compositions.

b) Instruments of all kinds were used to reinforce the voice in both sacred and secular music.

c) Instruments began to be used independently in the sixteenth century, particularly the organ and stringed keyboard instruments, the harpsichord and clavichord.

d) Ensembles of string or wind instruments were often used towards the end of the Renaissance. A consistency of tonal coloring was achieved by groups of instruments of a kind, for example, a group of viols or recorders in different ranges. In England this was called a *full* consort. A variety of tonal coloring was secured by using different kinds of instruments together. This was often referred to as a *broken* consort.

e) The lute, which held a place of importance parallel to the piano in the nineteenth century was the most popular single instrument.

f) See Appendix A for description of instruments.

IV. PRACTICE AND PERFORMANCE

Use of specific types of voices and instruments was left to the judgment of the performers, availability, and range demands of the particular voice parts.

Notation indicated only relative rather than absolute or fixed pitch. Accommodation to vocal and instrumental range determined the actual pitch of any given performance.

Clefs to designate the pitch names and relationships of the notes on the staff were used before the Renaissance. By the sixteenth century, however, regular use was made of the C and F clefs to designate the ranges corresponding to our modern soprano, alto, tenor, and bass voices. The G or treble clef began to displace the soprano C clef in the latter part of the sixteenth century.

No interpretive directions as to tempi, dynamics, or phrasing are to be found in the music of the period until the time of Giovanni Gabrieli.

Dependence on the common practice of specific periods and schools led to lack of notational directions in many cases. The use of sharps or flats written above the notes in modern editions indicates the editor's decision that these were included in performance, but not in notation, a practice known as *musica ficta,* as described in the chapter on Gothic music.

Another term which may have been applied to devices of performance was called *musica reservata.* There is little agreement as to its meaning but several of its interpretations suggest that performance was often regulated by commonly understood practices of improvisation for which no detailed directions were necessary at that time.

The 15th century French practice of using a succession of first inversion triads or sixth-chords was known as *fauxbourdon.* The composer duplicated a soprano melody at the sixth below, and a singer extemporized a fourth below the soprano. The result was a series of sixth-chords which marked the beginning of the use of the third and the full triad as a basic harmonic element (ex. 22).

Example 22. (Fauxbourdon)

A practice which was particularly cultivated in Venice, due in part to the architectural structure of St. Mark's Cathedral, was that of *polychoral* performance. The large choral compositions of the Venetian School of the late Renaissance lent themselves to a division of the choral forces into two or more groups which were placed in different parts of the church structure. The success of this practice gave rise to many compositions for divided choral groups, and their placement in various parts of the church was widely adopted by choir directors throughout Europe. When two choral groups merely alternate without joining forces it is called *antiphonal.*

V. VOCAL COMPOSITIONS

A. Single Movement Forms and Structural Devices.
1. *Motet.* Various types of motets were written in the fifteenth and sixteenth centuries. The isorhythmic motet (see the chapter on Gothic music)

continued in use until the middle of the fifteenth century.

Ex: Isorhythmic motet: *Veni Sancte Spiritus,* Dunstable
TEM, p. 87
Rec. HSE-9101

Many new methods of composition were applied to motet writing, but the cantus firmus in long held notes continued in use through the last half of the fifteenth century. However, the principal motet form of the Renaissance was that developed by Josquin Des Prez which consisted generally of a work in four to six voices with imitative treatment. The motet was usually made up of a number of sections, nonrepetitive, each of which treated a portion of the text. The texts were always in Latin and taken either from the liturgy of the Mass or from the Bible. The individual voices were most likely to overlap from one section to another, consequently well defined harmonic cadences were generally lacking except at such marked divisions as changes in meter, or at the final cadence.

Ex: *Parce, Domine,* Obrecht
MM, p. 55
Rec. HS-9038
Ex: *Tu pauperum refugium,* Des Prez
HAM, p. 92
Rec. Plei-252
Ex: *Tristis est anima mea,* Lassus
MM, p. 78
Rec. HS-9039
Ex: *Magnificat octavi toni,* C. Morales
TEM, p. 108
Rec. HSE-9101
Ex: Polychoral motet: *Laudate Dominum,* Hassler
TEM, p. 138
Rec. HSE-9101
Ex: *Sicut cervus,* Palestrina
HAM, p. 153
Rec. Plei-255

2. *Hymn.* These were polyphonic strophic settings of Latin poetic religious texts in which each verse of text was repeated to the same setting. The upper voice was generally predominately melodic.

Ex: *Ave maris stella,* Dufay
     SS, p. 63
     Rec. Tel, S-9439
Ex: *Beata de Genetrix,* Damett
     HAM, p. 69
     Rec. OR-438

3. *Chorale.* The hymn tunes and their four part chordal settings which were adopted for use in the German Protestant church by Luther and his musical collaborators are generally called chorales, German Protestant Chorales, or Lutheran Chorales. The texts were in the vernacular language, generally German. The tunes were often taken from older Latin hymns or specifically composed to appropriate texts, but a rich source was the secular folk melody. These chorales in their simple form are usually binary with the first section repeated. The melodies which are predominantly in the upper voice are slow moving, and the cadences very marked and strong.

Ex: *Komm, Gott Schoepfer, Heiliger Geist,* Walter
     TEM, p. 120
     Rec. HSE-9101
Ex: *Aus tiefer Not,* Walter
     HAM, p. 115
     Rec. Plei-253

4. *Psalm settings.* These were the hymns of the French Protestant movement, the Huguenots. They were simple settings, generally in chordal style, with some free polyphonic treatment. The dominant melody, as in the German Chorale, is in the upper voice. Rhythmically, these psalm settings were somewhat more lively than the German Chorales, and the texts were, of course, in French.

Ex: *Mon Dieu me paist,* Goudimel
TEM, p. 126
Rec. HSE-9101

Ex: *Two Settings of Psalm 35,* Goudimel and Claude le Jeune
HAM, p. 135
Rec. Plei-254

> 5. *Anthem.*   Anthems were the motets of the Anglican Church. They follow the structure of the Renaissance motet in the settings of the English texts. Two types were used, the *full* anthem which is like the traditional four part hymn, and the *verse* anthem which presents an innovation in the motet style in the late sixteenth century. In the verse anthem, soloists and chorus with instrumental accompaniments were used with an alternation between solo and choral sections.

Ex: Verse Anthem: *This is the Record of John,* Gibbons
HAM, p. 195
Rec. Plei-256

Ex: Anthem: *Heare the voyce and prayer of thy servants,* Tallis
TEM, p. 133
Rec. HSE-9101

Ex: Verse Anthem: *Christ rising again,* Byrd
HAM, p. 165
Rec. Plei-255

Ex: Anthem: *When David heard,* Tomkins
HAM, p. 191
Rec. Plei-256

> 6. *Frottola.*   This is a derivation from a dance form and represents the most important of the strophic forms developed in the late fifteenth and early sixteenth centuries in northern Italy. It is a kind of sophisticated folk song, generally chordal in structure, and characterized by variously arranged patterns of two contrasting musical ideas. One pattern commonly used is abaabab. The frottola was written in three or four voices. However, the lower voices were probably played on instruments, as well as sung.

Ex: *O mia cieca e dura sorte,* Cara
TEM, p. 97 and 99
Rec. HSE-9101

Ex: *Non vol aqua,* Tromboncini
HAM, p. 97
Rec. Plei-252

    7. *Madrigal.* The madrigal is the most highly developed of all the Renaissance secular vocal forms. Originating in Italy, composers of all schools set the lyrics of Italian poets to music in this form and it flourished in the latter half of the sixteenth century. Three stages of development are discernible. The chordal style represented by Arcadelt and Verdelot, the more highly developed imitative polyphonic style often in five voices represented by Palestrina, di Lassus and de Rore, and the highly dramatic and expressive madrigals of the late Renaissance: Monteverdi, Marenzio, and Gesualdo. The madrigal became very popular in England where an independent school of composers in a short time rivaled the Italians in quantity and quality of its production in the settings of English lyric poems. It was a through-composed (non-repetitive) polyphonic type of composition in contrast to the verse-refrain madrigal of the fourteenth century. It varied from a chordal type similar to the frottola to imitative polyphonic examples. In some respects the madrigal was a secular counterpart of the sacred motet, as were all these highly developed secular forms.

    There were also madrigals of a serious nature, though most of them were settings of lyrics which spoke of love—often unrequited love. Instances of the deliberate use of musically expressive devices to fit the text are not infrequent. These so-called *madrigalisms* consisted of textual interruptions by rests, chromaticisms, naive attempts to make the music illustrate the text by means of rhythmic and melodic tone painting. Frequent changes of rhythm are often used. Madrigals were written in three to five voices. Toward the end of the sixteenth century there was a distinct tendency to write madrigals in homophonic style with a predominating principal, or solo voice. The *ballet* madrigal, most common in England, was a strophic form with a "fa-la" refrain.

Ex: *S'io parto, i'moro,* Marenzio
MM, p. 100
Rec. HS-9039

Ex: *Thyrsis, sleepest thou?* Bennet
MM, p. 109
Rec. HS-9039

Ex: *Io pur respiro,* Gesualdo
HAM, p. 182
Rec. Plei-256

Ex: *Voi ve n'andat' al cielo,* Arcadelt
HAM, p. 141
Rec. Plei-254

Ex: *Hark, all ye lovely saints,* Weelkes
HAM, p. 193
Rec. Plei-256

8. *French chanson.* This term embraced the whole of the polyphonic secular writing to French texts of the fifteenth and sixteenth centuries. The fifteenth century chansons were generally in the repetitive fixed forms of the rondeau, or virelai. In the sixteenth century the fixed forms were abandoned and there is a truly polyphonic treatment in imitative style. Like the motet, the chanson is usually in sections and is constructed in a through-composed manner. The sections, however, are short and marked with simultaneous cadences in all voices. There is also a tendency to homophonic texture. Rhythms are faster and lighter than in the motet. Most of the sixteenth century chansons were in four voices and the top voice usually carried the principal melodic burden.

Ex: *Adieu m'amour,* Binchois
MM, p. 48
Rec. HS-9038

Ex: *Pour ung plaisir,* Crequillon
MM, p. 64
Rec. HS-9038

Ex: *l'Alouette,* Jannequin
HAM, p. 109
Rec. Plei-253

9. *Polyphonic lied.*   This is the German counterpart of the Italian and English madrigal and the French chanson. Almost without exception these were polyphonic settings of folk song melodies. In some instances these settings were almost strictly chordal. However, an imitative polyphonic treatment developed in the last half of the fifteenth and first half of the sixteenth centuries.

Ex: *Oho, so geb' der Mann ein'n Pfenning,* Senfl
TEM, p. 177
Rec. HSE-9102

Ex: *Zwischen Berg und Tiefem Tal,* Isaac
HAM, p. 91
Rec. Plei-252

10. *Quodlibet.*   The quodlibets were a type of polyphonic composition in which several popular or folk songs of the day were combined to make a humorous poly-textual unit.

Ex: *Fricaseé,* anon.
TEM, p. 170
Rec. HSE-9102

Ex: *Veni sancte spiritus, Veni creator spiritus,* Finck
HAM, p. 84
Rec. Plei-251

11. *Ayre.*   This was a late development in England and was a purely homophonic song in strophic style. The accompanying voices were usually played on the lute, though they could be either sung or played. Its most distinguishing characteristic was its strophic form.

Ex: *My Thoughts Are Winged with Hope,* Dowland
TEM, p. 189
Rec. HSE-9102

Ex: *Stay, cruel, stay,* Danyel
HAM, p. 184
Rec. Plei-256

12. *Other secular forms.*   A large body of traditional strophic forms such as the villancico, virelai, ballata, or rondeau, were employed both monodically and polyphonically in the fifteenth century.

They retained their fixed forms of the earlier period (see the chapter on Gothic music) though they were often more simple in formal and rhythmic structure. The principal melody was placed in the uppermost part, and settings were generally chordal with little imitation. The formal musical structure of these songs was determined by their strict poetic forms.

Ex: Villancico: *Soy contento y vis servido,* Encina
      TEM, p. 94
      Rec. HSE-9101

Ex: Meistersinger Melody: *Gesangweise,* Hans Sachs
      TEM p. 105
      Rec. HSE-9101

Ex: Virelai; *Ma bouch rit,* Ockeghem
      HAM, p. 79
      Rec. Plei-251

Ex: Rondeau; *De plus en plus,* Binchois
      HAM, p. 74
      Rec. Plei-251

B. **Composite Forms.**

  1. *Mass.* The Mass is the only important composite form used in the Renaissance, and as such is made up of a series of movements each of which is similar in structure and form to the motet. Each of these movements provides a musical setting for one of the five principal parts of the Ordinary of the Roman Catholic Mass: Kyrie, Gloria, Credo, Sanctus, and Agnus Dei. As in the motet, the composer employed secular, sacred, and freely invented cantus firmi, as well as imitative techniques for organizational purposes.

  The largest proportion of masses were those based on pre-existing material; plainsong, folk song, motets, or polyphonic secular works.

  One type often called the *plainsong* Mass, constructed on appropriate and different canti firmi for each of the parts of the Mass (the Kyrie on a plainsong Kyrie, the Gloria on a plainsong Gloria, etc.) continued to be used as in the single Mass composed by Guillaume de Machaut. (See chapter on Gothic music.)

The *cantus firmus* Mass using a single cantus firmus which appeared in each of the several parts of the composition was the most frequently composed style in the Renaissance. This cantus firmus might consist of an entire pre-existing melodic idea or only a portion of it. It might be quoted literally or paraphrased in all movements while reserved to the tenor voice, or it might be paraphrased throughout each movement and appear in all voices imitatively.

Ex: Cantus firmus Mass on a secular tune:
      Missa, L'Homme arme, Kyrie I and II, la Rue
      HAM, p. 95
      Rec. Plei-252
Ex: Cantus firmus Mass on a secular tune:
      Missa, Se la face ay pale, Kyrie I, Dufay
      MM, p. 43
      Rec. HS-9038
Ex: Cantus firmus Mass on a plainsong:
      Missa Pange Lingua, Des Prez
      Das Chorwerk, vol. 1, Möseler Verlag
      Rec. MCA-2507

A special type of Mass developed in the sixteenth century was called the *parody Mass.* This form is an even more complex extension of the technique of basing the parts, as well as the whole, on a preexisting condition. In the case of the parody Mass, a polyphonic motet was used as a basis for imitative development. The motet could be used in its entirety or in fragments throughout the several movements of the Mass. A motet was usually selected from among the composer's own works as the basis for a parody Mass.

Ex: Parody Mass: *Missa Veni sponsa Christi, Agnus Dei,* Palestrina
      MM, p. 86
      Rec. HS-9039

Names given to the preceding types of masses
were taken from the motets or canti firmi from
which they were derived, i.e., *Missa Pange Lingua.*
Relatively few masses were composed entirely on
original material freely invented.

Ex: *Missa Papae Marcelli,* Palestrina
Eulenberg Ed.
Rec. DDG ARC-198182

VI. INSTRUMENTAL COMPOSITIONS

A. **Single Movement Forms and Structural Devices**
   While instruments were popularly used in the performance of music during the Renaissance, there was
   actually no real independent instrumental writing
   until very late in the sixteenth century. Consequently, there are very few purely instrumental forms
   that are unrelated to the polyphonic style of vocal
   music. Except for dance music, the greatest amount
   of instrumental performance was either in duplication of, or substitution for, actual voice parts in polyphonic vocal works. Some works written specifically
   for instruments in the sixteenth century displayed a
   consideration for the special technical capabilities of
   those instruments then in use.

   1. *Ricercar.*   The ricercar is the instrumental equiv-
      alent of the vocal motet. Like the motet, it was
      constructed in several sections. Each section had
      a different musical theme which was treated im-
      itatively and contrapuntally. The ricercar written
      for instrumental ensemble was closely patterned
      after the vocal motet with numerous sections and
      melodic themes. The fact that many such works
      were published with instructions "to be sung and
      played" indicated their affinity to vocal forms.
      The organ ricercar, on the other hand, while ba-
      sically the same construction, tended to use fewer
      themes and sections, and therefore the treatment
      of the themes was much more elaborate and
      longer. Contrapuntal imitation was the principal
      element of form.

There was also a type of non-imitative ricercar for the lute, organ, and instrumental ensemble. These were unlike the imitative ricercar and motet and seem to have been written more for study purposes since they tend to exploit the technical possibilities of the instruments.

Ex: *Ricercar No. 7,* Willaert
 HMS, vol. 4, p. 51
 Rec. RCA, LM-6029–1
Ex: *Ricercar arioso,* Andrea Gabrieli
 HMS, vol. 4, p. 61
 Rec. RCA, LM-6029–1
Ex: *Ricercar,* Cavazzoni
 HAM, p. 121
 Rec. Plei-253

 2. *Canzona.* The instrumental canzona which appeared in the sixteenth century was at first a mere instrumental arrangement, or transcription, of the vocal chanson. It was written for either lute or keyboard performance. Subsequently, composers wrote original instrumental works in the style of the vocal chanson. Keyboard canzonas as well as canzonas for instrumental ensembles varied from the conventional imitation of the sectional character of the vocal chansons (see Chanson under Vocal Compositions) to the spectacular poly-choral type of the Venetian school, composition in which alternating sections in varying rhythms and textures were performed by alternating choirs of instruments.

Ex: Canzona francese: *deta Pour ung plaisir,* Gabrieli
 MM, p. 64
 Rec. HS-9038
Ex: *Canzona,* Maschera
 HAM, p. 201
 Rec. Plei-256

 3. *Cantus firmus form.* The *In Nomine* compositions were exclusively English in usage. They were instrumental works based on a cantus firmus originally taken from a mass by Tavener.

Ex: *In Nomine,* Gibbons
 TEM, p. 202
 Rec. HSE-9102

4. *Toccata.*   A form of keyboard composition deriving its name from the Italian *toccar,* to touch. The toccata exploited a rather improvisatory style of writing in which florid homophonic scale and chord passages were combined with imitative sections. Most characteristic of the toccata is its adherence to keyboard idiom and its unchanging tempo.

Ex: *Toccata Quinta, Seconda Tuona,* Merulo
TEM, p. 152
Rec. HSE-9102
Ex: *Toccata,* Merulo
HAM, p. 168
Rec. Plei-255

5. *Fantasia.*   This was a title of rather ambiguous nature, given to instrumental compositions in the sixteenth century. It was often used to indicate compositions in various forms. The name probably referred to the improvisatory nature of such works as the ricercar-like composition in very free form, but in strict contrapuntal style. The title was used to cover a wide variety of compositions published at the very end of the sixteenth century, many of which were free ricercars and chansons in tablature form.

Ex: *Three part Fantasia, No. 3,* Gibbons
HMS, vol. 4, p. 53
Rec. RCA, LM-6029-1
Ex: *Fantasia in Echo,* Sweelinck
HAM, p. 209
Rec. Plei-256

6. *Prelude.*   Another name which was applied very loosely to a variety of compositions which originally served to introduce a liturgical ceremony. In the fifteenth and sixteenth centuries it was used to designate a free type of idiomatic keyboard music, often very short and in a homophonic style. It usually exploited the technique of the keyboard. Unlike the canzona or ricercar, the prelude does not derive from any vocal form, but represents the first type of truly instrumental

music. The English virginal composers often used the term to describe a virtuoso type of keyboard composition.

Ex: *Praeludium*, Bull
HAM, p. 205
Rec. Plei-256

7. *Variation.* The variation is a form that is basically repetitive. It uses a newly invented, or a preexisting, melodic idea, which is presented in a succession of altered versions. The problem confronting the composer is to maintain the relationship between the successive versions and at the same time provide interest through the alterations. In the sixteenth century the beginnings of this form employed the device of altering the contrapuntal texture by the use of imitative figures, or by embellishing the melody by ornamentation and rapid scale passages.

Variations for lute and keyboard in the early sixteenth century Spanish school illustrates the contrapuntal type, while the keyboard variation of the English school is representative of the figured variation.

Ex: *Loth to depart*, Farnaby
MM, p. 115
Rec. HS-9039
Ex: *Goe from my window*, Munday
HAM, p. 204
Rec. Plei-256
Ex: *Diferencias sobra O gloriosa domina*, Luis de Narvaez
HAM, p. 130
Rec. Plei-254

8. *Dance forms.* There are only a few instrumental dances in polyphonic style to be found in the fifteenth century. Those which are known come from the *Muenchener Liederbuch* and the *Glogauer Liederbuch*, the two large collections of dances and songs dating from c. 1460. The sixteenth century, however, is a period dominated by dance forms and is often called "the century of the dance."

Sixteenth century dances are characteristically paired like the *pavane-galliard* and the *passamezzo-saltarello*. In these cases the first dance of the pair is in slow duple meter, followed by the second in a fast triple meter. In many instances the second dance is merely a rhythmically changed version of the first dance. This was particularly true of the German *Tanz* and *Nachtanz*, or *Tanz* and *Proportz*. In this case the second dance assumes the characteristics of a variation on the first. The structural form of the dance is basically binary.

Ex: *Pavana for the virginal,* John Bull
     TEM, p. 161
     Rec. HSE-9102
Ex: *Passamezzo d'Italie,* anon.
     TEM, p. 194
     Rec. HSE-9102
Ex: *Der Prinzen-Tanz; Proportz,* anon.
     MM, p. 74
     Rec. HS-9038
Ex: *Paduan and Intrada,* Puerl
     HMS, vol. 4, p. 51
     Rec. RCA, LM-6029-1

B. **Composite Forms.**
   The pairing of two dances and the actual grouping of several dances at the end of the sixteenth century indicated the desire to write instrumental works of a larger scope. These are among the first examples of the instrumental suite which was to become a standard form in the Baroque period.

Ex: *Three Dances,* Gervaise
     HAM, p. 148
     Rec. Plei-254

VII. IMPORTANT COMPOSERS

Because of the large number of composers found in the Renaissance, it is necessary to explain the basis upon which the following selection was made. The composers listed under this head represent important innovators in style and technical devices of composition. Moreover, they are often the leaders of a

Primavera (Allegory of spring)—Botticelli (c. 1460). Botticelli spent the greatest part of his creative life under the patronage of the Medicis of Florence. *Primavera* is a product of this period, and reflects his dependence on Grecian subject matter which served to delight the city rulers in their cult of neo-paganism and worship of beauty. Like the musician, the painter lacked Grecian models, but unlike the composer he could draw upon Grecian subject matter and depict in the central figures of this work the three graces of Greek mythology. In technique, Botticelli's matery of line rather than color parallels the polyphonic writing of his contemporaries, Dufay, Okeghem, and des Prez. (Courtesy Uffizi Gallery, Florence, Art Reference Bureau, Inc.)

particular school of composition or of a national group. During this period there were two distinctive schools, the Burgundian and the Flemish, the latter sometimes referred to as the Netherland School. The Burgundian School flourished during the first half of the fifteenth century and included Dufay and Binchois. The Flemish School, from about 1450 to 1600, included such composers as Ockeghem, Obrecht, Josquin Des Prez and many others who were to spread the Flemish innovations to various sections of Europe. While their works represent a high quality of Renaissance music their inclusion does not mean that their works were always superior to some composers who have been omitted from this list. There was also great activity in such countries as England, Spain, Germany and centers like Rome and Venice. These were also referred to as *schools*.

1. *John Dunstable* (c. 1370–1453) was an English composer and early master of counterpoint. He is especially noted for his interesting contrapuntal lines composed around the plainsong melody. He was an important influence on the composers of the Burgundian school.

Ex: *O rosa bella*
      HAM, p. 65
      Rec. Plei-251
Ex: Motet: *Sancta Maria*
      HAM, p. 66
      Rec. Plei-251

2. *Guillaume Dufay* (c. 1400–1474) is considered the master of the Burgundian school. His works show a strong preference for the upper voices, both melodically and rhythmically. The use of instruments is often indicated. He wrote in all the religious and secular forms of his time.

Ex: *Ave Regina Coelorum*
      HMS, vol. 3, p. 42
      Rec. RCA, LM-6016-2

3. *Gilles Binchois* (c. 1400–1460) was also one of the Burgundian group, and is best known for the excellence of his secular works, especially the chanson. Like others of his time, the stylistic features were essentially the same in both sacred and secular polyphony.

Ex: *Filles a marier*
     HMS, vol. 3, p. 45
     Rec. RCA, LM-6016-2

4. *Johannes Ockeghem* (1430–1495) was a pupil of Dufay
   and the leader of the Flemish school. His development of devices of imitation served as models for
   those who later perfected the *a cappella* style. He was
   also one of the first to write in four part polyphony.

Ex: Chanson: *Fors seulement*
     Collected Works, Breitkopf and Härtel
     Rec. M.H.-1003A
Ex: Mass: *Fors seulement*
     Collected Works, Breitkopf and Härtel
     Rec. M.H.-1003a
Ex: Sanctus from the *Missa Prolationum*
     MM, p. 51
     Rec. HS-9038
Ex: Virelai: *Ma maîtresse*
     HAM, p. 78
     Rec. Plei-251

5. *Josquin Des Prez* (c. 1450–1521) of the Flemish School,
   was one of the greatest composers of all time, and the
   first to make music a really expressive art. He was fortunate to have the majority of his compositions published during his lifetime. Because of this fact,
   coupled with his genius, he was well-known and had
   considerable influence on other composers. In general, his sacred works are contrapuntal in style, but
   many of the secular works tend toward homophonic
   practices, perhaps due to the influence of the Italian
   frottola.

Ex: Frottola: *El Grillo*
     HMS, vol. 3, p. 55
     Rec. RCA, LM-6016-2
Ex: Chanson: *Faulte d'argent*
     HAM, p. 93
     Rec. Plei-252
Ex: Motet: *Tribulatio et angustia*
     HMS, vol. 3, p. 58
     Rec. RCA LM-6016-2
Ex: Motet: *Ave Maria*
     MM, p. 58
     Rec. HS-9038

6. *Heinrich Isaac* (c. 1450–1517). While Isaac was a Flemish composer, he was at one time court composer to Maximilian in Vienna, bringing the Flemish style to Austria. While he wrote many masses and motets, it was his polyphonic settings of choral melodies that make his music memorable.

Ex: *Missa Carminum*
Das Chorwerk, vol. 7, Möseler Verlag
Rec. None, 71084

Ex: Polyphonic Lied: *Innsbruck ich muss dich lassen*
HMS, vol. 3, p. 75
Rec. RCA, LM-6016–1

7. *Jacob Obrecht* (1452–1505) was born in the Netherlands. He carried on the innovations of Okeghem, but added an expressive quality that followed the meaning of the texts. He also used four voices, the lower one becoming more a true bass line, leading to the frequent employment of the authentic cadence. He was also one of the first composers to have a large number of his works published during his lifetime.

Ex: Motet: *Si oblitus fuero*
HMS, vol. 3, p. 51
Rec. RCA, LM-6016–2

Ex: Motet: *Pater Noster*
HAM, p. 80
Rec. Plei-251

8. *Adrian Willaert* (c. 1490–1562) was a Flemish composer who became the founder of the Venetian school, numbering among his pupils such masters as Andrea Gabrieli and Zarlino. He held the post of Master of the Chapel at St. Mark's where he introduced a style of writing for two antiphonal choirs. While his sacred music is of a high quality, he is perhaps best known for his madrigals, a form which he raised far above the level of the popular frottola.

Ex: *Ricercar No. 7*
HMS, vol. 4, p. 51
Rec. RCA, LM-6029–2

Ex: Motet: *Victimae paschali laudes*
HAM, p. 116
Rec. Plei-253

9. *Ludwig Senfl* (c. 1490–1543) was Swiss, but held musical positions in Germany. He was known as a singer and a composer of church music. As a pupil of Isaac, he cultivated the Flemish style. He was also noted for the charm of his polyphonic settings of the German lied. Luther praised Senfl as the "Prince of all German music."

Ex: Polyphonic Lied; *Ach, Elslein, liebes Elslein*
     Antiqua Chorbuch, Teil II, Edition Schott, 4256, p. 82
     Rec. M.H.-929T
Ex: Polyphonic Lied: *Da Jakob nu das Kleid ansah*
     HAM, p. 114
     Rec. Plei-253

10. *Thomas Tallis* (c. 1505–1585) was an English organist and composer. He was the first to use the English language in settings of the liturgy of the Anglican church. He also wrote a large number of motets and masses, using Latin.

Ex: Motet: *Adeste nunc propitius*
     HMS, vol. 4, p. 34
     Rec. RCA, LM-6029-2
Ex: Responsorium: *Audivi vocum*
     HAM, p. 137
     Rec. Plei-254

11. *Jacobus Clemens* (non Papa) (c. 1510–c. 1556), a Flemish composer, was especially noted as one of the more progressive composer of the early sixteenth century in his use of chromatic harmonization. His best works are the masses and motets.

Ex: Motet: *Vox in Rama*
     HAM, p. 134
     Rec. Plei-254

12. *Antonio de Cabezon* (1510–1566), an important Spanish composer and organist, was a strong influence on many European composers for the organ and other keyboard instruments. He also made keyboard arrangements of the vocal music of Josquin Des Prez and other Flemish composers.

Ex: Variations: *Diferencias Cavallero*
     HAM, p. 145
     Rec. Plei-254

13. *Andrea Gabrieli* (c. 1520–1586) was an Italian composer of the Venetian school, a pupil of Adrian Willaert, and uncle and teacher of Giovanni Gabrieli. After extensive travel in Germany and Bohemia, Andrea became organist at St. Mark's in Venice where he achieved a great reputation as organist. He was a prolific composer of both choral and instrumental music, ranging from massive sacred works to the madrigal. Many larger compositions exhibit the polychoral tradition of the Venetian school established by Willaert.

Ex: Canzona Francese: *deta Pour ung plaisir*
       MM, p. 64
       Rec. HS-9038
Ex: Prelude: *Intonazione settimo tono*
       HAM, p. 146
       Rec. Plei-254

14. *Philippe de Monte* (1521–1603), a Belgian, was a friend of Roland de Lassus and was influenced by the Flemish style. He is best known for his expressive madrigals.

Ex: Mass: *Benedicta es*
       HMS, vol. 4, p. 24
       Rec. RCA, LM-6029–1
Ex: Parody Mass: *Missa super cara la vita*
       HAM, p. 160
       Rec. Plei-255

15. *Giovanni Pierluigi Palestrina* (c. 1525–1594), an Italian composer, was generally considered the greatest master of Renaissance Catholic music. His most important post was that of director of the Cappella Giulia at the Vatican. Palestrina is noted for the perfection of a purely vocal style, commonly known as the *a cappella* style. His music is characterized by a high degree of technical perfection with diatonic melody and a smooth texture that culminated in a rare beauty of sound that is almost transcendental in its implications. His *Missa Papae Marcelli* has become a model for the purest religious style of Catholic music.

Ex: Madrigal: *Alla riva del Tebro*
       HAM, p. 155
       Rec. Plei-255

Ex: *Missa Aetrna Christi Munera*
     Eulenberg, ed., AMA, p. 27
     Rec. DGG ARC 2533322
Ex: Motet: *Sicut cervus*
     HAM, p. 153
     Rec. Plei-255

16. *Roland de Lassus* (Orlando di Lasso) (1532–1594) was also a product of the Flemish school, but was international in his music. His fame rests mainly on his religious music, however he was equally effective in Italian and German madrigals and French chansons. He wrote over two thousand compositions. Historians rank him as the greatest of the Flemish composers, and along with Palestrina, one of the most important of the Renaissance composers.

Ex: Mass: *Ecce nunct benedicite Dominum*
     Breitkopf and Härtel, ed.
     Rec. None-71053
Ex: Chanson: *Bon jour mon couer*
     HAM, p. 159
     Rec. Plei-255
Ex: *Penitential Psalm III*
     HAM, p. 157
     Rec. Plei-255

17. *William Byrd* (1543–1623) was one of the greatest composers of English sacred music. He is best known for his superb polyphonic settings of sacred texts—music that won him the title of the *English Palestrina.* He was equally skilled in keyboard music for both the organ and virginal. His *Carmen's Whistle,* a set of variations for virginal, was very popular during his lifetime.

Ex: Motet: *Ego sum panis vivus*
     MM, p. 91
     Rec. HS-9039
Ex: Motet: *Non vos relinquam*
     HAM, p. 164
     Rec. Plei-255

18. *Thomas Luis de Victoria* (c. 1549–1611) was a leading representative of the Roman school in Spain. He studied in Rome, probably with Palestrina. His music has a dramatic intensity and spiritual fervor that is thoroughly Spanish. He is best known for the *Requiem Mass,* but he also wrote a large number of other works, including a book of hymns for four voices.

Ex: *Missa Quarti Toni*
     Breitkopf and Härtel
     Rec. M.H.-612H
Ex: Motet: *O vos omnes*
     HAM, p. 163
     Rec. Plei-255
Ex: Motet: *O Domine Jesu*
     HMS, vol. 4, p. 23
     Rec. RCA, LM-6029-1

19. *Luca Marenzio* (1553–1599) was an important Italian madrigalist. His works show that he was a very progressive composer who made many innovations in chordal relationships and chromaticisms.

Ex: *Scendi dal Paradiso*
     HMS, vol. 4, p. 14
     Rec. RCA, LM-6029-1
Ex: Madrigal: *Madonna mia gentil*
     HAM, p. 173
     Rec. Plei-255

20. *Giovanni Gabrieli* (c. 1554–1612) was a nephew and pupil of Andrea Gabrieli. He was the greatest composer of the Venetian school and one of the first to write for a combination of voices and instruments. One of his best known works in this medium was the *Sacre Symphoniae.* He achieved massive sonorities with his polychoral technique. He is often regarded as the first to develop orchestration and to use a wide range of dynamics as in his *Sonate Pian'e Forte.*

Ex: *Sacrae Symphoniae, in ecclesiis*
     HAM, p. 175
     Rec. Plei-255
Ex: *Sonata pian' e forte*
     HAM, p. 198
     Rec. Plei-256

21. *Thomas Morley* (1557–1602), an English composer and publisher, is best known for his madrigals and ballets. He was the publisher of the *Triumphs of Oriana*, a set of twenty-five madrigals by twenty-three composers—each madrigal in honor of Queen Elizabeth. He was also the author of the first English treatise on music, *A Plaine and Easie Introduction to Practicall Musicke.*

Ex: Madrigal; *Thyrsis and Milla*
     HMS, vol. 4, p. 48
     Rec. RCA LM-6029-2
Ex: Ballett: *My bonny lass*
     HAM, p. 180
     Rec. Plei-256

22. *Don Carlo Gesualdo* (c. 1560–1613) was an Italian madrigalist whose works represent the extreme of chromaticism reached in the last years of the Renaissance. The harmonic results achieved by Gesualdo, while often described as mannerism, are indicative of a growing consciousness of the strength of musical expression and of the ideals of the dawning Baroque era.

Ex: Madrigal: *Moro Lasso a mio duolo*
     TEM, p. 181
     Rec. HSE-9102
Ex: Madrigal: *Io pur respiro*
     HAM, p. 182
     Rec. Plei-256

23. *Hans Leo Hassler* (1564–1612) was a German who studied in Italy with Andrea Gabrieli. He adapted the Venetian style to the German lied and created a rather strong German musical style. He wrote in all the current and vocal and keyboard forms, both Renaissance and early Baroque, but was best known for his settings of German polyphonic songs and chorales.

Ex: Polyphonic Lied: *Ach Schatz*
     HAM, p. 187
     Rec. Plei-256
Ex: Motet: *Quia vidisti me*
     HAM, p. 186
     Rec. Plei 256

24. *Claudio Monteverdi* (1567–1643) not only spans the final years of one period and the beginning of another by virtue of his life span, but he was one of the first composers to employ consciously two different practices: a *prima prattica,* (stile antico), and a *seconda prattica,* (stile moderno). While he wrote works in the first practice which were typical of the Renaissance such as his sacred choral works and madrigals, it was his use of the second practice which marked his contribution to the emerging Baroque and made him historically important. This will be discussed more fully in the chapter on the Baroque.

Ex: Madrigal: *Amor*
Ricordi: Complete Works
Rec. DGG. ARC 2533146

25. *Thomas Weelkes* (c. 1575–1623) was one of the greatest of the English madrigalists. He was well in advance of his time in his characterization of text. He also wrote numerous anthems and services for the Anglican church.

Ex.   *O care thou wilt dispatch me*
HMS Vol. 4, p. 17
Rec. RCA LM-6029-1

VIII. OTHER COMPOSERS

A. Austria
   1. *Paul Hofhaimer* (1459–1537)
   2. *Jacobus Gallus (Handl)* (1550–1591)

B. England
   1. *John Taverner* (c. 1495–1545)
   2. *Giles Farnaby* (c. 1560–1640)
   3. *John Bull* (c. 1562–1628)
   4. *John Dowland* (1563–1626)
   5. *John Wilbye* (1574–1638)
   6. *Orlando Gibbons* (1583–1625)
   7. *John Farmer* (fl. 1591–1601)
   8. *John Bennet* (fl. 1599–1614)

C. Germany
1. *Conrad Paumann* (c. 1410–1473)
2. *Heinrich Finck* (1445–1527)
3. *Johann Walter* (1496–1570)
4. *Johannes Eccard* (1553–1611)
5. *Melchior Franck* (c. 1579–1639)

D. Italy
1. *Annibale (Il Padovano)* (c. 1527–1575)
2. *Claudio Merulo* (1533–1604)
3. *Marco Antonio Ingegneri* (1545–1592)
4. *Orazio Vecchi* (1550–1605)
5. *Giovanni Gastoldi* (d. 1622)

E. Burgundy-Netherland
1. *Pierre de La Rue* (d. 1518)
2. *Philippe Verdelot* (d. 1550)
3. *Nicholas Gombert* (c. 1490–1556)
4. *Thomas Crecquillon* (d. 1557)
5. *Clément Janequin* (c. 1485–c. 1560)
6. *Claudin de Sermisy* (c. 1490–1562)
7. *Jacob Arcadelt* (c. 1505–1565)
8. *Cipriano de Rore* (1516–1565)

F. Spain
1. *Louis Milan* (c. 1500–1561)
2. *Cristobal de Morales* (c. 1500–1553)

IX. IMPORTANT WRITERS ON MUSIC

A number of theoretical treatises on music were written during the Renaissance. These works were generally in Latin, the language of the scholar, and usually written in a learned style that often obscures rather than illuminates. However, these writings are the actual sources from which our knowledge of all musical matters not revealed by the actual music is drawn. Without these works many problems of reconstructing Renaissance music would be without authentic solutions, for they offer clues to, as well as the detailed explanations of, notation, tuning, performance, instrumental construction, rules of theory, and countless other areas puzzling to the present day scholar. Many of these works contain unique examples from the music literature of the times that would otherwise be unavailable. In several cases the authors wrote more than one work. In such cases the important one has been listed with its original title and date of writing or publication, as well as any modern edition or translation.

1. *Bartolome Ramos de Pareja* (c. 1440–1491) was a Spanish theorist. His *Musica Practica,* Bologna 1482, is a landmark in the science of harmony, particularly in its instruction concerned with intonation. Ramos, through his division of the monochord, established the ratios of 4:5 and 5:6 for the major and minor thirds.

2. *Johannes Tinctoris* (1436–1511) was a Belgian theorist and composer. His *Terminorum musicae diffinitorium,* Naples 1473, is the oldest known dictionary of musical terms. An English translation appeared in London in 1849. Another work was published during his lifetime and several manuscripts were published in Coussemaker's complete edition of the writings of Tinctoris in 1875.

3. *Franchino Gaforio* (1451–1522) was an Italian theorist. *Practica Musicae Franchino Gaforio Laudenis in IV libris,* Milan 1496, is Gaforio's magnum opus. It deals with rules of counterpoint and a discussion of practices in composition, as well as the current practices of performances.

4. *Pietro Aaron* (1480–1545) was an Italian theorist. *Toscanello in Musica,* Venice 1523, is one of a number of valuable works of Aaron who is considered among the most important theorists of the early sixteenth century. This work, his most important, contains descriptions of contrapuntal rules, chord formations as employed in his day.

5. *Martin Agricola* (1486–1556) was a German theorist whose *Musica instrumentalis deudsch,* Wittenberg 1529, is an authoritative work on the instruments of the time and a valuable source for the history of notation. Agricola wrote a number of other theoretical works as well.

6. *Henricus Glareanus* (1488–1563) was a Swiss philosopher, theologian, historian, poet, and musical scholar. His *Dodechachordon,* Basle 1547, advocated the completion of the modal series to twelve and greatly influenced the concept of modality and tonality. There is a German translation of this work published in 1888.

7. *Gioseffo Zarlino* (1517–1590) was an Italian theorist. In the *Instituzioni armoniche,* Venice 1558, Zarlino discusses various topics concerning music of his day in the four books that make up his major work. These include rules of counterpoint, intonation, text, treatment and the general excellence of music.

8. *Thomas Morley* (1557–1602) was an English composer and theorist. His *A Plaine and Easie Introduction to Practicall Musicke,* London 1597 (reprint 1937), is one of the earliest treatises on music published in England. A discourse on all phases of music making, this is the most important English book on musical theory in the Renaissance. A modernized edition was published in 1952.

Excerpts in English from several of the foregoing works can be found in *Source Readings in Music History* by Strunk.

Ramos	pp. 200–205
Tinctoris	pp. 193–200
Glareanus	pp. 219–228
Aaron	pp. 205–219
Zarlino	pp. 228–262
Morley	pp. 274–281

X. MANUSCRIPT SOURCES

Until music printing became a practicality in the sixteenth century, the manuscript collections constituted the most valuable source of actual music of the Renaissance. These manuscripts were usually made by anonymous copyists and were treasured in the libraries of monasteries, churches and royal courts. Of the countless manuscripts written before the end of the fifteenth century, when the printing of music had not yet displaced the collecting of musical works in handwritten form, certain monumental collections stand out as important. In many cases these are the sole sources of folk and composed music.

Old Hall MS, written about 1450 at the Catholic College of St. Edmunds in Old Hall, England, and reposing there at the present, contains a large number of Mass compositions and hymns. There is a modern edition of this work published in 1935–38 by Ramsbotham and Collins.

The *Trent Codices* are seven volumes of fifteenth century polyphonic music both sacred and secular. They represent one of the richest collections of representative works of about seventy-five fifteenth century masters of polyphony. A large part of this collection has been printed in the *Denkmäler Der Tonkust in Oesterreich*, volumes 7, 11, 19, 27, 31 and 40 in modern notation.

Among the collections of purely secular songs, the *chansonniers* and *liederbuecher* of France and Germany respectively are especially noteworthy. The *Copenhagen Chansonnier* of the fifteenth century contains thirty three polyphonic chansons and is representative of a number of such collections. It is available in modern edition also. Of the German collections, the *Glogauer Liederbuch*, the *Lochaimer Liederbuch*, and the *Muenchner Liederbuch* contain vocal and instrumental polyphonic and monophonic settings of German folk songs and composed works. All three of these are published in modern editions.

Supplementary Readings

Borroff	pp. 147–256
Cannon-Johnson-Waite	pp. 142–212
Crocker	pp. 143–220
Grout	pp. 145–292
Lang	pp. 168–313
Oxford, vol. 3	pp. 134–502
Oxford, vol. 4	pp. 1–514
Reese, R.	pp. 3–883
Schirmer	ch. 9– 12, 36
Wold-Cykler	ch. 7

Further References

Andrews, H. K. *An Introduction to the Technique of Palestrina.* London: Novello, 1958.

Bukofzer, Manfred. *Studies in Medieval and Renaissance Music.* New York: W. W. Norton, 1950.

Carpenter, Nan Cooke. *Music in the Medieval and Renaissance Universities.* Norman: University of Oklahoma Press, 1958.

Einstein, Alfred. *The Italian Madrigal.* Princeton: Princeton University Press, 1949.

Fellowes, E. H. *The English Madrigal Composers.* London: Oxford, 1950.
Gray, Cecil and Haseltine, Philip. *Carlo Gesualdo, Prince of Venosa. Musician and Murderer.* London: Paul, Trench, Trubner, 1926.
Jeppeson, Knud. *The Style of Palestrina and the Dissonance.* London: Oxford, 1927.
Lowinsky, Edward E. *Secret Chromatic Art in the Netherlands Motet.* New York: Columbia University Press, 1946.
Walker, Ernest. *A History of Music in England.* London: Oxford, 1952.

Monastery Church of Melk, Austria (1707–c. 1738). The highly ornate interior of the Roman Catholic Church of the eighteenth century in which the richly organized music of the Baroque echoed the
decorativeness of the architecture. Architectural elements were often
nonstructural as in the case of the arch and column which were often
used for purely decorative and expressive purposes, much in the same
way as deceptive cadences and modulations were used in music.
(Courtesy Marburg-Art Reference Bureau)

5
Chronology
of the Baroque

1547 Miguel de Cervantes
(1547–1616)
1548 Giulio Caccini
(c.1548–1618)
1557 Giovanni Gabrieli
(c.1557–1612)
1561 Francis Bacon
(1561–1626)
Jacopo Peri (1561–1633)
1562 Jan Pieterzoon Sweelinck
(1562–1621)
1564 Galileo Galilei
(1564–1642)
William Shakespeare
(1564–1616)
1567 Claudio Monteverdi
(1567–1643)
1571 Johann Kepler
(1571–1630)
Michael Praetorius
(1571–1621)
1577 Peter Paul Rubens
(1577–1640)
1578 William Harvey
(1578–1657)
1583 Giroloma Frescobaldi
(1583–1643)
1585 Heinrich Schütz
(1585–1673)
1586 Johann Hermann Schein
(1586–1630)

1587 Samuel Scheidt
(1587–1654)
1596 René Descartes
(1596–1650)
1598 Giovanni Lorenzo
Bernini (1598–1690)
1599 Francesco Borromini
(1599–1667)
Diego Velasquez
(1599–1660)
1602 Galilei discovers law of
falling bodies
Pier Francesco Cavalli
(1602–1676)
Jacques Champion
Chambonnières
(1602–1672)
1605 Giacomo Carissimi
(1605–1674)
1606 Rembrandt van Rijn
(1606–1669)
Macbeth written by
Shakespeare
1608 John Milton (1608–1674)
1609 Henrik Hudson explores
the Hudson River
1616 Johann Jakob Froberger
(1616–1667)
1618 Beginning of the Thirty
Years' War

1620 Pilgrims landed at
      Plymouth
1622 Jean Baptiste Molière
      (1622-1673)
1623 Marc' Antonio Cesti
      (1623-1669)
1626 Peter Minuit buys
      Manhattan Island
1628 William Harvey discovers
      circulation of the blood.
      Jean Henri d'Angelbert
      (c.1628-1691)
1630 Boston founded
1632 Jean Baptiste Lully
      (1632-1687)
      Baruch Spinoza
      (1632-1677)
      Christopher Wren
      (1632-1723)
1634 Taj Mahal begun
      Marc Antoine
      Charpentier (1634-1704)
1636 Harvard University
      founded
1637 Dietrich Buxtehude
      (1637-1707)
      First public opera house
      opened in Venice
1638 Louis XIV (1638-1715)
1640 Publication of the Bay
      Psalm Book.
1642 Isaac Newton (1642-1727
1648 End of the Thirty Years'
      War
1653 Arcangelo Corelli
      (1653-1713)
      Johann Pachelbel
      (1653-1706)
1659 Henry Purcell
      (1659-1695)

1660 Johann Kuhnau
      (1660-1722)
      Alessandro Scarlatti
      (1660-1725)
1661 Reign of Louis XIV
      (1661-1715)
1667 Milton writes *Paradise
      Lost*
1668 François Couperin
      (1668-1733)
1672 Newton propounds law
      of gravitation
1675 Christopher Wren begins
      St. Paul's Cathedral
1678 Antonio Vivaldi
      (1678-1741)
      First German opera house
      opens in Hamburg
1681 George Philipp Telemann
      (1681-1767)
1682 Philadelphia founded
1683 Jean Philippe Rameau
      (1683-1741)
1685 Johann Sebastian Bach
      (1685-1750)
      George Friederich
      Handel (1685-1759)
      Domenico Scarlatti
      (1685-1757)
1689 Peter I (The Great) Tsar
      of Russia
1700 Sauveur measures
      musical vibrations
1701 Yale University founded
1708 First German Theater
      opens in Vienna
1709 Christofori builds the
      first pianoforte
1710 Giovanni Batista
      Pergolesi (1710-1736)

1715 Louis XV reigns until
      1774
1719 Pompeii rediscovered
1730 Guarnerius family makes
      violins in Cremona
1738 First spinning machine
      patented
      Methodist Church
      founded by John Wesley
1740 University of
      Pennsylvania founded
      Frederick the Great rules
      to 1786
1745 Princeton University
      founded

5
Baroque
1575–1750

I. SOCIOCULTURAL INFLUENCES ON MUSIC

The word Baroque, probably derived from the Portuguese meaning an irregularly shaped pearl, was first used as a term of scorn for those art works, particularly architecture, produced from the end of the sixteenth century to the middle of the eighteenth century. While the word still carries with it some derogatory meaning, it is widely used to designate the arts and music of this era. Applied to such a long period and to such diverse countries as Italy, France, England and the vast territories that came under Germanic influence, it had various phases. Its division into early, middle, and late Baroque did not occur simultaneously in all areas. In general, Baroque art is considered excessively decorative, dramatic, flamboyant, and emotional. There is a tendency to fuse the arts wherever possible. Architecture, painting and sculpture, for example, are combined in the domed ceilings of the seventeenth and eighteenth century churches. Music, literature, painting, architecture, and sculpture are all combined in the opera or *drama per musica*. Consequently, there is often a confusion of media; painting tries to portray what sculpture can do better; music tries to be literary. The intense desire to express an idea, a feeling, the artists' own deep convictions and emotions often led to excesses in all forms of art. The tendency to ascribe these violent expressive qualities to lack of taste or to the desire to cover poor workmanship placed the Baroque forms in a position of disfavor in the late eighteenth and nineteenth centuries. A reappraisal of the Baroque in the twentieth century as representative of a period of violent and revolutionary upheavals, however, gives a new insight into the deep-lying motives which find expression in what seems at first a very superficial kind of art.

The whole Baroque movement had its inception in Italy as a part of the Counter Reformation. Its influence and spirit spread rapidly into all parts of Europe, particularly into southern Germany and Austria where the Catholic Counter Reformation was most successful in its struggle with the Protestant North. Despite its first association with the Catholic Counter Reformation, the Baroque spirit became an equally vital part of the Protestant Reformation, and in fact pervaded all forms of artistic expression both spiritual and secular. Some important movements in religion, government, economics and science that were partially responsible for the activity of the Baroque are as follows:

The struggle between Roman Catholicism and Protestantism known as the Thirty Years' War dominated the first half of the seventeenth century, especially in northern and central Europe. This devastating struggle delayed the development of the Baroque musical life in the German lands for better than a generation. However, both the Catholic church, which in this series of wars partially regained its political influence, and the Protestant church which developed a clear cut form of its own, adapted the prevailing magnificence of style to their own purposes.

The rise of absolute monarchies and the unification of national states played an important part in the creation of national styles, since the monarchs and princes were among the most important patrons of a lavish musical life. The courts of the Louis of France and Hapsburgs of Spain and Austria were examples of centers that stimulated the production of the larger and more spectacular forms of musical expression like the opera. Smaller courts, such as those of the German princes and dukes, were influential in cultivating an intimate kind of music for both salon and chapel. The courts of the Dukes of Weimar and the Princes of Anhalt-Cöthen are examples of these smaller but highly cultural courts.

World-wide intensive colonization during the seventeenth and eighteenth centuries gave rise to a wealthy merchant class. This wealth supplied the basis for the rich independent cites that were to provide a suitable climate for the establishment of a commercial theater and its musical production, the opera. Cities like Venice and Hamburg are good examples of such a concentration of merchant wealth and their musical theaters became internationally famous during this period.

There was a great interest shown in all fields of scholarly inquiry in the Baroque era. Discoveries through the application of inductive reasoning were most spectacular in the field of the sciences—physiology, astronomy, mathematics, physics. The success of scientific examination in these fields influenced musicians to apply methods of science to problems of music and led to a systematic development of the techniques and materials of musical art. Such works, discoveries and devices as Bach's *Art of the Fugue*, Rameau's *Treatise on Harmony*, Morley's *A Plaine and Easy Introduction to Music*, the practice of well-tempered tuning and the perfection of the violin family are all examples of the urge to systematization and scientific inquiry.

A phenomenon of the Baroque is that the plastic arts, literature and music abound in examples of affectations and expressive feeling. Architecture achieves these affectations by means of such devices as the arch without a keystone and the twisted stone columns as decorative elements whose function no longer is architectural but expressive. Music discovers the way to effect these same qualities in the tension created by dissonance within the tonal system of Baroque harmony. In music the use of affectations, calculated and planned emotional expression, is referred to as the *doctrine of affections*.

II. FUNCTION OF MUSIC

While a great deal of religious music was written for purely liturgical purposes, especially in the Lutheran church, an increasing amount of religious music for instruments was used for nonliturgical purposes. Some of this nonliturgical music was used for preludes, postludes, and to provide a musical background for quasi-religious purposes: marriage ceremonies, the dedication of a new building, the elevation of a civil or religious official to office.

A great amount of music in the latter part of the Baroque period was written for amateur performers in the households of the aristocracy and the wealthy class. While most of this music was instrumental, vocal music also was included. Music of this type was truly chamber music, meant more for the pleasure of the performer than for an audience.

Music for private entertainment was cultivated in the households of the aristocracy where small bands of musicians provided both the compositions and performances of dinner music, dances and even ensemble concerts that ranged in style from the purely utilitarian to that of real aesthetic quality.

In the large wealthy courts, ballet and opera were first performed as a special kind of entertainment for the princes and the courtiers. The opera soon developed into a very popular form of public entertainment, first in Italy and soon over all of Europe. Performances of purely instrumental character were rarely given for the general public.

The oratorio was the religious counterpart of the opera. Because of the subject matter and manner of presentation it did not assume as popular a position as opera, but it did find importance in public performance as a kind of choral concert.

Special festive occasions often called for vocal music as well as instrumental music. The secular cantata was often employed for such events with texts that referred directly or allegorically to the occasion.

There was no institutional organization for teaching the musical arts. Young boys who showed interest and talent either were taught by their own musical fathers or relatives or were attached to the household of a composer-performer. Without doubt many compositions were written for the teaching of such prospective musicians. Such works as the *Little Organ Book* by J. S. Bach was undoubtedly in part, at least, the result of providing exercise material for his four musical sons. Geminiani's *Art of Violin Playing* was a more systematic approach to instrumental pedagogy. Instruction in performance and composition was restricted to the aspiring musician and to the households of the aristocracy and wealthy burghers.

III. CHARACTERISTICS OF STYLE

For the first time in the history of western European music two styles flourished side by side: (1) the Renaissance style, the *stile antico* which carried over into the Baroque period; and (2) the new Baroque style itself, often called *stile moderno*. The following characterizations apply to the stile moderno or *nuovo musiche*, which is typically Baroque. It must be realized, however, that many composers, sometimes some of the most important, continued to use characteristics of Renaissance style.

The stile moderno was characterized by several stylistic compositional devices peculiar to the Baroque itself. One of these devices was given the Greek name of *monody*. This was a manner of writing in which melodic line was supported by a very simple chordal accompaniment. Originally the melodic line, or monody, was something midway between speech and song and was called *stile rappresentativo*. It was characterized by freedom of rhythm, pauses, and asymmetric phrases. The alleviation of the monotony of this form of musical declamation by means of passages that were more melodic in character eventually gave rise to the distinction in monodic style between recitative and aria.

Another characteristic of the Baroque music was the *stile concertato*. In the concertato style the composer used various forces, instrumental and vocal, in compositions which are both the result of harmonic or contrapuntal cooperation and also the planned contrast of instruments or voices against one another either as soloists or as groups. Many of the vocal and instrumental forms of the later Baroque are derived from this style of writing.

The *stile concitato* or excited style was another device of writing whereby the music interpreted the words or moods of the dramatic action: the use of tremolo in the strings of the orchestra or rapidly sung syllables to a repeated note by the voice are typical of this style.

1. *Formal Organization*

   a) In the newly devised recitative the text dominated the formal structure.

   b) Contrapuntal development of the thematic material continued to be used in works which were wholly or partially contrapuntal—the fugue, toccata, and the chorale prelude.

   c) Homophonic forms generally depended upon simple statement and contrast of melodic material.

   d) The variation principle was used in both homophonic and contrapuntal forms such as theme and variation, passacaglia, or chorale variation.

   e) Sequential patterns were a frequent device of formal organization.

   f) A great number of solo instrumental works for the keyboard instruments, both organ and harpsichord, were written in a style which suggested improvisation. Rapid scale passages, decorations, or chordal figuration, in a free fantasy-like vein were characteristic of such compositions. Sometimes such improvisatory passages were obviously used for a display of a brilliant technique, and were dictated by this consideration rather than purely musical ones.

g) The establishment of major-minor tonality led to clear cut phrase and period construction in formal design.

2. *Melody.*   Melodic writing varies from the declamatory style of the recitative, which might be regarded as almost a negation of melody, to the extremely florid style of the late Baroque arias and instrumental melodies.

a) The recitative, an invention of the early Baroque composers, represented a melodic idea whose structure was determined solely by verbal considerations. Two forms of recitative were employed. One was known as *recitativo secco* (dry recitative) in which only a thorough bass accompanied the voice (ex.23).

The other type of recitative was *recitativo accompagnato* (accompanied recitative) in which the voice was more dramatic and accompanied by an ensemble of instruments (ex.24). Accompanied recitative style was usually used to introduce an aria in the dramatic forms of opera and oratorio.

b) Melody gradually assumed vocal and instrumental idiomatic styles, but these were often interchangeable. It was not uncommon to find purely vocal design applied to instrumental writing and vice versa. Both instrumental and vocal music employed melodic line of extended range. The desire for vocal display and the use of homophonic style account for this phenomenon in vocal music, while the continued perfection of keyboard instruments and the strings made an extended instrumental range possible.

Example 23. St. Matthew Passion   J. S. Bach

Example 24

c) The *bel canto* (beautiful singing) style emphasized beauty of vocal sound and brilliant florid
   technique. Composers provided for this demand
   by writing melodies which were musically scin-
   tillating but not necessarily dramatically expressive. In conformity with this demand, melodies
   often deteriorated into spectacular vocalises with
   ornamentation either written in or left to the discretion of the singer.

d) Melody in homophonic music was essentially one
   of balanced phrase and period, usually in four or
   eight measures.

e) Melody was often based on chordal outline.

f) While the upper melodic line was dominant in
   the homophonic style, there existed a kind of polarity between the melody and the bass line

Example 25   J. S. Bach

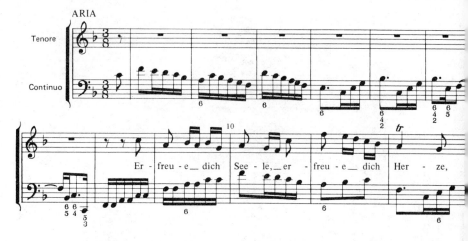

which was in itself a melodically conceived part
(ex.25).

3. *Rhythm*
    a) Rhythm was generally simple and tempo con-
       stant.
    b) The importance of the moving basso continuo
       gave a certain driving, almost motoric, feeling to
       both instrumental and choral works written in
       contrapuntal style.
    c) The rapid change of harmony induced by the
       melodic basso continuo also made for a driving
       harmonic rhythm, the movement given to music
       by changes in harmony, which added its force to
       the total rhythmic motion.

4. *Harmony*
    a) There was a distinct break from the modal to the
       major-minor system of tonal relationship.
    b) Harmony's chordal nature was determined by a
       system of numbers placed under the notes of the
       bass line. The harmony so specified was then re-
       alized by the keyboard performer. This device
       was called by various names: thorough bass, fig-
       ured bass, basso continuo, or merely continuo.
       Example 26 illustrates the use of figured bass and

Example 26

J. S. Bach

Example 27

example 27 is a possible realization of the same bass.

c) The melodic character of the bass line suggested rapid changes of harmony, especially in the works of the late Baroque (ex.26).

d) Chromaticism, and use of dissonance was freely employed in early Baroque for expressive purposes in vocal works. In the late Baroque both instrumental and vocal composition made use of chromaticism. Tempered tuning of keyboard instruments was introduced and made possible the chromatic changes that were necessary for extended modulations, which were changes from one key to another. Bach's *Forty Eight Preludes and*

The Ecstasy of St. Theresa (1646) Bernini. Every possibility of height-ened expression of which sculpture is capable is used in this work: the facial expression of the saint, the contortion of the bodies of both figures, the one in thrusting the arrow, the other in its reception; the folds of the clothing which weave an exciting pattern of moving lines, all these are captured in this dramatic moment of ecstasy. The har-monic and formal contrast in musical composition, especially in mu-sical drama, the opera, is a typical counterpart of this sculptured work. (Courtesy Alinari/Art Resource, NY)

Fugues (The Well Tempered Clavier) illustrates how tempered tuning made it possible to play in all keys both major and minor without retuning the instrument.

e) Even in works which were essentially contrapuntal, Baroque counterpoint was based on major-minor tonality rather than the modality of the Renaissance.

5. *Texture*

a) Homophonic texture was employed exclusively in the opera and in solo arias of all kinds. Many instrumental forms such as the sonata da camera, keyboard sonatas, and suites were also predominately homophonic.

b) Polyphonic texture was achieved by tonal counterpoint. It was used in religious choral works as well as in many types of instrumental compositions such as the fugue, chorale prelude, or variations on a ground.

c) The tendency in purely homophonic forms to include contrapuntal techniques and the harmonic richness of contrapuntal forms tended to make the texture of most Baroque music rather thick and opaque.

d) There was great emphasis on contrasting textures, especially in the concertato style. The common contrast of large massed groups with small ones was enhanced by the general use of contrapuntal treatment for the large and homophonic treatment for the smaller groups.

6. *Media and tone color*

a) Many of the instruments in use in the Baroque era were in forms which were forerunners of modern instruments.

b) The violin family was perfected and gradually displaced the viols by the end of the period.

c) There was a real idiomatic feeling in writing for specific instruments. Examples are especially evident in works for the harpsichord and clavichord.

d) One of the most popular chamber music groupings of instruments is that known as the *trio-son-
ata*, a name applied both to the instrumental
group and to the literature written for it. It consisted of four instruments despite its title: two
treble melodic instruments (often interchangeable), a bass instrument to play the continuo part
(wind or string instrument) and a keyboard instrument to realize the figured bass (usually a
harpsichord).

e) Another chamber group was the *solo sonata* whose
name again belies the instrumentation. It consisted of three instruments—one melodic, one
bass, and a keyboard instrument for the harmony.

f) There was as yet no fixed orchestral group, although orchestras were used both as accompanying groups in vocal dramatic works and as
independent musical organizations. The Baroque
orchestra consisted mainly of strings with a number of wood-wind instruments.

g) One of the special Baroque instrumental practices was the use of the high trumpet called *clarino*. The skill developed by clarino players
prompted many Baroque composers to use the
trumpet as a solo instrument.

h) The Baroque organ was a small instrument with
great clarity and mellowness of tone, but it lacked
the ability to execute a crescendo. All contrasts in
dynamics had to follow the Baroque idea of contrasting sonorities of tone, achieved on the organ
by changes in registration. The limited size and
pureness of tonal quality made the Baroque organ
an ideal instrument on which to realize the
transparent contrapuntal texture of the organ
forms of the period. Practically all of the great
composers of the Baroque wrote for the organ and
most of them were organ performers.

i) The term *clavier* referred to all types of keyboard
instruments, especially the harpsichord and the

The inner principal group of the high altar in the Augustin Church of Freibourg, Switzerland (1592–1601), by Peter Spring. Four of the angelic host are playing instruments which are clearly identifiable; left upper, a harp; left lower, a zink (cornetto); right upper, a harp; right lower, a sackbut (trombone). The sculptured group represents the acceptance of secular music into the church art and music in the Baroque era. (Courtesy of Bärenreiter-Bildarchiv)

clavichord. The former, known variously as *cla-vecin, cembalo, gravicembalo, spinet,* and *virginal,* was the more widely used instrument and was only displaced by the *piano* which was invented in 1709 by Cristofori, but not universally adopted until after the Baroque era. Much solo and ensemble music was written for the harpsichord, especially in the last half of the Baroque period.

j) For solo purposes voices came to be used in the modern classification of soprano, alto, tenor, and bass. Since vocal solos and ensemble used instrumental accompaniment, a work written for a specific voice range could not readily be performed by a different voice. As a result certain characteristic vocal parts came to be assigned to specific vocal ranges, especially in dramatic writing.

k) A vocal phenomenon unique to the Baroque was the male or artificial sopranos known as *castrati.* The power, range, and technical facility of the castrati voices made them a great favorite with the Baroque opera audience and accounts for many soprano arias in Baroque operas of extreme difficulty for the modern singer.

l) See Appendix A for description of instruments.

IV. PRACTICE AND PERFORMANCE

The Baroque was the last period in which improvisation was a definite requisite of every performer. Such improvisatory techniques as the realization and actual addition of ornaments in both vocal and instrumental performance were not only tolerated but expected. In fact, in both instrumental and vocal music composers often only outlined the melodic line with the full expectation of having the performer add not only ornamentation but passing tones, scale passages and even melodic fragments to the notated melody. Vocal music was particularly given to such improvisatory additions at highly expressive points, often as dictated by the texts, and these were known as *gorgia.* In the later Baroque brilliant rapid ornamentation of a virtuoso type was known as *coloratura,* used especially by the soprano voice.

In both vocal and instrumental compositions performers were expected to extend cadences, especially climactic cadences near the end of a movement or work, with elaborate improvisation. Such improvisations came to take the name of *cadenzas*. In the solo arias of operas and in the solo instrumental concertos, cadenzas came to be an integral part of the work, and performers used them not only to exhibit their ability at improvisation but also their command of technical skill. Organists practice improvisation to the present day.

Closely allied to pure improvisation was the realization or completion of the harmonies indicated in the figured bass by keyboard performers. Where the figuration was present the realization consisted of improvising suitable chordal and rhythmic patterns or even contrapuntal lines (ex.27). Much music, however, was not even figured so that the keyboard realization demanded the choosing of both the proper harmony and its patterns.

Tempered systems of tuning were universally used. Meantone temperament was the most consistently employed, but by the end of the Baroque period the tendency toward a system of equal temperament was indicated by the ever increasing modulatory practice of composers. Tuning of some instruments varied, such as the altered tuning of the violin, known as *scordatura*, a device used to achieve unusual chordal effects.

While writing for instruments became more and more idiomatic, there was still freedom given to the choice of instruments in certain compositions. Flutes, both recorder and the new transverse or German type, as well as oboes and violins were often interchangeable in ensemble music.

Tremolo and pizzicato were string instrument performance techniques introduced in this period.

Dynamic markings such as *p., f., cresc., dim.,* were introduced but were used very sparingly. Most dynamic variations were achieved by contrasting instrumental groups of varied size or quality.

Designation of ornamentation by the use of abbreviations and signs was increasingly used in the Baroque. While performers were at liberty, in fact were expected, to improvise ornamentation even though it was not marked by the composer, composers used a large variety of signs to indicate their personal wishes in the matter. While some of the ornamentation directions were in common usage, many of them took on the personal meaning of the individual composer or school to which he belonged. This has given rise to many differences of interpretation in the works of the Baroque.

Tempo designations such as *allegro, andante, grave,* were also introduced but had a wide range of meaning.

Almost all composers were recognized as virtuoso performers as well as composers. This was especially true in the area of keyboard performance. Both Bach and Handel were celebrated as skillful performers on the organ. Corelli, Tartini and Biber made notable advances in the technic of violin playing, with double stops, triple stops, arpeggios, etc. In the performance of opera, Farinelli became internationally known as a virtuoso castrati.

V. VOCAL COMPOSITIONS

A. Single Movement Forms and Structural Devices.

1. *Recitative.*   Short as well as long passages written in a style of highly inflected declamation are known as recitatives. This is the declamatory form of the *stile rappresentativo* which came to be separated from the lyrically melodic parts of the monody. By the end of the seventeenth century the clear distinction between recitative and aria had been accomplished. The recitative served to carry the narrative and acted both as a prelude to and the connecting material between the highly emotional points represented by the arias. Recitatives took no formal structure such as the aria. They were rhythmically free and served merely as a vocal vehicle for the prose dialogue.

    In more serious situations, recitative might be accompanied by full orchestra. In quick moving operatic narrative, it was often accompanied only by the harpsichord in realization of the figured bass. In the former case, it was known as *accompanied recitative;* in the latter, *secco* or *dry recitative.*

Ex: Accompanied Recitative: *Comfort Ye* from *The Messiah,* Handel
NS, p. 117
Rec. Col. MS-6928

Ex: Secco Recitative: *Al valor del mio brando,* from *Rinaldo,* Handel
      MM,p. 189
      Rec. HS-9040

2. *Aria.* The more melodic passages of the *stile rappresentativo* took on a formal character and finally separated from the declamatory parts as arias. The most typical form which these arias assumed was the three part or *da capo aria* developed by the Neopolitan opera school. This form was almost universally adopted by the writers for all musical dramatic works, secular and religious. The aria form was often applied to ensembles such as duets or trios.

Ex: Aria: *Cara sposa* from *Rinaldo,* Handel
      MM, p. 189
      Rec. HS-9040

Ex: Aria: *Every Valley* from *The Messiah,* Handel
      NS, p. 120
      Rec. Col. MS6928

3. *Arioso.* A free vocal form for solo voice that mixes the declamatory style of the recitative with the lyrical style of the aria. Like the aria, the arioso was accompanied by full orchestra. The arioso was often used to express rapid changes of mood by means of the vocal line and the orchestral accompaniment. Unlike the aria, the arioso was not cast in a formal design.

Ex: Air: *O jour affreux* from *Dardanus,* Rameau
      HMS, vol. 5, p. 23
      Rec: RCA, LM-6030

Ex: Arioso: *Ach Golgotha,* from the *St. Matthew Passion,* J. S. Bach
      MM, p. 226
      Rec. HS-9040

4. *Chorus.* Choral and ensemble passages took on no specific formal character. Contrapuntal texture generally prevailed in the oratorio and mass settings, while homophonic texture was the rule in operatic writing. Because of the emphasis on solo singing, choral passages were infrequent in Baroque opera and occurred only because of the

dramatic incident required as a necessary part of the action.

Ex: Scene from *Venus and Adonis,* Blow
L'Oiseau Lyre Press
HMS, vol. 5
Rec. RCA, LM-6030-2

> 5. *Motet.*   The Baroque composers continued the tradition of the unaccompanied choral motet of the Renaissance. The texture, however, was the typical tonal counterpoint of the Baroque period and not the modal counterpoint of the Renaissance. The motet was generally of liturgical nature and was used in both the Roman Catholic and Lutheran churches.

Ex: Motet: *Ich lasse dich nicht,* J. C. Bach
Möseler Verlag
HMS, vol. 5
Rec. RCA, LM-6030-1

> 6. *Spiritual concerto.*   Works variously known as *concerti ecclesiastici* and as *Geistliche konzerte* were frequently composed in the concertato style. They were restricted to a few voices with continuo or sometimes a few concerted instruments. Many of them were for only a single voice. The German composers of the seventeenth century used this type of composition most frequently since it could be used in much the same manner as a cantata in the Lutheran service.

Ex: Sacred Cantata: *O Herr, hilf,* Schütz
MM, p. 135
Rec. HS-9040
Ex: Chorale concerto: *Erschienen ist der herrliche Tag,* Schein
TEM, p. 217
Rec. HSE-9102

> 7. *Anthem.*   Baroque composers continued to write anthems (see Renaissance Vocal Compositions) for the Anglican church. The verse anthem with an introduction of dramatic style was most typical of the Baroque era.

Ex: Verse Anthem: *Hear, O Heavens,* Humfrey
      HMS, vol. 5, p. 38
      Rec. RCA, LM-6030-2

8. *Solo song.*   Solo songs, though not constituting a
major form were frequently written, especially
by the German composers. They were strophic,
usually of folk-like character in binary or ternary
form of arias with instrumental accompaniment.

Ex: *Meine Seufzer meine Klagen,* Erlebach
      HMS, vol. 5, p. 18
      Rec. RCA, LM-6031-1

B. Composite Forms

1. *Opera.*   The most significant composite vocal
form originating in the Baroque period was the
dramatic opera, first called *drama per musica.* The
first impulse toward this form was given by certain intellectuals, noblemen, poets, and musicians who met in Florence. They formed a group
known as the Florentine Camerata. They wished
to create a drama in which words should domi-
nate the music and dictate the rhythm. This was
a seventeenth century attempt to recreate what
was thought to be the role of music in the classical tragedies of the ancient Greeks. The expression of this desire came to be called the *monodic
style.* Opera generally concerned itself with secular themes shaped into dramatic form. Early
opera was based on Greek myths but later works
dealt with historical, legendary, and fictional heroes and heroines. A distinction between *opera
seria* (serious or grand opera) and *opera buffa*
(comic opera) came into existence at the end of
the seventeenth century.

Opera employed orchestra, chorus, and soloists.
The performances were staged with appropriate
scenic settings and dramatic presentation. Elaborate stage machinery was often a dominant part
of the stage decor. While the first operas were
performed for private showings in such surroundings as palace halls, theaters or opera

houses were soon built for public presentation and made provision for the *stage mechanic.*

Musically the opera used a variety of formal sections such as arias, choruses, dances, duets, and other ensemble numbers. The music was exclusively homophonic in texture. Choral passages, generously used in the early operas, were finally reduced to insignificant proportions, while the solo arias received more and more attention.

Because of the great public appeal of opera by the end of the seventeenth century, certain characteristics were attached to it by virtue of its place of composition and performance. Four general schools of opera can be discerned, namely Italian, French, English, and German.

The Italian school was the first and most widely disseminated. Its main centers were Florence, Venice, Rome, and Naples, from which it spread to all the great political and economic centers of Europe. By the end of the seventeenth century most Italian opera had become little more than an elaborate display of solo singing. Arias in *bel canto* style, displaying elaborately embellished and virtuoso passages were loosely held together by dramatic narrative sung in *secco* recitative. The orchestra provided an overture in Italian form and an inobtrusive accompaniment for the vocal passages which added little to the dramatic intensity of the work.

Ex: *Orfeo,* Monteverdi
     Bärenreiter, ed. No. 2031a
     Rec. DGG ARC. 270015

Ex: Opera Buffa: *La Serva Padrona,* Pergolesi
     Ricordi, ed.
     Rec. None. 71043

Ex: *Julius Caesar,* Handel
     Aria and Recitative: *V'adoro, pupille*
     HMS, vol. 5, p. 17
     Rec. RCA, LM-6030–1

French opera whose centers were the courts of the Louis of France differed from the Italian in language and general emphasis. The French composers, influenced by the great popularity and prestige of the classic French drama, tended to emphasize dramatic sincerity and action, and wrote arias of simpler melodic line with less demands on virtuoso technique. The inclusion of ballet episodes was an attempt to give national character to the French opera by continuing the tradition of the ballet de cour (see Glossary). In the French opera the orchestra provided an overture in the French style. It also provided the music for the dances as well as accompaniment for the singing.

Ex: *Scene infernale* from *Alceste*, Lully
      HMS, vol. 5, p. 20
      Rec. RCA, LM-6030–2
Ex: Scene from *Castor et Pollux*, Rameau
      MM, p. 172
      Rec. HS-9040
Ex: *Chaconne* from the opera-ballet, *Les Fetes Venitiennes*, Campra
      TEM, p. 270
      Rec. HSE-9103

English opera is represented by very few works. The general characteristics were adopted from French and Italian models. The tradition of the English dramatic form of the masque to which music was often added was influential in the few operas written.

Ex: *Dido and Aeneas*, Purcell
      Oxford University Press, Piano Score
      Rec. DGG, ARC-198424

In Germany, opera found wide acceptance and while the Italian style was well entrenched, a considerable number of important German composers were active. Most of their works were in the Italian style, even when written to German texts. The *Singspiel*, a German native form, in which songs of a popular nature were combined into a form of musical entertainment, was the only original form comparable to opera.

Ex: Scene: *Ach! Nero ist nicht Nero mehr,* from *Octavia,* Keiser
HMS, vol. 5, p. 26
Rec. RCA, LM-6030-2

Ex: Aria from *Croesus,* Keiser
TEM, p. 277
Rec. HSE-9103

2. *Oratorio.* The oratorio employed the same forces as the opera, but was distinguished from it in that it usually did not use dramatic action or stage settings for presentation. Originally performed in the oratory of the church in Italy, by the end of the Baroque era it had become a musical dramatic form based on a religious but nonliturgical theme, and presented in concert form. The oratorio, while it employed soloists, tended to emphasize the chorus and usually contained a number of large choral movements.

The forms of the solo and small ensemble movements were identical with those of opera though often of more reserved character. The choral movements, however, were almost exclusively contrapuntal in style, ranging from strict to free fugal forms. The oratorio frequently used a dramatic character known as the narrator (*storicus or testo*) who introduces and often narrates the story of the work by means of recitative. In this case the other dramatic characters use recitative only in introducing their aria and ensemble numbers.

Ex: *Jephte,* Carissimi
GMB, p. 244
Rec. M.H.-3137H

Ex: *Draw the Tear,* from *Solomon,* Handel
MM, p. 200
Rec. HS-9040

Ex: Oratorio scene: *Rappresentatione di Anima e di Corpo,* Cavalieri
TEM, p. 208
Rec. HSE-9102

3. *Passion music.* The settings of the passion of Christ as narrated in the four gospels of the New Testament were frequently set for both Catholic

and Lutheran church use. These settings were actually oratorios whose texts were restricted to the Biblical quotations concerning Christ's trial and crucifixion, and such other commentary as the composer might select in keeping with this subject. A narrator took the part of the Evangelist and sang all the narration that was not in direct quotation in recitative style. Other soloists took the parts of the Biblical characters and sang those solos which were commentary on the story. The chorus represented the people, soldiers, priests and also sang choruses based on the commentary. In some Passion settings for the Lutheran church, the German Protestant Chorales were also used. Other than these deviations the work was constructed in the same manner as the oratorios of the period.

Ex: *St. Matthew Passion, S.244, J. S. Bach*[1]
Eulenburg, ed.
Rec. DGG, ARC-2712001

4. *Cantata.* The cantata was used in several forms and for several purposes. There were both solo and choral cantatas written for liturgical and nonliturgical religious purposes, as well as secular occasions.

The structure of the cantatas was essentially the same in all instances. Small instrumental groups were employed for accompaniment with solo instruments often used in obligato fashion with the voice. Soloists and chorus provided the vocal forces. The forms of the aria, ensembles and choruses were those used in the opera and oratorio. Cantatas might be regarded as miniature, intimate types of oratorio of a chamber music variety. The only difference between the solo cantatas and the choral cantatas was the forces employed. Solo cantatas were written for a single solo voice. Choral cantatas used a chorus and usually some soloists.

1. The letter "S" refers to the numbering of Bach's works in the Schmieder thematic catalog.

While both Roman Catholic and Protestant composers wrote cantatas, those written by the Lutheran composers in the sixteenth and seventeenth centuries comprise the greatest wealth of
church music of this period. These were liturgical cantatas and might be said to represent a kind
of musical sermon since most cantatas were written for specific holy days in the church calendar.

Ex: *Laudate Dominum*, Buxtehude
     Bärenreiter, ed.
     Rec. None. 71258

Ex: *Wachet Auf*, Cantata No. 140 J. S. Bach
     N.S., p. 219
     Rec. None 71029

Ex: *Ein feste Burg*, Cantata No. 80 J. S. Bach
     OM, p. 149
     Rec. Sera. S-60248

Ex: Chorale and Chorus from *Christ lag in Todesbanden*, Cantata
     No. 4, J. S. Bach
     MM, pp. 208, 215
     Rec. HS-9040

Ex: Recitative and aria from *Stravaganze d' Amore*, Marcello
     TEM, p. 304
     Rec. HSE-9103

5. *Mass.*   The Catholic Mass continued to be set by
composers. In typical Baroque style it takes on a
dramatic character with addition of orchestral accompaniment and the frequent division of the
various sections into solo and ensemble as well
as choral settings. Even the da capo aria form is
employed in some instances.

Ex: *Messe de Minuit*, Charpentier
     Concordia Publishing House
     Rec. ANG-S-36528

VI. INSTRUMENTAL COMPOSITIONS

In general there were no specific instruments designated
for much of Baroque instrumental music. Instruments were interchangeable, for example, keyboard compositions could be
performed on the harpsichord, clavichord, or even the organ.

In ensembles violins, flutes and oboes were interchangeable, as were the bassoon, cello and string bass. In some works instruments such as the clarino trumpet, oboe d'amore, etc., were specified, but could be substituted by other instruments of the same range.

A. **Single Movement Forms and Structural Devices.**

1. *Toccata.*   The toccata, frequently called *prelude*, grew out of the improvisatory style and was a continuation of the Renaissance toccata. (See Renaissance Instrumental Compositions). In the mature Baroque style the improvisatory toccata was coupled with section in imitative contrapuntal style. A final crystallization of form was revealed in the toccata which framed a fugal middle section between two rhapsodic improvisatory parts. The toccata frequently was treated as a single movement independent of the fugue with which it was often paired. In this case it was likely to be of purely improvisatory nature.

Ex: *Toccata in e minor for Organ,* Pachelbel
MM, p. 156
Rec. HS-9039

2. *Prelude.*   This name is freely used to describe an introductory movement, usually one of improvisatory character. It is often applied to the toccata form itself. In the late Baroque, preludes coupled with fugues were usually rhapsodic in character.

Ex: *Prelude and Fugue in E flat major for Organ,* S.552 J. S. Bach
Peters, ed.
Rec. Col. MS-6748

Ex: *Toccata and Fugue in d minor for Organ* S.565 J. S. Bach
Peters, ed.
Rec. Col, MS-6261

Ex: *Prelude and Fugue in c minor* from the *Well Tempered Clavier,* S.846/893 J. S. Bach
NS, p. 207
Rec. DGG, 2714004

3. *Ricercar.* An imitative contrapuntal form for harpsichord or organ, the Baroque ricercar, in contrast to that of the Renaissance, is a work without contrasting sections in which one theme is developed imitatively. The distinction between ricercar and fugue is more a distinction of rhythmic drive than that of formal organization. The ricercar is inclined to be more modal in harmonic structure, exploits its thematic material with less climactic contrast, makes less use of sequential treatment, and uses thematic material that is slower moving and potentially less rhythmically significant.

Ex: *Ricercar dopo il Credo,* Frescobaldi
      MM, p. 144
      Rec. HS-9039

4. *Fugue.* The fugue is an imitative contrapuntal form built on a single theme known as the subject imitated in two or more individual voices. The exposition of the subject alternately on the tonic and the dominant pitch levels (the latter form of the subject is known as the answer), emphasizes the tonic-dominant relationship as a means of achieving formal developent. Fugues, in contrast to the ricercars from which they were developed, used subjects of more melodic and rhythmic character. They often employ a persistent counter-subject along with the principal subject and develop the subject through various key changes, rhythmic treatment, or sequential appearances. Episodes, or sections in which the subject does not appear in its entirety, alternate with repeated appearances of the subject in some or all of the voices. While the fugue is generally a single movement of comparatively brief duration, it is possible to present the fugal material in a great variety of key relationships so that the single movement could be drawn out to considerable length. A fugue with two subjects is called a double fugue.

While the fugue is essentially an instrumental form, especially well adapted to organ and other keyboard performance, the principle of fugal development is found in many of the other instrumental forms and also in the large choral works of the Baroque period. It represents the highest development of the harmonic contrapuntal technique of the period.

Ex: *Well Tempered Clavier, S.846/893* J. S. Bach
OM, p. 182; AMA, p. 100
Rec. DGG, 2714004

Ex: *Contrapunctus III*, from *The Arts of Fugue, S.1080* J. S. Bach
MM, p. 230
Rec. HS-9040

Ex: *Capriccio über dass Hennengeschrey*, Poglietti
TEM, p. 232
Rec. HSE-9102

5. *Fantasia.* A keyboard composition usually for organ, the fantasia was a larger and more complex kind of ricercar. It employs a single theme which is often presented in a series of sections so that the entire work takes on the form of contrapuntal variations on a theme.

The term *fancy* was used in England to designate works of this general nature written for an ensemble or consort of viols or wind instruments. It should be noted that the name fantasia was also given to improvisatory single movement works which were paired with the later fugues like the prelude and toccata.

Ex: *Fantasies for 3, 4, 5, 6, 7, Viole da Gamba*, Purcell
Nagels Musik-Archiv
Rec. DGG ARC 2533366

Ex: *Fantasie*, Telemann
TEM, p. 297
Rec. HSE-9103

6. *Orchestral overture.* While this term was used in various connotations, two forms growing out of the Italian and French opera are typical of the multiple section work under this heading, the French overtures and the Italian overtures. They

differ mainly in the order of the three sections that make up the complete work. The French overture consists of a slow, pompous, richly harmonic section that is followed by a lively, driving fugal section, and concludes with a return to the opening slow section or at least a part of it. The Italian overture reverses the order of movements to fast, slow, fast. Both types were used as pure orchestral forms as well as orchestral openings to operas.

Ex: *Overture to Armide,* Lully
MM, p. 152
Rec. HS-9039

Ex: *Sinfonia* to the opera, *La Caduta de Decem Viri,* A. Scarlatti
Rec. HSE-9103

7. *Theme and variation.*   An extension of the same form used in the Renaissance in which a melody either original, or pre-existing (more often the latter), is presented in a number of variations. In the Baroque such compositions became more idiomatic for the particular instrument for which they were written, often exploiting the technical aspects of instrumental performance. Two kinds of variation were employed. One type is of a contrapuntal character in which the melody remains intact as it wanders from voice to voice while the counterpoint changes in each variation. The other type is essentially homophonic; the harmony remains the same throughout while the melody above the harmony is ornamented or changed in the subsequent variations.

Ex: *La Follia,* Corelli
Schott, ed.
Rec. DGG ARC 2533133

Ex: *Goldberg Variations,* S.988, J. S. Bach
Eulenburg, ed.
Rec. DGG, ARC-198020

8. *Passacaglia and chaconne.*   While there are those who contend these two names designate different forms, both are basically variations on a repeated bass line (ostinato bass) of four to eight

measures. Sometimes this ostinato melody can be found in voices other than the bass so that the basic theme assumes the character of a harmonic pattern. Passacaglias and chaconnes were written for all types of instruments and combinations although those for keyboard are the more frequent.

Ex: *Passacaglia and Fugue in c minor* S.582, J. S. Bach
     NS, p. 158
     Rec. Col. MS-6261
Ex: *Chaconne for Violin,* Vitali
     Schirmer, ed.
     Rec. DGG ARC 2533086

9. *Chorale prelude.* A generic type of organ music in which a chorale tune is the basis of the composition. In some instances the chorale tune acts as a theme for a set of variations. Such works are known as *chorale partitas* or *chorale variations.* In other instances the chorale tune is used as the basis for a fantasia, and the work is then known as a *chorale fantasia.* By far the most popular, however, is a single setting of the chorale tune which might vary from a highly developed fugal treatment to a rather simple homophonic presentation. This form probably originated as a prelude to the actual singing of the chorale by the congregation in the Lutheran church.

Ex: *Chorale Prelude, In dulci jubilo* S.599/644, Buxtehude and J. S. Bach
     HMS, vol. 6, p. 26
     Rec. RCA, LM-6031-2
Ex: *Chorale Prelude, Christ lag in Todesbanden,* S.599/644, J. S. Bach
     MM, p. 212
     Rec. HS-9040
Ex: *Chorale Prelude, Nun komm, der Heiden Heiland,* Buxtehude
     TEM, p. 237
     Rec. HSE-9102

B. **Composite Forms**

Compositions with several independent sections or movements with contrapuntal texture are:

1. *Church sonata (Sonata da chiesa).* This composition evolved from the sectional canzona of the

Renaissance (see Renaissance Instrumental Compositions) into a rather freely designed composite form which became one of the most important in the chamber music of the Baroque period. While there are no definite forms for each of the movements, this type of composition generally uses alternating slow and fast tempos with contrapuntal or fugal style in one or more movements. The church sonata was written for various instrumental combinations: (1) any solo melodic instrument with continuo (see solo sonata); but (2) it was most frequently written for two violins or other melodic instruments and continuo (trio sonata). While dance forms were regularly found in the chamber sonata, movements of the church sonata were sometimes in dance forms though not necessarily so named. The church sonata often went by the simple name *sonata*, especially in the late Baroque.

Ex: *Sonata da chiesa in e minor*, op. 3, No. 7, Corelli
      MM, p. 162; NS, p. 77
      Rec. HS-9040

Ex: *Violin Sonata in g minor*, Tartini
      Schirmer, ed.
      Rec. None. 71361

2. *Chamber sonata (Sonata da camera).*   This is the ensemble form of the suite written as a solo sonata or trio sonata, but often using larger groups. Adherence to the basic four dances was less likely to be found in the chamber sonata. Additional and substitute dances were often used. A prelude frequently prefaced the chamber sonata, and movements other than dances, such as the aria, are often found.

Ex: Trio Sonata: *Concert Royal*, Couperin
      Editions de l'Oiseau Lyre, *Complete Works of Couperin*, vol. 7
      Rec. DGG ARC 2712003

Ex: *Violin Sonata in E Major*, S.1006, J. S. Bach
      Schirmer, ed.
      DGG—2709028

3. *Concerto.* Two forms of the concerto, the solo concerto and the concerto grosso, were the final instrumental contributions of the Baroque period. These two forms differed only in that the solo concerto used a single instrument as soloist, while the concerto grosso used a group of soloists, generally three, in contrast to the larger mass of orchestral sound.

Three movements are most frequently employed: an allegro, a slow movement in a closely related key, and a shorter fast movement in the original key. Each of the movements is constructed on the plan of alternating soloist (or soloists-concertino) and full orchestra (tutti or ripieno). While soloists and orchestra may be given different themes, usually the entire thematic material is presented by the full group and then developed by the soloist or soloists in turn. The solo concerto and the concerto grosso were never designed to display the technical virtuosity of the soloists. However, they offered the Baroque composer the possibility of combining the concertato idea, the polarity of bass and treble melody, the concept of clear major-minor tonality and the use of a number of separate movements, into a single idealized instrumental form.

Ex: *Violin Concertos, nos. 1 and 2,* S.1041/2, J. S. Bach
Schirmer, ed.
Rec. DGG ARC 2533075

Ex: *Concerto Grosso in C major* (first movement), Handel.
MM, p. 182
Rec. HS-9040

Ex: *Brandenburg Concerto no. 2,* S.1046/51, J. S. Bach
NS, p. 171
Rec. Ang. S-3627

Ex: Concerto: *La Primavera, Op. 8, no. 1* (first movement), Vivaldi
TEM, p. 286
Rec. HSE-9103

4. *Suite.* The idea of extending an instrumental piece by joining a number of dance movements of different rhythms and tempos was an extension of the Renaissance device of pairing dances.

(See Renaissance Dance Forms). The most con-
ventionalized suite was written for the harpsichord (keyboard suite) in which four dances were
combined to form a complete work. These dances
are the *Allemande, Courante, Sarabande,* and *Gigue.*
Each dance is generally in a binary form with the
first part ending in the dominant key and the second half returning to the tonic. The dances have
no thematic relationship to one another and the
only unifying factor is the constancy of key between all the dances. While the four dances
named were considered the basic dances of the
suite (*partita* in German, also *ordre* in French),
other dances, even those in current ballroom use,
were often added to, or substituted for, the original ones. This is especially true of the French
ordre. Each dance retains its original rhythmic
character but is cast in an idealized form with no
practical use in mind.

Ex: *Suite in e minor,* Froberger
     MM, p. 147
     Rec. HS-9039
Ex: Lute piece: *Tombeau de Mademoiselle Gaultier,* D. Gaultier
     TEM, p. 227
     Rec. HSE-9102

> 5. *Orchestral suite.*   As in the chamber sonata, there
> was no definite adherence in the orchestral suite
> to the basic four dances, and additional move-
> ments both dance and otherwise were freely used.
> The orchestral suite was often called an overture
> since the first movement is frequently in the form
> of the French overture.

Ex: *Suite no. 3 in D major for Orchestra,* S.1066/9, J. S. Bach
     Eulenburg, ed. NS, 211
     Rec. DGG 924005

> 6. *Keyboard sonata.*   The original use of the term
> sonata to differentiate instrumental from vocal
> works was often retained in the Baroque period.
> A number of keyboard compositions therefore
> bear the names sonata, though they do not re-
> semble either of the two typical sonata types of

the Baroque, the chamber or church sonatas. Some of these sonatas were in a number of movements and some were single movement works. Generally simple binary or ternary forms were used for the individual movements which varied from dance-like character to song types, usually homophonic in texture.

Ex: *Sonata in c minor*, D. Scarlatti
MM, p. 179
Rec. HS-9040

VII. IMPORTANT COMPOSERS

1. *Giulio Caccini* (c. 1546–1618) was an Italin singer and composer associated with the Florentine Camerata. His performance of the new type of monodic composition, *musica in stile rappresentativo*, was looked upon as the ideal of this style. His most important work was the collection of madrigals and arias published under the title *Nuove Musiche*, the preface to which gives one of the clearest and most detailed descriptions of the manner of performance of the new monodic style.

Ex: Madrigal: *Dovro dunque morire*
MM, p. 120
Rec. HS-9039

2. *Jacopo Peri* (1561–1633) was a member of the Florentine Camerata. His *Dafne* may be considered the first opera in the new monodic style. He was noted for his masterly handling of pedal-point basses, a device which suited his delight in somber subject matter.

Ex: Three pieces from the opera *Euridice*
GMB, p. 186
Rec. Tel. 2635014

3. *Jan Pieterzoon Sweelinck* (1562–1621) was a celebrated Dutch organist and composer. Two contributions to organ literature are outstanding—his development of the organ chorale variation which led to the organ prelude, and his use of

monothematic treatment in the ricercar which resulted in the form known as the fugue. While he also wrote a great number of vocal works in the Renaissance style, his organ compositions are early Baroque. His numerous pupils, mostly Germans, made him the founder of the famous north German organ school.

Ex: *Chorale Variation: Ach Gott, von Himmel sieh' darein*
HMS, vol. 4, p. 62
Rec. RCA-6029-1

4. *Claudio Monteverdi* (1567–1643) was the greatest of the early Italian Baroque composers and the creator of the first great operatic masterpiece in modern style. In his *Orfeo* he adapts the Florentine recitative style to the use of closed forms such as the aria and dance song. He was equally at home in the Renaissance polyphonic and the Baroque monodic idioms. His madrigals are among the finest of the Italian school, but even here he shows his association with the modern school of the Baroque through his close attention to word and mood expression. Monteverdi also used an enlarged orchestra and made some specific selection of instruments in his dramatic works. His harmonic usages for expressive purposes caused much adverse criticism, particularly by one Giovanni Artusi. Among his works are eight books of madrigals, a number of operas the most important of which are *Orfeo, Il Ritorno Di Ulisse, L'Incoronazione Di Poppea,* as well as dramatic scenes and religious music.

Ex: *Orfeo*
Chester, ed; OM, p. 72; NS, p. 46
Rec.Tel. 3635020

5. *Michael Praetorius* (1571–1621), a German composer and theorist who devoted himself entirely to the writing of Lutheran choral works. His most important contribution to music history was made in his treatise, *Syntagma Musicum.*

Ex: *Wie schön leuchtet der Morgenstern*
     HMS, Vol. 4, p. 39
     Rec. RCA, LM-6029-2
Ex: *Vater unser im Himmelreich*
     HAM, p. 189
     Rec. Plei-256

6. *Girolamo Frescobaldi* (1583–1643), an Italian organist and composer was an important link in the history of fugal form. While he wrote no works actually called fugues, his monothematic ricercars were among the most important forerunners of this form. As a teacher of Froberger his influence in the development of composition and performance of the south German organ schools was paralleled only by Sweelinck's influence in the north. He was recognized as one of the greatest organists of his day, having been appointed organist at St. Peter's in Rome. His compositions include the typical organ forms of the early Baroque such as toccatas, capriccios, ricercars, and canzonas. A collection of such works composed for church use in his *Fiori Musicali* (Musical Flowers).

Ex: *Organ Music*
     Bärenreiter, ed.
     Rec. Col MG 32311

7. *Heinrich Schütz* (1585–1672) was the greatest German composer before Bach. Evidence of his importance is the oft repeated designation of Schütz as the father of German music. His contacts with Italian music of the late sixteenth and early seventeenth centuries led him to write a great number of vocal works to German texts of a dramatic religious nature that introduced the new Baroque style into Germany. He adapted recitative, thorough-bass, concertato idiom to works for the Lutheran service, and laid the foundation for the great art of dramatic church music in his *Sacred Symphonies, Sacred Songs,* and *Little Sacred Concerti* which finally blossomed into the cantatas and passion musics of Bach and his contemporaries.

A recent revival of Schütz's work has revealed a
starkness and simplicity of dramatic presentation
that make such works as *The Seven Last Words, The
Christmas Story, The Resurrection of Our Lord*, and
his *Passion Music* extremely popular after three
hundred years.

Ex: *Seven Last Words*
Eulenburg, ed.
Rec. Turn-34521

8. *Johann Hermann Schein* (1586–1630) was another
German who helped introduce Italian monody
and instrumental music into Germany. His choral adaptations for the organ were representative
of the great interest in this form. A collection of
twenty suites for strings called the *Banchetto Musicale* represented some of the earliest instrumental works written in Germany. He also wrote a
great number of sacred and secular vocal compositions.

Ex: *Banchetto musicale, Suite no. 5*
Moeck, ed.
Rec. DGG, ARC-198166

9. *Samuel Scheidt* (1587–1654) is often considered the
most important German organ composer of the
first half of the seventeenth century, particularly
in his treatment of the chorale in true organ style.
His greatest published work, *Tabulatura Nova*, was
a collection of figured chorales, toccatas, fantasias, hymns, and other works for the organ.
Though his main contribution was in organ compositions, he wrote many choral works as well.

Ex: *Tabulatura Nova*
Ugrino, ed.
Rec. Orion 77264

10. *Pier Francesco Cavalli* (1602–1676) was celebrated
as an opera composer in his native Italy, where
he held the position as maestro di Cappella at St.
Mark's in Venice. He was also well known in
France and Austria. While he wrote church works
his forty-one operas gained him wide recogni-

tion. His greatest operatic successes were *Jason, Cerce,* and *Hercules, The Lover.* Cavalli's wide recognition attests to the rapid rise and acceptance of Italian opera in countries other than Italy.

Ex: Duet: *Musici della selva* from *Egisto*
HMS, vol. 5, p. 11
Rec. RCA, LM-6060-1

11. *Jacques Champion Chambonnieres* (c. 1602–1672) is regarded as the founder of the French clavecin school. As the teacher of Couperin the Elder, d'Angelbert, and others, his influence was felt not only in France but throughout Europe. He was first chamber musician to Louis XIV. His wide recognition influenced the German harpsichord composers from Froberger to J. S. Bach. His compositions were exclusively for the harpsichord.

Ex: *Keyboard Music*
HMS, vol. 6, p. 20
Rec. RCA, LM-6031-2

12. *Giacomo Carissimi* (1605–1674) was an Italian composer who applied the new devices of the monodic style to religious music, particularly the oratorio. His masterpiece, *Jephte,* is an example of his position as the founder of the oratorio.

Ex: *Afferte gladium,* from *Judicium Salomonis*
MM, p. 129
Rec. HS-9039

13. *Johann Jakob Froberger* (1616–1667) was a German organist and pupil of Frescobaldi whose techniques he introduced into Vienna. He wrote many works for the organ, and is credited with having created the keyboard suite and established the order of dances within it: Allemande, Courante, Sarabande and Gigue.

Ex: *Suite in e minor*
MM, p. 147
Rec. HS-9039

14. *Marc' Antonio Cesti* (1623–1669) was a well-known Italian opera composer whose works gained him wide recognition. *Il Pomo D'Oro* (The Golden

Apple) produced in Vienna in 1667 is regarded as his masterpiece.

Ex: *E dove t' aggiri* from *Il Pomo d' oro*
HMS, vol. 5, p. 12; OM, p. 81
Rec. RCA, LM-5030-1

15. *Jean-Henri d' Angelbert* (c. 1628–1691) was a French composer and a pupil of Chambonnières. His collection, *Pieces de clavecin avec la maniere de les jouer—Pieces for the Harpsichord with Instructions for their Performance,* contains suites, arrangements of airs from Lully's operas and variations as well as instructions on how to play figured bass.

Ex: *Prelude, Allemande, Sarabande* from a suite for harpsichord
HAM, vol. 2, p. 96
Rec. Vic, Vics-1370

16. *Jean-Baptiste Lully* (1632–1687) was the most distinguished opera composer of the seventeenth century in France though he was actually an Italian by birth. He succeeded in establishing a true French opera which was in effect a reform of the traditional Italian opera of his time with its many musical excesses. He was able to give the French opera a greater measure of dramatic sincerity through his handling of dramatic recitative, arias, and instrumental accompaniment. He established the ballet as a part of the French opera as well as the French overture. His musical production was not exclusively operatic, however, since he composed a great number of ballets for Molière's plays, and even some independent instrumental music and religious choral works. Among his operatic masterpieces are *Cadmus et Hermione, Alceste, Armide et Renaud, Thésée,* and *Perseé.*

Ex: *Scene infernale* from *Alceste*
HMS, vol. 5, p. 20
Rec. RCA, LM-6030-2

17. *Marc-Antoine Charpentier* (1634–1704) was a French composer, pupil of Carissimi, and mostly concerned with writing religious works—masses, motets, and oratorios. He also wrote operas and

smaller dramatic works for the stage, but suffered disfavor at the hands of Lully.

Ex: Oratorio scene: *Le Reneiment de St-Pierre*
TEM, p. 242
Rec. HSE-9103

Ex: Motet: *Ave Regina Coelorum*
SS, p. 175
Rec. None-71040

18. *Dietrich Buxtehude* (c. 1637–1707) was a famous German organist and composer. Buxtehude influenced J. S. Bach who made a two-hundred mile journey on foot from Arnstadt to Lübeck to hear Buxtehude play in 1705. Buxtehude's works include all the current forms of organ music, much choral music and a variety of chamber and harpsichord compositions.

Ex: Chorale Prelude: *In Dulci jubilo*
HMS, vol. 6, p. 26
Rec. RCA, LM-6031-2

19. *Johann Pachelbel* (1653–1706) was a middle German organist and composer mainly of organ works though he also wrote for the other keyboard instruments. His fugues are of utmost importance not only because of their influence on Bach's writing in this form, but for their intrinsic artistic value.

Ex: *Toccata in e minor*
MM, p. 156
Rec. HS-9040

20. *Arcangelo Corelli* (1653–1713) was Italian, one of the first great violin virtuosos, and a composer of great importance. He is looked upon as the founder of modern violin technique with its intricacies of bowing, performance of double stops, and chord effects. He was not a prolific composer. His entire output consisted of six opus numbers or collections of which four are devoted to trio sonatas, one to violin and keyboard, and one to the concerto grosso. The latter represents a new form of composition of which Corelli is recognized as

the creator. Handel was acquainted with Corelli
and was undoubtedly influenced by his instrumental writing.

Ex: *Concerto grosso Op. 6, no. 8 "Christmas Concerto"*
      Eulenburg, ed.
      Rec. DGG 2530070
Ex: *Violin Sonatas Op. 5,*
      Schott, ed.
      Rec. DGG ARC 2533132/3

21. *Henry Purcell* (c. 1659–1695) was England's most
    famous Baroque composer, and his death in 1695
    brought to an end any important musical contri-
    bution from a native English composer for the
    next two hundred years. Despite a very short life
    his works are numerous and representative of all
    areas of composition, church, dramatic, and in-
    strumental. He was equally gifted as an instru-
    mental and vocal composer. Among his most
    important works are the numerous anthems and
    religious choral compositions; the collection of
    twelve trio sonatas published during his life-
    time, and his one opera, *Dido and Aeneas*, a work
    still frequently performed. Purcell was singu-
    larly gifted in his ability to compose on a ground
    bass and a number of the famous arias from his
    opera, notably Dido's aria, *When I am Laid in Rest,*
    are constructed in this form.

Ex: *Dido and Aeneas*
      Oxford University Press, ed., OM, p. 102
      Rec. DGG, ARC—198424
Ex: *A New Ground*
      MM, p. 159
      Rec. HS-9040

22. *Johann Kuhnau* (1660–1722) was a German com-
    poser whose works for the harpsichord are the
    most important among his other instrumental and
    vocal compositions. He was J. S. Bach's immedi-
    ate predecessor as cantor at St. Thomas Church in
    Leipzig. His most important works are his sona-
    tas for harpsichord, especially the group of six
    entitled *Biblical Sontas* which are early examples

of program music in which Biblical stories are illustrated by means of musical allusion.

Ex: *Biblical Sonata No. 2*
Broude, ed.
Rec. M.H.-879T

23. *Alessandro Scarlatti* (1660–1725) was known mainly for his contributions to the style of the Neapolitan opera of which he wrote over one hundred. He also added a rich literature of chamber and orchestral music as well as religious cantatas and masses to Italian music of the Baroque. Scarlatti established the da capo aria in the Neapolitan opera, a form which was generally adopted for all dramatic arias.

Ex: Quartet: *Idolo mio ti chiamo Tito* from *Tito Sempronio Gracco*
HMS, vol. 5, p. 16
Rec. RCA, LM-6030–1

24. *François Couperin* (1668–1733) was a member of a famous French family of musicians. He was known as Couperin le Grand, because of his enormous skill as an organist. His religious compositions, mainly for the organ, constitute a large part of his works. His most numerous and renowned compositions, however, are those instrumental works which he wrote for the harpsichord during the last part of his life. The many *ordres* or suites for clavecin consist of dances which are often programmatic in nature. He also wrote *The Art of Playing the Clavecin* which was of wide influence. Among his best known works are the *Concerts Royaux*, the four volumes of *Piéces De Clavecin*, and *Les Gouts Réunis*, the latter consisting of a number of concerted pieces written for strings and clavecin. Couperin's works are characterized by the polarity of bass and melodic line and use of ornamentation typical of the gallant style of his time.

Ex: *Concerts Royal*
Editions de l'Oiseau Lyre. Complete edition, vol. 7
Rec. DGG ARC 2712003

Ex: *La Galante*
      MM, p. 169
      Rec. HS-9040

>   25. *Antonio Vivaldi* (c. 1678–1741) was the most cele-
>   brated of all the Baroque Italian masters and
>   probably the most musically prolific. While he
>   wrote a large number of operas, oratorios, secular
>   cantatas, and church music, his present fame rests
>   in his concerti grossi and solo concertos. These
>   number over four hundred. Vivaldi was a priest
>   in the Roman Catholic church and for many years
>   was in charge of the musical program of the Os-
>   pitale della Pieta in Venice, a home for orphaned
>   and foundling girls. It was in discharge of this
>   duty that he wrote most of his instrumental and
>   smaller choral works which were performed by
>   the girls in the institution. Among the most fa-
>   mous of the concerti grossi are the works known
>   as *L'Estro Harmonico* (Harmonical Whim), *Cimento
>   dell' armonia e dell' invenzione* (The Struggle be-
>   tween Harmony and Invention) and *Le Stagioni*
>   (The Four Seasons). J. S. Bach was especially in-
>   fluenced by Vivaldi's concertos and transcribed
>   several for clavier.

Ex: *Concerto for Flute and String Orchestra*, Op. 10, no. 3 "Il Gar-
      dellino"
      Schott, ed.
      Rec. DGG 2533044
Ex: *Concerto Grosso Op. 3 no. 11 in d minor*
      NS, p. 84
      Rec. LON. STS. 15364

>   26. *Georg Philipp Telemann* (1681–1767) was perhaps
>   the most prolific of German composers of the late
>   Baroque era. His compositions covered every
>   conceivable field of musical performance. Some
>   concept of his enormous output can be gained
>   from the fact that he wrote some forty operas,
>   about three thousand cantatas and motets with
>   orchestra or organ, six hundred overtures, forty-
>   four passion settings, and equally numerous
>   works for special occasions such as funerals,
>   weddings, coronations, consecrations. His fame

was considerably greater during his lifetime than that of J. S. Bach whose life-span was contained within that of Telemann. The last forty-six years of his life were spent in Hamburg where he was city director of music. He took this position in preference to that of cantor of St. Thomas Church in Leipzig. The latter position was then assumed by Bach who was second choice to Telemann in the eyes of the church council. Telemann remained relatively unknown during the nineteenth and early part of the twentieth centuries. However, the revival of interest in Baroque music during the past thirty years has brought his music to the fore again, particularly the orchestral and chamber music.

Ex: *Concerto in D major for Trumpet, 2 Oboes and Continuo*
Sikorski, ed.
Rec. None. 71132

Ex: Opera: *Pimpinone*
Bärenreiter, ed.
Tel. 2635285

27. *Jean Philippe Rameau* (1683–1764) was well known in his day as a musical theorist, organist and composer. His early career was that of organist in several of the great cathedrals of France. While serving in this capacity at Clermont-Ferand, he wrote his famous *Treatise of Harmony* in 1722. In this work he stated his system of chord building on superimposed thirds; the conception of a chord in all its inversions as one and the same entity; and the idea of a fundamental bass by which chord progressions are determined. His fame as a composer, however, is based mainly on his dramatic compositions, of which the works *Les Indes Galantes* (The Gallant Indians) and *Castor and Pollux* are his masterpieces. Besides a long list of dramatic works—ballets, operas, and incidental music for drama—Rameau wrote a considerable amount of works for clavecin and chamber groups typical of the Baroque period. Rameau's dramatic works were exceptional for their expressive melodic line, originality of instrumentation, and richness of harmonic idiom. Rameau's

ideas aroused violent interest both antagonistic and favorable, first between those who favored him and those who favored Lully, and later between his adherents and the *Encyclopedists*. The latter exchange was known as the "War of the Buffoons." The perennial charges against the operatic innovator that were leveled against Monteverdi before him and Gluck and Wagner after him were leveled at Rameau. His critics found his works lacked melody, were filled with illogical harmony, and used orchestral instruments in a noisy fashion.

Ex: *Pie'ces de Clavecin*
      Durand et Fils, ed.
      Rec. Turn-34243
Ex: *Les Indes Galantes*
      Durand et Fils
      Rec. Col. M-32973

28. *Johann Sebastian Bach* (1685–1750) is recognized as one of the greatest composers of all times. He was a member of what is, perhaps, the most interesting musical family in history. Over one hundred members of the Bach family in Thuringia were occupied in musical activities. Of this number some twenty were performers and composers of special significance, including both ancestors and offspring of Johann Sebastian.

At fifteen years of age Bach spent a short time of study with his brother Johann Christoph in Lüneburg. A year as violinist in the orchestra of the Duke of Saxe-Weimar was followed by his first real post as organist in Arnstadt in 1704. He left Arnstadt in 1707 to take the post of organist in Mülhausen. In 1708 he moved again, this time to Weimar where he was made court organist and chamber musician to the Duke of Weimar. In 1714 he was raised to the rank of chamber musician and remained in this post until 1717. During this time he made a reputation for himself as one of the great organists of his day as well as a composer of a wide variety of works in both secular and religious fields. In 1717 he accepted the post of chapelmaster and director of chamber music to the Prince of Anhalt at Cöthen. Here Bach composed most of his orchestral and chamber music. His wife Barbara died in 1720, and in 1721 Bach married Anna Magdalena Wülken, a gifted musician whose handwriting is often found in early manuscripts of Bach's works.

In 1723 Bach succeeded Kuhnau as cantor of the Thomas School in Leipzig, a post he held until his death in 1750. As organist and director of music at the two principal churches in Leipzig, Bach composed most of his great church music during the next twenty-seven years.

Among the many visits he paid to other cities in the capacity of organist, organ installer, and composer, none was more famous than the one to the court of Frederick the Great in Potsdam where his second son, Karl Philipp Emanuel, was chamber musician. It was during this visit that Bach improvised upon a theme given him by Frederick, a theme which he later used as the basis for his work known as *The Musical Offering*. An unsuccessful eye operation in 1749 caused Bach to become totally blind, and in 1750 he died from a stroke of apoplexy. Bach represents the culmination of an era, particularly through his great emphasis on contrapuntal style. He was a master of the art of tonal counterpoint and his *Art of the Fugue* is a veritable exhaustive treatise dealing with all manners of contrapuntal devices illustrated in the canons and fugues which comprise the work. His skill in handling fugal treatment is evident in all types of compositions, instrumental, vocal, secular, and religious. In his use of instruments he foreshadowed the future in music. He composed in every conceivable form except that of the opera. While the great preponderance of his works were written for the church, there is much of his instrumental output that is strictly secular in nature. Even the smallest works, however, demonstrate his care and attention to compositional excellence. His mastery of counterpoint within the tonal system is comparable to that of Palestrina within the modal idea.

It was more than half a century after his death before any measurable appreciation of his great contribution to the history of music was realized. Mendelssohn brought Bach to the attention of the musical world of the nineteenth century with a performance of the *Saint Matthew Passion* in Leipzig in 1829.

A great number of Bach's works were lost in manuscript. A comparatively small amount was published during his lifetime. Despite the great loss the complete edition begun in 1850 by the Bach Gesellschaft contained forty-seven volumes. A second complete edition is now in process of publication. Bach's works were not given chronological opus numbers. Wolfgang Schmieder published a thematic-systematic catalog in 1950 (6th edition, 1969). Bach's works are now listed with these numbers preceded by "S."

Among the great masterpieces remaining today are the following works listed under vocal and instrumental headings:

Vocal works: *Mass in b minor, The Saint Matthew Passion, The Saint John Passion, The Christmas Oratorio,* two *Magnificats,* approximately one hundred and ninety church cantatas, over twenty-five secular cantatas, and many other short works.

Instrumental Works: *The Art of the Fugue, The Musical Offering, The Italian Concerto for Harpsichord, The Goldberg Variations for Harpsichord, The Well Tempered Clavier,* suites, partitas, and inventions for harpsichord, *Four Overtures (Suites) for Orchestra, The Brandenburg Concertos, Six Solo Suites for Violoncello, Three Sonatas and Three Partitas for Solo Violin,* numerous works for organ, including chorale preludes, toccatas, preludes, fantasias and fugues, and concertos for harpsichord and violin as well as numerous sonatas for instrumental combinations.

Ex: *Goldberg Variations for Harpsichord,* S.988
       G. Schirmer, ed.
       Rec. DGG, ARC-198020
Ex: *The Art of the Fugue,* S.1080
       Peters, ed.
       Rec. DGG, ARC-2708002
Ex: *The Brandenburg Concertos,* S.1046/51
       Eulenburg, ed.
       Rec. DGG, ARC-2709016
Ex: Cantata: No. 21 *Ich hatte viel Bekümmernis,*
       Eulenburg, ed.
       Rec. Tel. 2635032
Ex: *Saint Matthew Passion,* S.244
       Eulenburg, ed.
       Rec. DGG, ARC-2712001

29. *Domenico Scarlatti* (1685–1757), the greatest of the Italian composers for the keyboard, was one of the most original composers in the history of music. While he wrote works for the church and for the operatic stage, his greatest contribution was his more than five hundred compositions for the harpsichord. He was the son and pupil of Alessandro Scarlatti. After a very productive youth in Italy he took a post with the Portuguese court in Lisbon where he became music master to the Princess Maria Barbara. It was for her that he composed the works that were to make him famous, the *Esercizi per gravicembalo (Exercises for the Harpsichord),* which usually go by the name sonatas today. When the princess married the heir to the Spanish throne, Scarlatti moved to Madrid where he spent the remainder of his life from 1729 to 1757 as master of the salon. His sonatas are the finest example of late Baroque writing for the harpsichord. Scarlatti managed to exploit the instrument to the utmost in these works and in so doing laid the foundation for future keyboard technique. Many of the works call for such innovations in performance as the crossing of the hands. The sonatas of Scarlatti reflect the whole gamut of moods from the gay and dance-like,

which often include Spanish rhythms, to the songlike and romantic.

Ex: *Sonatas*
G. Schirmer, ed.
OM, p. 92; AMA, p. 144; NS, p. 278
Rec. DGG, ARC-2533072

30. *Georg Friedrich Handel* (1685–1759) was a compatriot of Johann Sebastian Bach, and one who shares with him the distinction of bringing an era to a close.

In contrast to Bach, Handel was a cosmopolitan composer who added to his German heritage a wide study and firsthand knowledge of the Italian musical style, and practiced these accomplishments during most of the last fifty years of his life in England. Handel was something of a musical prodigy, for after instruction on organ, oboe, and harpsichord as well as in counterpoint and fugue, he assumed the position as assistant organist in Halle, his native city, at the age of twelve. During this year he also composed a number of choral and instrumental works. In 1702 Handel went to Hamburg where he was associated with the opera until 1706. In the same year he went to Italy where he became successful as a composer of Italian opera and dramatic oratorios. In 1710 he returned to Germany as chapel master to the Elector of Hanover, a relationship that resulted in his going to England when this prince took over the throne of England.

From this time on Handel was occupied with a variety of activities: teacher, director of the Royal Academy of Music (an institution whose prime purpose was the production of Italian opera in London) composer, opera impresario, and traveler. His main compositional area was that of opera until 1741, when he turned to the composition and production of oratorios. It is in the latter field that he achieved a lasting fame.

In general it might be said that Handel reflects the past in his emphasis on the vocal media, but foreshadows the future in his predominantly homophonic style. His compositions, both secular and religious drama, reveal a spirit of grandeur, for there is always something of the pomp of the court about all his works. He wrote twenty-seven oratorios and over forty operas as well as a great quantity of other vocal forms such as anthems, masques, cantatas, and vocal solos and ensembles. Handel was also a prolific composer of instrumental compositions which include all the Baroque forms: concerti grossi, harpsichord suites, organ concerti, chamber music for strings, winds, and keyboard, and large orchestral works. Among his vast number of works a few stand out as masterpieces: the oratorios, *The Messiah, Samson, Judas Maccabaeus, Solomon, Israel in Egypt, Saul;* the operas, *Alcina, Julius Caesar, Rinaldo, Xerxes;* for orchestra, *The Water Music, The Fire-works Music,* and *Twelve Concerti Grossi for Strings.*

Several incomplete and often inaccurate editions of the works of Handel have been issued from time to time. In 1955 work was begun on a new complete edition issued by the Georg Friedrich Handel Gesellschaft of Halle.

Ex: *Concerti Grossi,* Op. 6,
      Bärenreiter, ed.
      Rec. Vox-SVBX558(Q)

Ex: *The Messiah*
      G. Schirmer, ed.; NS, p. 113
      Rec. ANG-S-3657

Ex: *Julius Caesar*
      Bärenreiter, ed.; NS, p. 110
      Rec. RCA LSC-6182

31. *Giovanni Battista Pergolesi* (1710–1736) whose short life fell entirely within the eighteenth century was, however, still representative of the Baroque style of composition. He wrote both instrumental and vocal music, but it was his opera buffa compositions which were to bring him fame. Pergolesi wrote three of these works which were performed between the acts of his serious operas. The most famous of these *La Serva Padrona* which was the rival opera to Rameau's works that were

the focus of the 'War of the Buffoons' (1752), is still found in the modern opera repertoire. While a large number of trio sonatas, solo sonatas, and concertos in the Baroque style are ascribed to Pergolesi, it is doubtful that many of them are his work. A number of religious works were published, the best known today being the *Stabat Mater*.

Ex: Opera Buffa: *La Serva Padrona*
      Ricordi, ed.
      Rec. None. 71043
Ex: *Recitative and Aria* from the opera Buffa; *Livietta e Tracollo*
      TEM, p. 314
      Rec. HSE-9103

VIII. OTHER COMPOSERS

A. Austria
1. *Heinrich Ignaz Franz von Biber* (1644–1704)
2. *Johann Joseph Fux* (1660–1741)

B. England
1. *Henry Lawes* (1596–1662)
2. *Matthew Locke* (c. 1630–1677)
3. *Pelham Humfrey* (1647–1674)
4. *John Blow* (1648–1708)

C. France
1. *Robert Cambert* (1628–1677)
2. *Michel-Richard de Lalande* (1657–1726)
3. *Jean Marie Leclair* (1697–1764)

D. Germany
1. *Melchior Franck* (c. 1579–1639)
2. *Franz Tunder* (1614–1667)
3. *Johann Caspar Kerll* (1627–1693)
4. *Nikolaus Adam Strungk* (1640–1700)
5. *Johann Christoph Bach* (1642–1703)
6. *Johann Krieger* (1651–1735)
7. *Georg Muffat* (1653–1704)
8. *Philipp Heinrich Erlebach* (1657–1714)
9. *Georg Boehm* (1661–1733)
10. *Reinhard Keiser* (1674–1739) .
11. *Christof Graupner* (1683–1760)

12. *Johann Gottfried Walther* (1684–1748)
13. *Johann Friedrich Fasch* (1688–1758)
14. *Johann Adolph Hasse* (1699–1783)

E. **Italy**

1. *Emilio del Cavalieri* (c. 1550–1602)
2. *Adriano Banchieri* (1568–1634)
3. *Salomone Rossi* (1587–1630)
4. *Stefano Landi* (1590–1655)
5. *Domenico Mazzochi* (1592–1665)
6. *Biago Marini* (1595–1665)
7. *Giovanni Legrenzi* (1626–1690)
8. *Alessandro Stradella* (1642–1682)
9. *Giovanni Battista Vitali* (1644–1692)
10. *Agostino Steffani* (1654–1728)
11. *Giuseppe Torelli* (1658–1709)
12. *Antonio Lotti* (1667–1740)
13. *Giovanni Bononcini* (1670–1747)
14. *Tomaso Albinoni* (1671–1750)
15. *Evaristo Felice dall' Abaco* (1675–1742)
16. *Francisco Durante* (1684–1755)
17. *Nicola Porpora* (1686–1768)
18. *Benedetto Marcello* (1686–1739)
19. *Francesco Geminiani* (1687–1762)
20. *Francesco Maria Veracini* (1690–1750)

IX. IMPORTANT WRITERS ON MUSIC

1. *Giovanni de' Bardi* (1534–c. 1612) was an Italian aristocrat who through his philosophical and literary interest founded the Florentine Camerata, the group whose investigation led to the first operatic composition. His writings, all in Italian, are concerned with speculations concerning the *new music.*

2. *Giovanni Maria Artusi* (c. 1540–1613) was an Italian writer on music. *L'Artusi ovvero dello imperfezioni della moderna musica, Venice 1600* (Artusi, concerning the imperfections of modern music) is a representative critical essay. Artusi was very conservative in his musical philosophy and is remembered mainly for his criticism against the *new style* as represented by Monteverdi at the opening of the seventeenth century.

3. *Michael Praetorius* (1571–1621) was a German musician, composer, and theorist. His *Syntagma Musicum*

(Musical encyclopedia), Wittebergae (1615–1618), appeared in three volumes. The first, written in Latin, deals with ancient church music and secular instruments. The second volume, in German, is an exhaustive treatise on the instruments of the Baroque period and represents the most important source of information in this area. Forty-two woodcuts depicting the principal instruments add to its importance. The third volume contains accounts of secular music. This total work is, perhaps, the most valuable treatise written during the Baroque period. Reprints of the second and third volumes were made in 1929 and 1916 respectively.

4. *Marin Mersenne* (1588–1648) was a French theorist. His *Traite de l' Harmonie Universelle* (Treatise Concerning Universal Harmony), Paris 1627, was published in an expanded form in 1936 and 1937 as *Harmonie Universelle.* It includes a discourse on harmonic theory and an especially valuable description, both verbal and pictorial, of all the instruments of the seventeenth century. An English version of this work was published under the title *Harmonie Universelle: The Books on Instruments,* 1957.

5. *Christopher Simpson* (c. 1610–1669) was an English violist and composer. *The Division Violist or an Introduction to the Playing Upon a Ground,* London 1659, is a book of instruction in the playing of the viol and improvisation. A modern edition was published in 1958.

6. *Johann Joseph Fux* (1660–1741) was a German composer and theorist whose most important work was *Gradus ad Parnassum* (Steps to Parnassus), Vienna 1725. An English translation was published in 1943. This work became a standard text in contrapuntal instruction and was studied by such masters as Mozart and Haydn, and used by such distinguished teachers as Cherubini and Albrechtsberger. It was of great influence in the teaching of counterpoint for well over a century.

7. *François Couperin* (1668–1733) was a French composer, organist and clavecinist. *L'Art de toucher le clavecin* (The art of playing the harpsichord), Paris 1716, described Couperin's manner of performance of his clavecin pieces and is of greatest importance in its description of the manner and style of playing the keyboard literature of the seventeenth and eighteenth centuries.

8. *Johann Mattheson* (1681–1764) was a German composer and writer. His *Grundlage einer Ehren-Pforte, woran der tüchtichsten Capelmeister, Componisten, Musikgelehrten, Tokünstler, etc., Leben, Werke, Verdienste, etc., erschienen sollen* (Foundation for a triumphal arch on which the lives, works and success of the greatest directors, composers, learned musicians, and artists shall be inscribed) Hamburg 1740, was a biographical dictionary which is a source of historical information of the period.

9. *Jean-Philippe Rameau* (1683–1764) was a French composer and theorist. His *Traité de l' Harmonie* (Treatise on Harmony) Paris 1722, presented the revolutionary idea of a harmonic system in which the chords were built on thirds and were classified in all their inversions as the same chord. Rameau's treatise also established the primacy of chords on I, IV, and V in a given key.

10. *Francesco Geminiani* (1687–1762) was an Italian violinist, composer and writer. *The Art of Playing the Violin*, London 1730, was first published anonymously and was the first method for violin instruction to be written. In 1751 it was published under Geminiani's name as *The Compleat Tutor for the Violin*. A facsimile edition was published in 1952. This work is of utmost importance in the study of principles of violin playing of the Baroque era.

11. *Giuseppe Tartini* (1692–1770) Italian violinist, composer and theorist, wrote a number of theoretical works dealing with his discovery of combination tones and other theories concerning harmonic structure.

12. *Jacques Hotteterre* (d. c. 1760) was a French flutist. His *Principes de la flûte traversière ou flûte d'Allemagne, de la flûte à bec ou flûte douce et du hautbois* (Principles of playing the tranverse or German flute, the recorder or sweet flute and oboe), Paris 1707, is the earliest work on the performance of the three wood wind instruments.

Excerpts in English from several of the foregoing works can be found in *Source Readings in Music History* by Strunk.

Bardi:	pp.	290–301
Artusi:	pp.	393–404
Fux:	pp.	535–563
Rameau:	pp.	564–574

Supplementary Readings

Borroff	pp. 257–360
Bukofzer	*Music in the Baroque Era*
Cannon-Johnson-Waite	pp. 247–286
Crocker	pp. 223–352
Grout	pp. 293–447
Lang	pp. 314–550
Oxford, vol. 5	pp. 1–776
Schirmer	ch. 13–17, 37
Wold-Cykler	ch. 8

Further References

David, Hans T. and Mendel, Arthur. *The Bach Reader*. New York: Norton, 1945.

Flower, Newman. *Handel*. London: Cassell and Co., 1959.

Geiringer, Karl. *The Bach Family*. New York: Oxford, 1954.

Grout, Donald J. *A Short History of Opera*. New York: Columbia University Press, 1947.

Hutchings, Arthur, *The Baroque Concerto*. New York: Norton, 1965.

Newman, William S. *The Sonata in the Baroque Era*. Chapel Hill: University of North Carolina Press, 1959.

Palisca, Claude V. *Baroque Music*. Englewood Cliffs: Prentice-Hall, 1968.

Salon of Marie Antoinette (1762–1764)
Elegantly decorated salons, such as this, were the centers of intellectual and artistic activity during the eighteenth century. It was in this kind of setting that the young Mozart performed for royalty. (Courtesy Keystone View Company)

6
Chronology
of the Classic

1684	Antoine Watteau (1684-1721)	1735	J. C. Bach (1735-1782)
1694	François Voltaire (1694-1778)	1739	Karl von Dittersdorf (1739-1799)
1696	Giovanni Tiepolo (1696-1770)	1743	Luigi Boccherini (1743-1805)
1701	Giovanni Sammartini (1701-1775)	1748	Jacques Louis David (1748-1825)
1703	François Boucher (1703-1770)	1749	Johann Wolfgang Goethe (1749-1832)
1710	Louis XV (1710-1774)	1751	Benjamin Franklin experiments with electricity
1714	Willibald von Gluck (1714-1787) K. P. E. Bach (1714-1788)	1755	Marie Antoinette, Queen of France (1775-1793)
1716	Etienne Maurice Falconet (1716-1791)	1756	Wolfgang Amadeus Mozart (1756-1791)
1717	Johann Stamitz (1717-1757) Maria Theresa Empress of Austria (1717-1780)	1757	Antonio Canova (1757-1822)
1723	Sir Joshua Reynolds (1723-1792)	1760	George III of England reigned until 1820 Luigi Cherubini (1760-1842)
1724	Immanuel Kant (1724-1804)	1769	Watt's steam engine patented Napoleon Bonaparte (1769-1821)
1726	Charles Burney (1726-1814)		
1732	Jean Honoré Fragonard (1732-1806) Franz Joseph Haydn (1732-1809)	1770	Ludwig van Beethoven (1770-1827) First New York performance of *Messiah*

1771   First Edition of the
Encyclopedia Britannica
1774   Discovery of oxygen
1776   American declaration of
independence
Burney's *History of Music*
published
Discovery of hydrogen
1788   Steamboat invented
1789   Beginning of the French
revolution

1792   White House built
1793   Louis XVI of France
beheaded
1794   Haydn's second trip to
London
1795   Paris Conservatory
founded
1799   Beethoven's First
Symphony finished

6
Classic
1725-1800

I. SOCIOCULTURAL INFLUENCES ON MUSIC

The term *Classic* is used here to designate the music of the eighteenth century. This term has also been used by historians to describe all the arts that are concerned mainly with problems of form, logic, balance and restrained expression, and that were also based on models of Greek and Roman art. Unfortunately, there are no such models for Classic music to emulate. Consequently the term, as applied to music, refers to the works of those eighteenth century composers whose music gives the impression of clarity, repose, balance, lyricism and restraint of emotional expression. The Classic period is one of the high points of music history and was nourished by a number of important developments in the patronage and function of music during this time.

Austria and Germany became the center of a very vital musical activity. It must be noted that in these countries there were a large number of courts that were able to maintain their independence. This was in contrast to France and England, where almost all aristocratic life had come under the influence of a central power. In Austria and Germany, however, these small courts gave up much of their political and economic independence, but maintained their artistic and social status. There was even greater rivalry among them in artistic and social matters. Moreover, a long tradition of instrumental music, an abundance of talent, a natural love of music among all classes, great artistic ambition combined with great wealth—together these made the perfect conditions for an enthusiastic patronage.

Composers depended upon the patronage of a court or aristocratic society that was very discriminating in its tastes. This society was not only sophisticated and elegant, but disclaimed any affinity for being profound, or showing its emotion. The Age of Reason had placed a premium on intellectual pursuits and looked with a good deal of suspicion on any reliance upon feelings.

The concert hall and opera house became established institutions. This made it possible for all classes to enjoy the fruits of creative activity, whether aristocratic or not.

Publishing houses became well established and exerted a strong influence on both composers and the public. They not only made performances of musical works more widespread, but publishers were in a position to champion certain composers—often at the expense of others.

There was a general decline in the patronage of the church toward serious music. While there were certain reform movements in both Protestantism and Catholicism during the eighteenth century, none of them provided a suitable climate for a continuous growth of religious music. Certainly, the rather shallow attitude of aristocratic society did little to maintain the religious music at the level of the Baroque.

II. FUNCTION OF MUSIC

Music in the Classic era served a highly sophisticated and aristocratic society. Its most common function was to provide delightful entertainment for guests in exclusive salons. Unlike Baroque music which often had a descriptive character, Classic music was more abstract and tended to avoid representation.

A larger but still discriminating audience patronized public concerts of orchestral music and the elegant spectacle of opera.

Music also served an important function in the home, for this was an era of amateur musical performances, both vocal and instrumental. Many serious composers were called upon to write chamber music as well as vocal solos and ensembles for amateur consumption.

Naturally, music for dancing was in popular demand for a society that loved gaiety and entertainment.

While the church was not a major consumer of serious music, it still demanded that composers write sacred music for its services in the spirit of secularism that prevailed.

III. CHARACTERISTICS OF STYLE

All the characteristics of style applied to all forms in the Classic era. All of the following stylistic qualities were present to some extent in all of the classic forms, vocal or instrumental.

1. Formal organization
   a) Musical form was predicated on the idea of one melody being contrasted homophonically with a second melody, leading to the A B A formula. This was partly in protest against the complications of polyphony and partly an effort to create a form that could be grasped and enjoyed by all—aristocrat with discriminating taste and middle-class bourgeois.
   b) Forms are precise and clear, with sections being clearly marked off by cadences.
   c) Classic music is characterized by a symmetry of form. Musical periods tend to be balanced often in units of four measure phrases.
   d) Folk music in all its forms and idioms was gradually introduced into serious music. This was especially true of Haydn, who used some Croatian melodies and rhythms in his music. No doubt this reaching into folk music was due to the rather wide range of the Classic audience. Folk elements also appeared in opera and song.

2. Melody
   a) There was an emphasis on lyricism with smooth melodic contours. Ornaments were often written out and became a lyric part of the melody.
   b) Chordal structure was often the basis for melodic configuration. In fast tempos ascending chordal patterns were often referred to as *rocket figures* (ex. 28).
   c) Melodies were extended to the double phrase and more. This was in contrast to the generally short, cryptic melodic devices of earlier music.
   d) Melodic devices such as ornaments, sequential patterns, became formalized to a point of being clichés.

Example 28   Stamitz

3. Rhythm

a) Classic composers usually used very simple and constant rhythmic patterns that were clearly punctuated by rhythmic cadences.

b) There is a tendency toward uniformity of rhythmic patterns. Polyrhythms were no longer used as in earlier music.

c) An important formal device of rhythm was the Alberti bass which is the breaking up of the triad into broken chord figures with a repeated rhythmic pattern (ex. 29).

Example 29

d) Silence became a part of the element of rhythm. Strong cadences are sometimes followed by a measure of silence in order to heighten the effect of the cadence.

e) The tempo of a movement, or section, is always constant from beginning to end.

4. Harmony

a) Harmony is tonal with a harmonic rhythm that moves slowly and subordinate to the melody. This results in a predominately homophonic style (ex. 30).

b) Because the bass no longer served a melodic function, the Baroque polarity between soprano and bass disappeared. Consequently, the device of the basso continuo was discontinued.

c) Harmony is generally simple, rarely using anything more complicated than primary and various sevventh chords (ex. 30).

xample 30   W.A. Mozart

d) There is a formal key relationship between themes and between movements of forms. This key relationship serves to provide contrast and interest without introducing new material. In the exposition of the sonata-form the first theme is in the tonic. The second theme is in the dominant of the original, or the relative major if the first is in a minor key. The development usually contains a number of modulations away from either the tonic or dominant with a return to the tonic. In the recapitulation the second theme is in the tonic, thus reconciling the key relationships and enabling the movement to end in a tonic cadence. The key relations between movements are less varied. In general all movements are in the same key with the exception of the second movement, which is in the sub-dominant, dominant, or relative minor. If the first movement is in minor, the last movement is sometimes in the parallel major.

e) The most commonly used cadence was the IV, V, I with the final tonic on a strong beat (ex. 31).

Example 31

IV   V   I

The feminine cadence was also frequently employed. This is the usual authentic cadence, but with the final tonic on a weak beat (ex. 32).

Example 32

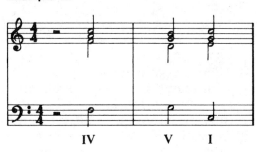

IV   V   I

5. Texture
   a) The texture of Classic music is essentially hom-
      ophonic, with lyric melody predominating.
   b) Even when polyphonic texture is present, there
      is a clarity and transparency of line that gives the
      music an almost filigree effect. In orchestral music
      this clarity of texture is emphasized by means of
      contrasting tonal coloring.
6. Media and tone color
   a) The most popular means of musical expression
      was instrumental—the orchesta, chamber music
      (both strings and winds) and solo instruments.
   b) The orchestra in the Classic period usually con-
      sisted of two flutes, two oboes (two clarinets), two
      bassoons, two horns, two trumpets, two tympani,
      and a complement of strings that numbered about
      twenty five. The orchestra was divided into four
      major groups—strings, wood-winds, brass, and
      percussion. With the exception of the percussion,
      each group became a complete choir in itself.
      Though the harpischord was still frequently used
      for the bass line and to supply harmonic texture,
      in general its use for this purpose diminished
      significantly toward the end of the eighteenth
      century.
   c) While the lute and harpischord had been the
      household instruments during the Renaissance
      and the Baroque, they were superceded by the
      piano during the late eighteenth century.
   d) Instrumental chamber music became very pop-
      ular. The large number of amateur performers
      and the intimacy of artistocratic society supplied
      a suitable climate for its development. Some of
      the finest of all Classic music can be found in the
      literature of the string quartet, piano quintets,
      trios, or sonatas.
   e) Another medium very much in demand was
      opera. Testimony of this can be seen in the large
      number of operas composed by both major and
      minor composers.

f) Aside from opera, vocal music was of minor importance, but remained in the form of religious music, folk songs, and the lied.

g) See Appendix A for description of instruments.

IV. PRACTICE AND PERFORMANCE

Dynamics became commonplace. This was another means of achieving contrast, but instead of changing the sonority as in the Baroque tutti and concertino, the Classic composer employed crescendo and diminuendo as well as sudden changes from *ff* to *pp*.

Composers gave explicit directions in dynamics, tempi, phrasing, and all other interpretive matters, leaving little for the performer's imagination.

While ornaments were not always written out, there was a precise formula for the designation of each figure. It is in this area that the Classic composer depended upon tradition and consequently the correct interpretation of ornaments is a serious problem for today's performer.

In the Classic period composers wrote for specific instruments and combination of instruments such as the string quartet, woodwind ensembles, etc. Composers designated the instrumentation to be used, contrary to the Baroque practice which permitted the performers to choose suitable instruments.

Among the important performers of the Classic period Mozart stands out as a virtuoso pianist with numerous performances as both pianist and conductor. While Haydn was not a virtuoso performer, he was a formidable conductor, scoring great success both at the Court of Esterhazy and, in his later years, in London with his Salomon symphonies. Luigi Boccherini was a notable cellist, as shown by his numerous celli concerti, which still remain as an important segment of the literature for this instrument.

V. INSTRUMENTAL COMPOSITIONS

A. Single Movement Forms and Structural Devices

1. *Sonata-form.* The sonata form is by far the most representative single movement form. It is almost always used as a first movement of a composite sonata or symphony, but may also be used as a slow movement or a final movement. It was also used as the structure of some single movement compositions. Its organization is basically threefold, consisting of: 1. The presentation of two contrasting harmonic sections, each of which may have the same or contrasting themes or theme groups (the exposition or statement). 2. The development of these themes through harmonic and motivic exploration and transformation (development section), and 3. their reconciliation harmonically, melodically, and rhythmically (the restatement or recapitulation section).

The following is the plan of the Classic sonata-form:

Exposition ‖:Th. I. (maj.) trans. Th. II. Dom. trans. Cl. Th.:‖
           ‖:Th. I. (min.) trans. Th. II. Rel. trans. Cl. Th.:‖

Development Varied treatment of material of the exposition
             in distant keys followed by a cadence.

Recapitulation Th.I. (maj.) trans. Th.II. tonic trans.
                Th.I. tonic min. trans. Th.II. tonic min. trans.
                Cl. Th. tonic, Coda.
                Cl. Th. tonic min., Coda

(Th. I is first theme; trans. is transition; Th. II is second theme; Cl. Th. is closing theme. The outline below the line is the pattern when the movement is cast in a minor key.)

Composers sometimes prefaced the sonata-form with a slow introduction which was a carry-over from the French overture and also served as a musical device to quiet the audience and gain attention. There was usually no connection between the musical material of the introduction and the thematic material of the sonata-form. This introductory section was most often used in the first movement of the symphony.

Most larger sonata-form movements added a Coda to the re-statement section. This was a section in the tonic key which strengthened the finality of the closing cadence.

Ex:[1] *Symphony no. 101, D major (Clock), first movement,* Haydn
Piano Sonata no. 14, c minor, K. 547, first movement, Mozart
String Quartet no. 1, F major, Op. 18, first movement, Beethoven

2. *Rondo.* The rondo is also predicated on the idea of repetition of a theme after a contrasting melodic idea. It differs from the sonata-form in that it has no development section and that the principal theme is always repeated in the tonic. The typical form is as follows: A B A C A B A. In a major key B is usually in the key of the dominant. If A is in a minor key, B is in the relative major. C which is in the tonic is usually a melodic idea of minor significance or merely an episode between the repetitions of A. Late eighteenth century composers frequently combined aspects of the sonata and rondo forms, resulting in an expansion of the middle section (C) through use of development techniques. This modification is often referred to as the "sonata-rondo form."

Ex.   *String Quintet in g minor, K. 516, last movement,* Mozart
Piano Sonata no. 2, A major, Op. 2, last movement, Beethoven

3. *Variation-form.* The variation was still popular in the Classic period. It was used extensively as the second movement of keyboard sonatas and also in some quartets and symphonies. In the Classic period, the variation-form was primarily homophonic. Variations were both harmonic and melodic, using contrasting tempi and rhythmic patterns as well as changes in tonal coloring.

Ex: *Clarinet Quintet, A major K. 581, last movement,* Mozart
String Quartet in C major, Op. 76, second movement, Haydn
Variation for piano in f minor, Haydn

I. Because a large number of scores and recordings by numerous publishers and recording companies exist for almost all music from the classic era to present day, specific editions and recordings will be omitted. Scores may be found in the anthologies suggested in the Introduction.

4. *Three-part song form.* The three-part song form is more instrumental than its name indicates. It is based on lyric melody in a simple A B A, and was often used as the second movement of a sonata.

Ex: *Piano Sonata no. 1 in f minor, second movement,* K. P. E. Bach
Symphony no. 101, D Major (Clock), second movement, Haydn

5. *Minuet, trio, and other dance forms.* While there were numerous single dance forms written specifically for ballroom dancing, the minuet is practically the only one which succeeded in achieving a place in the art music of the Classic period. In general the dance forms retained their two-part form of the Baroque, but the minuet became a three-part form in its Classic guise. Its plan is as follows (note that each of the sections is a three-part form):

A Minuet (A repeated, B plus A repeated)
B Trio (C repeated, D plus C repeated)
A Minuet (A B A all without repetition)

Ex: *Eine Kleine Nachtmusik, Serenade for String Orchestra,* K. 525, *Menuetto,* Mozart
Symphony no. 101, D major (Clock) third movement, Haydn

6. *Overture.* The eighteenth century overture was usually a sonata-form type structure. It was associated almost exclusively with the opera and was used as an expression of mood preparatory to the first scene. In the late eighteenth century composers began to incorporate material from the main body of the opera into the overture.

Ex: *Overture to Orfeo ed Euridice,* Gluck
Overture to Marriage of Figaro, Mozart

7. *Polyphonic instrumental forms.* The polyphonic forms of the Baroque were not completely discarded during the Classic period. They were, however, most often used as musical devices rather than complete forms. For example, the first theme of a sonata-form was sometimes cast as a *fugato* (fugal passage). Fugal passages were also often used in the development sections of the

sonata-form. Both Haydn and Mozart made extensive use of the fugue in this manner and used polyphonic forms both as single works and as complete movements in some of their later works. In contrast to the Baroque fugue, however, the subjects were usually longer and of a more lyric quality.

Ex.   *String Quartet, B major, K. 387, last movement,* Mozart
Symphonie no. 41, C major, K. 550, last movement, Mozart

B. **Composite Forms.**

1. *Sonata.* The most important composite form of the Classic era is the sonata, an abstract instrumental form of large dimensions in three or four separate movements. It was developed from the seventeenth century dance suite and trio sonata. It was also influenced by the Italian operatic overture. A Classic sonata usually consists of (1) a fast movement in sonata-form, (2) a slow movement in three-part song form, variation form, or sonata-form, (3) a minuet and trio, and (4) a very fast movement in rondo or sonata-form. On occasion this last movement is a variation-form, but in any event it is always in a fast tempo. If there are only three movements, the minuet is omitted. A sonata is the name used for this composite form when written for one or two instruments. When written for more than two instruments, it takes the name of the particular ensemble, such as a symphony, or trio. There is a potential universatility about the sonata. It is the only form that is divorced from religion, drama, and the dance. It also has more universal appeal than the polyphonic forms such as the fugue because it is less complicated intellectually. K. P. E. Bach is the composer who was mainly responsible for the sonata, although he cannot be credited with its invention.

Ex: *Piano Sonata no. 10, C major, K. 330,* Mozart
Sonata for Violin and Piano, G major, K. 301, Mozart
Piano Sonata no. 44, Haydn

2. *Symphony.* The symphony is a sonata for orchestra and is normally in four movements. The use of a larger group of instruments called for a much more extended composition. The varied tonal possibilities of the orchestra made it possible to have a greater variety of style, more extended climaxes, and a more complex development section. The first movement of the symphony was often preceded by a slow introduction.

There were two important "schools" of Classic symphony composers: the Mannheim school with Stamitz as its most important composer and the Viennese school of Haydn, Mozart, and Beethoven.

Ex: *Symphony no. 1, Op. 21, in C major*, Beethoven
Symphony no. 92, (Oxford), Haydn
Sinfonia a 8 in D major, Johann Stamitz

3. *Concerto.* This is a work for solo instrument (more rarely for two or more solo instruments) and orchestra in the pattern of the sonata, but generally omitting the minuet and trio thus making it a three-movement composition. In the first movement the orchestra presents an abbreviated exposition in the tonic, followed by the solo instruments direct statement of the thematic material. This device is designated as a double exposition. The development follows with the solo instrument pitted against the orchestra. Following the recapitulation, there is usually a brilliant cadenza—a free improvisation on the themes by the performer, although this was sometimes written out by the composer. The second and third movements follow that of the sonata with optional cadenzas.

Ex: *Cello Concerto in B flat major*, Boccherini
Piano Concerto, no. 20, d minor, K. 466, Mozart
Ex: *Concerto no. 10 in E flat major for Two Pianos,
K. 365*, Mozart.

4. *Chamber music.* All kinds of small instrumental ensembles, using the forms of the sonata come under this heading. These forms were called Trios, Quartets, Quintets, and Sextets and were for various combinations of string and wind instruments. However, the String Quartet was the most common. When the piano was used in combination with string instruments, the form was designated as a Piano Trio, Piano Quartet, Piano Quintet.

Ex: *Piano Trio, no. 1 in G major,* Haydn
Piano Quartet, no. 2 in E flat major, K. 493, Mozart
String Quartet, no. 19 in C major, K. 465 Mozart

5. *Serenades, divertimenti, cassations, notturni.* These works constituted a rather large body of literature usually written for specific occasions. They were often a continuation of the earlier suites and sinfonia of the Baroque, but were now based on the Classic characteristics of form and style. They were written for any number of instruments from small chamber groups to the full orchestra and in many instances consisted of a large number of separate movements.

Ex: *Divertimenti, Op. 31, Haydn*
Serenata Notturna, D major, K. 239, Mozart

VI. VOCAL COMPOSITIONS

A. Single Movement Forms and Compositional Devices

1. *Recitative.* This is not a form but a device of composition carried over from the Baroque period. Recitatives were both secco and orchestrally accompanied and had considerable musical interest, apart from carrying the narrative portions of the drama. The accompaniment itself was often highly suggestive of the atmosphere of the text.

Ex: *Cosi fan tutte,* Mozart

2. *Aria.*   The aria in the Classic opera of Gluck and Mozart avoided the spectacular virtuosity of the Baroque opera. While the principle of the da capo aria still prevailed, it was a much more expressive musical realization of the text. As in the recitative, the orchestra created the proper mood by means of lyric melody and tonal coloring.

Ex: *Alceste,* Gluck

3. *Choruses and ensembles.*   The operas of Gluck and Mozart use the chorus as an effective part of the drama. Ensembles, especially in Mozart, are marvelous examples of subtle musical dramatization. In contrast to the homophonic texture of the aria, these choruses and ensembles are usually polyphonic. Each member of the ensemble is often declaiming elements of counterplots and intrigue along with the main story. In essence this is both musical and dramatic counterpoint.

Ex: *Marriage of Figaro,* Mozart

4. *Vocal polyphony.*   While homophony was the basic texture of Classic vocal as well as instrumental music, polyphony as a compositional device still prevailed in some forms. This was especially true in operatic ensembles and in the chorus sections of the Mass and oratorios. Examples can be found in the ensembles of the *Marriage of Figaro* and *Don Giovanni* by Mozart. Haydn's *Creation* and Mozart's *Requiem Mass* show examples of polyphonic texture in religious vocal music. Polyphonic forms such as the canon and motet were still composed, often on light comic texts for social singing. Both Haydn and Mozart wrote many of these delightful works.

Ex: *Der Greis,* Haydn
Piu non si trovano, K. 549. Canzonetta for two sopranos and bass, Mozart.

5. *Lied.*   The Classic lied replaced the ornamented pathos of seventeenth century arias and songs. The lied was characterized by simple folk-like melodies and was usually strophic (the same

melody and harmonic substance for each stanza of the poem). Some of the finest strophic songs were written in the late eighteenth century by Mozart and Haydn to the poems of Goethe.

Ex: *An Chloe K. 524*, Mozart
      My Mother Bids Me Bind My Hair, Haydn

B. **Composite Forms**

   1. *Opera.*   Opera in the eighteenth century underwent considerable reform from the stereotyped practices of the Neapolitan school. These reforms were realized in the works of Gluck, who thought of himself as a reformer of opera, and by Mozart. In general, it can be said that the structure of opera in the late eighteenth century became much more fluent and subtle than that of the Baroque. The relation between music and drama was somewhat restored. No longer were singers left to their own devices in improvising dazzling vocal effects that had little to do with the story. No longer was the stage mechanic more important than the composer. There was a strong emphasis upon skillful characterization of the protagonists, together with a greater dramatic force. The principle of the sonata-form structure was applied with great success to operatic scenes and arias. Each became a closed form, complete in itself. In addition to *opera seria* there was further development of comic opera in the eighteenth century: opera buffa, opera comique, ballad opera and singspiel. Each represented a national style and all were characterized by spoken dialogue along with recitative and aria.

Ex: *Orfeo ed Euridice*, Gluck
      Don Giovanni, Mozart
      Abduction from the Seraglio, Mozart

   2. *Oratorio.*   The oratorio was continued in the tradition of the Baroque, but with emphasis on classic characteristics of style. The best-known Classic oratorios are by Haydn. *The Creation* was based on a text from the Book of Genesis and the *Seasons*,

a secular work on poetry by the Scottish poet, James Thomson, and translated into German. Both of these works have become successful concert pieces.

Ex: *The Creation,* Haydn
      The Seasons, Haydn

   3. *Mass.*   There was a general decline in the quality of religious music composed during the Classic era. Much of what was composed was written for liturgical use, but was also appropriate for the concert hall. The Mass was the favorite of these forms and consisted of the setting of the Ordinary of the Mass with soloists, chorus, and orchestra, and was symphonic in nature.

Ex: *Missa Solemnis in d minor, (Nelson Mass),* Haydn
      Mass in C major (Coronation), K. 317, Mozart

VII. IMPORTANT COMPOSERS

   1. *Giovanni Sammartini* (1701–1775) was a pioneer in the development of the Classic sonata. He is also known for his chamber music in the Classic style. He was Gluck's teacher. The principal works that survive today are a number of sonatas for chamber ensemble, especially the string quartet and symphony.

   2. *Christoph Willibald Gluck* (1714–1787) was an opera composer who initiated many reforms that eventually laid the foundations for the later opera composers. However, his reforms had little immediate effect on the composers of his own time. Gluck, after writing in the traditional Italian style, finally came to the conclusion that the dramatic force of the libretto must be the most important aspect of opera. To achieve this he made the following innovations: (1) He eliminated virtuosity, substituting lyric simplicity; (2) he strove to create musical portraits of his characters and their feelings; (3) he returned to the use of plots taken from mythology—plots that avoid the complex counterplots and minor intrigues of Neapolitan

opera; (4) he made the recitative more musically expressive; (5) he used the instruments of the orchestra as a tonal palette, creating the proper mood and atmosphere by tonal coloring; (6) he used the chorus as a dramatic device to intensify the dramatic force; (7) he made the overture an introduction to the mood and spirit of the opera. His most important works were *Orfeo ed Eurydice*, 1762; *Alceste*, 1767; *Armide*, 1777; *Iphigenie en Tauride*, 1779.

3. *Karl Phillip Emanuel Bach* (1714–1788) was the son of J. S. Bach and sometimes was known as the *Berlin* Bach. He was well-known as a performer on keyboard instruments as well as a composer. He was very influential in establishing the form and style of Classic composing, and is often credited with being the first to write in the sonata-form. There is no doubt but that both Haydn and Mozart were influenced by his style. He wrote more than 200 sonatas-and solo works for the piano, in addition to numerous concerti and chamber music works. His sonatas show the basic form of the sonata, but there was little, if any, development of the themes in the sonata-allegro movement.

4. *Johann Wenzel Anton Stamitz* (1717–1757) was the founder of the Mannheim school and made a number of important contributions to both orchestral playing and writing for orchestra. The most important of these were: (1) The first use of extensive dynamic shading in orchestral performance. (2) The introduction of the clarinet into the orchestra. (3) The introduction of the minuet into the symphony as the third movement. (4) The creation of what was known as the finest orchestra in all of Europe. He wrote about 74 symphonies, but because the symphony was perfected by Haydn and Mozart, these works are seldom performed today.

Oath of the Horatii.—David (1785). The classic balance and linear form
of this painting suggests the classic sonata forms of such composers
as Haydn and Mozart. (Art Resource, NY)

5. *Franz Joseph Haydn* (1732–1809) was one of the
   most prolific composers of the eighteenth century. Haydn's career is a fine example of the patronage system functioning at its best. Born in
   lower Austria, he received his early training as a
   choirboy at St. Stephens in Vienna. Aside from
   this schooling he was largely self-taught in music,
   drawing heavily upon the style of such Classic
   composers as K. P. E. Bach. Haydn was finally
   given a post as assistant Kappelmeister at the
   Court of Prince Esterhazy in 1761 and was to
   enjoy an ideal patronage for a period of over
   thirty years. His duties were to provide music re-
   quested by the Prince for any and all occasions.
   Consequently, he was called upon for every conceivable form of music from sonatas through

opera and including all forms of Catholic religious music. A most important factor in the development of his orchestral music was the fact that he had an orchestra at his disposal at all times. This enabled him to experiment with various orchestral instruments and orchestral timbres. It was Haydn who brought unity to late eighteenth century music and perfected the Classic style. Haydn wrote an enormous amount of music; much of it has been lost and the remainder is only now being published in a complete edition. His more important works are the symphonies (well over 100 of which 104 are published) and the 82 string quartets. His main contributions to the Classic style consist of (1) the use of a slow introduction to the first movement of the symphony, (2) enlarging the development section of the sonata-form and developing fragments of themes, (3) using the variation-form for the slow movement of symphonies and quartets, and (4) using a more flexible orchestration that permitted melodies to be imitated in contrasting tonal coloring. Of his total creative output, the following works are his most representative: (1) the *London Symphonies* (nos. 93–104); (2) the later quartets, especially the *Emperor, Op. 76, no. 3; and the Lark, Op. 65, no. 5;* (3) two oratorios, the *Creation* and the *Seasons;* and (4) the piano sonatas.

6. *Johann Christian Bach* (London Bach), (1735–1782) was also a son of J. S. Bach. Johann Christian Bach lived and studied in Italy for a time after studying in Berlin with his brother, K. P. E. Bach. He later went to England where he became music master to the Queen of England. He was an important composer of the light homophonic genre and his music was an important source of the Classic style. He wrote numerous operas in addition to piano sonatas, symphonies and various kinds of chamber music.

7. *Karl von Dittersdorf* (1739-1799) was a successful composer of Classical symphonies, church music and opera, although he was eclipsed by both Haydn and Mozart. One opera, the *Doctor and Apothecary*, still survives, as well as numerous string quartets and a few symphonies.

8. *Luigi Boccherini* (1743-1805) was a composer and cellist who was a great admirer of Haydn's music and who copied his style. He wrote a great quantity of chamber music, including 102 quartets and 125 quintets. His six cello sonatas and four cello concertos are still prominent in the present day repertory of music for cello.

9. *Wolfgang Amadeus Mozart* (1756-1791) was a composer whose creative inventiveness and lyric genius place him among the three or four giants of music. Born in Salzburg, Mozart showed evidence of a great creativity from infancy. His youth was spent in the atmosphere of the Salzburg Court where his father was a violinist. His genius was recognized early and his talents as a performer and as a composer were displayed to almost all of Europe through tours to the important courts and musical centers. In spite of almost ideal conditions for a successful career and despite his superior talents, Mozart's life was one of struggle and disappointment. In contrast to Haydn, Mozart never really had a patron. He was one of the first independent composers who had to struggle for recognition and commissions without the security of a permanent post. Without patronage, Mozart was forced to write in every popular form of his day in order to interest people in his music. His death and burial in a pauper's grave came just as he was gaining some public acclaim for his opera, *The Magic Flute*, a recognition that might have brought him the security of a permanent position. In style, Mozart was a conformist. He refined and polished the Classic forms, but made no major innovations over those made by Haydn. It should be noted that Mozart knew Haydn and their friendship probably influenced Mozart's

mature works. While there are many similarities between their styles, Mozart is distinctive in the following ways: (1) in general, his melodies are more lyric, more extended, and more subtle in their lyric expressiveness; (2) he seldom repeats phrases note for note, but makes some minute change in ornaments, rhythm, harmonic structure, or dynamics; (3) he seldom uses the slow introduction to his symphonies; (4) he indulges in more chromaticism in both melody and harmony, thus foreshadowing the romantic style; and (5) in his chamber music especially, all parts become equal in importance.

While he did not follow the devices of Gluck's reforms, his refined classic taste, his innate feeling for, and love of the theater led him to write what was perhaps the happiest solution to the problems of combining pure music and extra-musical ideas. Mozart's operas can be placed in three general classifications: (1) opera buffa, the most important of which are *Marriage of Figaro, Cosi fan Tutte* and *Don Giovanni*; (2) The German operas—*The Magic Flute* and *The Abduction from the Seraglio*; (3) The Italian style operas—*La Clemenza di Tito* and *Idomeneo*.

It is difficult to pick out the major works from Mozart's total output of over 600 compositions. However, there are a few that can stand out from the rest as monuments to his creative genius. Mozart did not number his works chronologically by the usual opus numbers, but Ludwig von Köchel compiled a chronological catalog in the middle of the nineteenth century. This catalog was recently brought up to date by the late Alfred Einstein and this numbering system is used today. Mozart's works are designated by the letter K and the appropriate number.

Of his total number of works, attention is called to the following: (1) the last three symphonies, *E flat major, No. 39 (K.543), g minor, No. 40 (K.550); C major, No. 41 (K.551). (2)Among the string quartets there is a group known as the Ten Celebrated Quartets*

(Köchel numbers 387, 421, 428, 458, 464, 465, 499, 575, 589, 590). The *Clarinet Quintet in A major* (K.581) must also be included in the great works of chamber music. (3) Mozart also wrote chamber music for winds and strings. Among these are: *Serenade in D major for winds and strings (K.320), Divertimento in D major for String quartet and 2 horns (K.334), Sextet for String Quartet and 2 Horns (K.552). (4) Violin Concertos in G major (K.216), D major (K.218), A major (K.219).* (5) Of the 25 piano concertos, the following are performed most often: *C major (K.415), B flat major (K.450), G major (K.453), and d minor (K.466).* (6) His most representative piano sonatas are those in *c minor (K.467), C major (K.545), B flat major (K. 570), and D major (K.576).* (7) While he wrote a number of religious works, his *Requiem Mass* is his crowning achievement in this medium.

10. *(Maria) Luigi Cherubini* (1760–1842) was the last important composer to show the classical restraint that identifies him as a Classic composer even though he lived well into the nineteenth century. He was born in Italy where he became a successful Italian opera composer. He soon made Paris his permanant home and devoted his creative life and conducting duties to the French style. His operas were influenced by Gluck's reforms, but never achieved a great success. Perhaps his best opera is *Médée* which has been revived in recent years. Other French operas are *Lodaiska* and *Les Deux journées*. Two *Requiem Masses* show a high quality of church music that is noted for its superb counterpoint.

11. *Ludwig van Beethoven* (1770–1827) must be considered as both a Classicist and a Romanticist and will be discussed more fully in the chapter on Romanticism. While the greater portion of his compositions reveal the characteristics found in the Romantic style, his earlier works conform to the pattern of the Classic. It is generally accepted that those works written before 1802 are patterned after the traditions of Haydn and despite

an occasional outburst of impatience with the harmonic and dynamic simplicity of Classicism, his acceptance of the tradition is fairly complete. The important earlier works included the piano sonatas up to Opus 53; the first three piano concerti; *String Quartets, Opus 18;* and the First and Second symphonies.

VIII. OTHER COMPOSERS

A. Austria
1. *F. X. Richter (1709–1789)*
2. *Christopher Wagenseil (1715–1777)*
3. *George Matthias Monn (1717–1750)*
4. *Michael Haydn (1737–1806)*

B. **England**
1. *Thomas Arne (1710–1778)*
2. *William Boyce (1710–1779)*

C. **France**
1. *Jean Jacques Rousseau (1712–1778)*
2. *François Gossec (1734–1829)*
3. *André Grétry (1741–1813)*

D. **Germany**
1. *Johann Joachim Quantz (1697–1773)*
2. *Wilhelm Friedemann Bach (1710–1784)*
3. *Christian Cannabich (1731–1798)*

E. **Italy**
1. *Niccolò Jommeli (1714–1774)*
2. *Niccolò Piccini (1728–1800)*
3. *Domenico Cimarosa (1749–1801)*

F. **United States of America**
1. *William Billings (1746–1800)*

IX. IMPORTANT WRITERS ON MUSIC

Because Classicism was concerned mainly with form there was little philosophizing about music. Most of the writers were seeking to formalize musical performance and consequently gave detailed instructions as to how to play instruments and also how to interpret the various devices of musical practice. A few of the more important writers and their works are listed following. Note that in most cases the writers were also creative artists, or at least performers.

1. *Johann Joachim Quantz* (1697–1773) was a composer and flutist as well as the author of *Versuch einer Anweisung, die Flöte Traversiere zu spielen* (Essay on Instruction for playing the Transverse Flute) Berlin 1752. While the title suggests a method for flute, Quantz deals with problems and questions of the general musical practice of his time.

2. *Jean Jacques Rousseau* (1712–1778) was a French writer, philosopher, and sometimes music scholar and composer. His *Dictionaire de musique* was published in 1767. This work contains many of Rousseau's articles written originally for the *Encyclopedie* to which he was a major contributor.

3. *Christoph Willibald Gluck* (1714–1787) wrote an important treatise on opera, the *Preface to Alceste*, Vienna 1769. *Alceste* was composed in 1767 but the printed score appeared in 1769. It is in this preface that Gluck seeks to establish the aesthetics of his musical theories concerning opera. He also gives an account of what he believed to be serious abuses of the true purpose of opera in the Italian school.

4. *Karl Phillip Emanuel Bach* (1714–1788) wrote *Versuch über die wahre Art, das Clavier zu spielen* (Essay on the True Art of playing Keyboard Instruments) Berlin 1753–1762, (New York 1949). This work is still an authoritative source of information on the traditions of performance of Classic music for the keyboard. It is also very valuable in the realization of classic ornaments and embellishments.

5. *Leopold Mozart* (1719–1787) was the author of *Versuch einer gründlichen Violinschule* (Treatise on the Fundamental Principles of Violin Playing) Augsburg 1756, (London 1951). Leopold Mozart was the father of Wolfgang Amadeus and an eminent violinist and teacher. This work is one of the first successful methods of violin playing. Along with K. P. E. Bach and Quantz, he gives us an account of the musical practice of the classic era.

6. *Sir John Hawkins* (1719–1789) was an English music historian who wrote *A General History of the Science and Practice of Music,* London 1776, republished in 1875. Hawkins' history, published about the same time as Burney's history, is filled with reliable information, especially about the musical scene in eighteenth century London.

7. *Charles Burney* (1726–1814) was the most important English music historian of the eighteenth century. *A General History of Music,* London 1776, reprinted New York 1957, is the first important history of music in English. It contains many interesting comments on the contemporary musical trends that reveal the general attitude of both the creative musician and the public during Burney's time. Burney made extensive trips to the musical capitals of Europe and wrote two volumes concerning the musical scene on the Continent.

Excerpts in English from several of the foregoing works can be found in *Source Readings in Music History by Strunk.*

Quantz	pp. 577–598
Gluck	pp. 673–675
Bach, K. P. E.	pp. 609–615
Mozart, L.	pp. 599–608

Supplementary Readings

Borroff	pp. 361–452
Cannon-Johnson-Waite	pp. 287–340
Crocker	pp. 355–411
Grout	pp. 448–519
Lang	pp. 530–733
Schirmer	ch. 18–22, 38
Wold-Cykler	ch. 9

Further References

Burney, Dr. Charles. *An Eighteenth Century Musical Tour in Central Europe and the Netherlands.* New York: Oxford, 1959.

Burney, Dr. Charles. *An Eighteenth Century Music Journey in France and Italy.* New York: Oxford, 1959.

Carse, Adam. *The Orchestra in the Eighteenth Century.* Cambridge, England: W. Heffer, 1940.

Dent, E. J. *Mozart's Operas,* rev. ed. New York: Oxford, 1947.

Einstein, Alfred. *Mozart: His Character and Work.* New York: Oxford, 1945.

Geiringer, Karl. *Haydn, A Creative Life in Music.* New York: W. W. Norton, 1946.

Geiringer, Karl. *The Bach Family.* New York: Oxford, 1954.

Grout, Donald J. *A Short History of Opera.* New York: Columbia University Press, 1947.

Helm, Ernest E. *Music at the Court of Frederick the Great.* Norman: University of Oklahoma Press. 1960.

Hutchings, Arthur. *Mozart, the Man, the Musician.* New York: Schirmer, 1976.

Landon, H. C. Robbins. *Haydn's Chronicle and Works.* Bloomington, Univ. of Indiana Press, 1976.

Newman, William S., *The Sonata in the Classic Era.* Chapel Hill: University of North Carolina Press, 1963.

Pauly, Reinhard G. *Music in the Classic Period.* Englewood Cliffs: Prentice-Hall, 2nd ed., 1973.

Rosen, Charles. *The Classical Style.* New York: Viking, 1971.

Paris Opera House (1861–1874). There is an opulence about this
structure that reflects the tastes of the newly rich of the nineteenth
century Industrial Revolution. This opera house and others like it
were the setting for the Romantic opera with their extravagant spec-
tacles dealing with heroic and epic subjects, supernaturalism, mystery, and passion. (Courtesy National Monuments Record, London—
Art Reference Bureau)

7

Chronology
of the Romantic

1746 Francisco Goya
(1746–1828)

1770 Ludwig van Beethoven
(1770–1827)

1776 John Constable
(1776–1837)

1782 Niccolò Paganini
(1782–1840)

1786 Carl Maria von Weber
(1786–1826)

1791 Jean Gericault
(1791–1824)

1792 Gioacchino Rossini
(1792–1868)

1796 Camille Corot
(1796–1875

1797 Franz Schubert
(1797–1828)
Gaetano Donizetti
(1797–1848)

1798 Eugene Delacroix
(1798–1863)

1801 Vincenzo Bellini
(1801–1835)

1803 Hector Berlioz
(1803–1869)

1804 Napoleon becomes
Emperor

1806 Lewis and Clark reach
the Pacific

1808 Honoré Daumier
(1808–1879)

1809 Felix Mendelssohn-
Bartholdy (1809–1847)
Abraham Lincoln
(1809–1865)
Charles Darwin
(1809–1882)

1810 Frederic Chopin
(1810–1849)
Robert Schumann
(1810–1856)

1811 Franz Liszt (1811–1886)

1812 Charles Dickens
(1812–1870)
Fairy Tales by Grimm
Brothers
War of 1812 between
England and United
States

1813 Guiseppe Verdi
(1813–1901)
Richard Wagner
(1813–1883)

1815 Battle of Waterloo

1816 Froebel founds the first
kindergarten

1818   Karl Marx (1818–1883)
First steamship, the
Savannah, crosses the
Atlantic
Charles Gounod
(1818–1893)

1819   Gustave Courbet
(1819–1877)
Walt Whitman
(1819–1892)
Victoria, Queen of
England (1819–1901)

1822   Cèsar Franck (1822–1880)
Louis Pasteur (1882–1895)

1823   Monroe Doctrine
promulgated

1824   Bedřich Smetana
(1824–1884)
Anton Bruckner
(1824–1896)

1831   Beginning of Antislavery
movement

1832   Edouard Manet
(1832–1883)

1833   Alexander Borodin
(1833–1887)
Johannes Brahms
(1833–1899)

1834   Edgar Degas (1834–1917)
Mechanical reaper
invented by McCormick

1837   Morse invents telegraph

1838   Georges Bizet
(1838–1875)
First photographs taken
by Daguerre

1839   Modeste Moussorgsky
(1839–1889)
Paul Cézanne
(1839–1906)

1840   Piotor Ilyitch
Tchaikovsky (1840–1893)
Auguste Rodin
(1840–1917)
Claude Monet
(1840–1926)
First electric light

1841   Antonin Dvořák
(1841–1904)
Auguste Renoir
(1841–1919)
Saxophone invented by
Adolphe Sax

1843   Edvard Grieg (1843–1907)

1844   Friedrich Nietsche
(1844–1900)
Rimsky-Korsakov
(1844–1908)

1845   Gabriel Fauré (1845–1924)

1846   Ether used for frist time
as anesthetic

1848   Marx and Engels
pronounce the *Communist
Manifesto*

1851   George Seurat
(1851–1891)

1853   Vincent Van Gogh
(1853–1890)
Japan opened to the West

1854   Thoreau's *Walden*
published

1858   Giacomo Puccini
(1858–1924)

1859   Darwin's *Origin of Species*
published

1860   Hugo Wolf (1860–1903)
Gustave Mahler
(1860–1911)

1861   American Civil War
(1861–1865)

1862   Claude Debussy
       (1862–1918)
1864   First Atlantic Cable
       Richard Strauss
       (1864–1949)
1865   Jean Sibelius (1865–1957)
1867   Alaska purchased from
       Russia
1869   First transcontinental
       railway in the United
       States
       Suez canal opened

1876   Bell invents the
       telephone
1877   Edison invents the
       phonograph
1883   Automobile engine
       patented by Daimler
1884   Universal adoption of
       solar day as unit of time
1866   American Federation of
       Labor organized
1895   Discovery of X-ray by
       Roentgen
1898   Spanish-American War
       starts

7
Romantic
1800-1910

I. SOCIOCULTURAL INFLUENCES ON MUSIC

The early nineteeth century saw the rise of a style of music, literature and art that we refer to as Romantic. The nineteenth century was a time of dramatic thought and action. It was also a time of strong contradictions between capitalism and socialism, freedom and oppression, logic and emotion, science and faith. The consequence of these contradictions was a change in the thinking of people, especially creative artists. An intellectual change took place in the minds of composers that was many sided, complex and often confused. Consequently it is impossible to say there is a definite Romantic style. Other periods of the past had a core of accepted beliefs and practices that drew composers together with a similarity between their music. Romanticism, on the other hand, had the tendency to isolate creative personalities—for their practices and beliefs were often in opposition and, like Romanticism itself, complex. However, the following are a few of the important sociocultural events and ideas which influenced composers to display Romantic qualities.

The revolutionary spirit that finally exploded in the French Revolution infused artists with the ideals of liberty and individualism. In terms of music, there were several Romantic results. There was a general impatience with the rules and restraints of Classicism. Just as the Revolution opposed the eighteenth century status quo, so music revolted against the practices of Mozart and Haydn. To be different was the goal and the Romantic period was to witness a great variety of musical experiments to achieve individualism. Moreover, to implement the ideals of liberty, composers sought to express their own personal convictions and to portray events and ideas as they understood them. The expression of emotion and the evocation of imagination became the primary goal of most Romantic music. In an effort to stimulate the imagination there arose a predilection for the strange and the remote, a fascination for the mysteries of the universe.

The Industrial Revolution caused a major change in the economic and social life of the common man and also gave rise to a wealthy capitalistic middle class. There was a general leveling of society and, while the composer did not write for the lower classes, his music was addressed to the masses to a far greater degree than before in the history of music. The wealthy middle class was the potential patron for the composer who had all but lost aristocratic patronage because of the increasing decline in the power and influence of the court. Literature and the visual arts were quick to use the injustices of the Industrial Revolution, the exploitation of the workers, the low standards of living and the social abuses of the lower classes as subjects for their works. Music, however, seems to have denied the existence of these pressing problems. While Wagner wrote a few scenes which may have revealed the bitterness of industrial exploitation, the avoidance of this theme is worthy of note. Music became more and more disassociated from real life. Composers expressed the splendor and pride of the human spirit in what seems to be an escape from reality for those who could afford the luxury of music.

The development of the *business* of music was also an important influence on the direction composers took in their writing. In order to cultivate the patronage of a wider and unorganized public, the composer, together with his publisher and concert manager, had to *sell* music to the public. Publication was on a different basis than it had been. In the effort to capture audiences a dynamic and colorful personality came to be an important asset, as can be noted in such individuals as Liszt, Berlioz, and Wagner. The concert manager, or *impresario* as he was often called, was also an important figure in the business of music. His opinion as to what the public would accept and be enthusiastic about was a strong motivation for many a composer and performer. Another important person behind the scenes of music was the music critic. He was a sort of liaison between the public and the composer. His writing served not only to interpret the composer to the public, but to set standards of musical taste. Needless to say the composer was usually in conflict with most of the critics, but the critic was still often responsible for the acceptance or rejection of a composer's works.

While the revolutionary spirit had its origin in France, it was in Germany and Austria that Romanticism had its strongest foothold and where it flourished. The French almost abandoned the Romantic ideal because of their affinity for the classic. Germany and Austria, however, were younger; they had never known the oppression of a strong central absolutism and they were also more concerned with the things of the spirit. Because of their youthfulness there seemed to be a conscious emphasis on folklore and historical epics in their desire to achieve a cultural heritage equal to the older and longer established countries. Whatever the reasons, the seeds of musical romanticism were to fall upon very fertile ground, particularly in Vienna.

II. FUNCTION OF MUSIC

Romantic music still served a sophisticated and aristocratic society as had been the case with the Classic music. Aristocratic patronage was considerably smaller than it had been in the eighteenth century and there were practically no opportunities for the kind of patronage enjoyed by Haydn. The intimacy of the exclusive salon was still the ideal setting for chamber music and solo forms. Performance, however, was no longer by amateurs, for Romantic music was usually too technically demanding for unskilled performers.

Outside the patronage of the exclusive salon was a large, but unorganized and unsophisticated, concert-going public which loved music. Romantic composers were constantly striving to gain the recognition of this vast audience and, in an effort to win acceptance, they were very sensitive to the likes and dislikes of these music-lovers. This middle-class listener searched for new excitement or relaxation from everyday life in music. To stir up or calm down his feelings was the function of the composer. There were two general types of music that appealed to these patrons—symphonic music and the extravagant spectacle of opera and ballet.

Performers, as well as composers, had the urge to be acceptable and to dazzle audiences. Composers, who were often also fine performers themselves, like Liszt and Paganini, wrote a large number of virtuoso pieces to thrill the public with technical display.

Because the Romantic composer expressed his own feelings and convictions, some music was written without patronage in mind. He wrote to express himself in personal documents of art. These were often experimental in nature and uncompromising so far as public taste was concerned. The last piano sonatas and string quartets of Beethoven and many songs by Schumann and Hugo Wolf are examples of this kind of expression.

Social dancing by all segments of society gave the composer a large market for dance music. The great popularity of the waltz made fame and fortune for composers like Johann Strauss and his son and, in addition, aroused the envy of many who may have been artistic successes, but never gained public favor.

The Church can no longer be considered a patron of music. There was very little music written for liturgical purposes. The small amount of sacred music written during this time contained the personal religious feelings and convictions of the composer, expressed in music for the concert hall.

The teaching of music became an established profession. Many fine conservatories and schools of music were founded for the education of the performing and creative musician. Research in music history and theory was introduced into the programs of many universities by the end of the nineteenth century. A great number of prominent composers and performers such as Liszt, Mendelssohn, Rimsky-Korsakov and Schumann achieved wide recognition as teachers. To meet pressing needs for pedagogical material composers wrote etudes and other short pieces for teaching purposes. Many of these works, like the *Etudes* of Chopin, are of a very high level of artistry and form an important segment of the repertory for the piano.

Research at the universities led to the beginning of the great complete editions of composers including Bach, Mozart, Beethoven, etc., as well as the large anthologies, such as the *Denkmäler der Tonkunst in Oesterreich*, and the *Quellenlexikon der Musiker und Musikgelehrten* of Robert Eitner.

III. CHARACTERISTICS OF STYLE

Because Romanticism is so personal and so filled with contrasting concepts of music, not all characteristics of style are present in all forms. There are contradictions in style between groups of composers and even within the works of individual composers. There were Romantic idealists and Romantic realists. The idealists were absolutists, who insisted music must exist for its own sake without extramusical devices. The realists were the champions of program music, who believed music could and should tell a story, imitate sounds of nature, or express a visual scene. Preoccupation with literary forms is seen in the importance of the text in solo-song.

There was a contradiction between virtuosity and intimacy. Some Romantic composers excelled in spectacular virtuosity, which was expressed by brilliant technical performances and often by the resources of a vast number of performers. On the other hand, there were those who emphasized the intimacy of miniature forms and delicate textures to express their personal feelings in solo songs, chamber music, and lyric piano works.

There was also a contrast between nationalism and internationalism. There were composers whose aim was to extol national characteristics and evoke patriotic feelings by using folklore, folk songs, and dances. They often used realistic devices to evoke expressiveness associated with national, or ethnic subjects. Nationalism became strong in such countries as Russia, Poland, and Bohemia. In Russia a group called the *Russian Five,* whose members were César Cui, Mily Balakirev, Modest Mussorgsky, Alexander Borodin and Nikolai Rimsky-Korsakov, made a special effort to break away from the dominance of the Italian and German tradition. There were also Romanticists who avoided nationalistic devices in the search for a universal musical language. In general these composers were the so-called *absolutists* who believed that music should express itself and not be contaminated by extramusical ideas.

There was one concept that all Romanticists had in common which gave their music a sense of unity: their music was aimed at the evocation of emotion as its primary function. The concept is based on the premise that a feeling of musical tension is necessary to achieve a corresponding intensification of emotional response. All Romantic music, therefore, concerns itself with the problem of achieving this tension. Most Romanticists revolted against the restraints and formalism of the Classic era. However, some Romantics, such as Schubert, Mendelssohn and Brahms, cast their Romantic expressions in molds of Classic forms.

As the nineteenth century came to a close there was also a revolt against Romanticism by writers, painters and composers called Impressionism. Impressionism was the connecting link between Romanticism and the experimentalism of the early twentieth century. It was a cult of suggestive colors, lines, words, melodies and harmonies. The listener, viewer and reader were called upon to supply the details and complete the impressions. The movement was strongly influenced by the painters Monet and Manet and by the symbolic imagery of the poets Verlaine and Mallarmé, among others. Led by Debussy, composers denied both the objectivity of programmatic composers and the pathos of the Romantic idealists. Impressionistic music was a music of coloristic effects, of vague harmonies and loosely knit forms.

1. *Formal organization*
    a) Musical form was still predicated on the idea of contrasting melodies in the homophonic style, making the sonata still the most important type of formal organization. Rather than two contrasting melodies, there were often contrasting theme groups and sometimes only motives pitted against each other.
    b) In addition to the Classic forms that were still in use, there were free forms, such as the ballad, nocturne, or fantasy. These were most common in piano music. The free forms, however, were still based on contrasting themes, but usually without development sections. Sometimes, in the very short preludes or etudes, only one theme or melody might be used with changes in harmony or rhythm for the contrast.
    c) Forms are not precise and clear as in the Classic, but are often overlapping, vague, and without strong cadences. Sections and even movements of the longer works often melt one into the other by means of subtle and mild cadential effects, both harmonically and rhythmically.
    d) It was a common practice, especially in the larger forms, to use some of the same thematic material in each movement as a means of maintaining a constant expressive character. This is sometimes called *cyclic*, or psychological form.
    e) Forms are not always symmetrical or balanced. Musical phrases and periods often use uneven numbers of measures and different numbers of

beats in each measure. Development sections of the sonata form have a tendency to be lengthy. It was here that the composer could use his imagination and ingenuity to best advantage.

f) Folk melodies, or at least folk-style melodies, were used extensively in Romantic music. This was especially true in nationalistic music, but was also a common practice in the music of the Romantic idealists. Folklore was especially popular in Romantic opera, where it was no doubt aimed at arousing enthusiasm among the general public.

2. *Melody*

a) Romantic melody has a tendency to grow out of harmonic progressions and is less independent than previously. Chromaticism is frequent and helps to create harmonic tension.

b) Melodic themes are not stylized as to length or form. They are frequently fragmentary with rhythmic interruptions and irregular phrases. They can also be extremely long, with many deceptive cadences which give a feeling of continuous "spinning out." There is also a tendency to use many rising and falling melodic curves.

c) Melody is characterized by an intensity of personal feelings. Dynamic climaxes and frequent changes in dynamics serve to build the tension necessary for its expression.

d) The whole-tone scale was sometimes used by the Impressionists for both melodic and harmonic purposes. This scale, which does not have the perfect fourth, fifth, or leading tone, denies a sense of tonic, or center, thus permitting each tone to move without creating tension to any other tone of the scale (ex. 33).

Example 33   Debussy

3. *Rhythm*

   a) In the early Romantic period, the element of
   rhythm remained much as it had in the Classic.
   From about the middle of the century, however,
   rhythm comes to be more irregular and more interesting. There are often changes in the number
   of beats in a measure, cross-rhythms and synco-
   pations (ex. 34).

Example 34   Chopin

   b) Rhythm is often complex and rhapsodic. It sometimes avoids strong stresses in order to increase
   the sense of tension, especially in slower movements.

   c) Tempo in Romantic music is not always constant.
   There are frequent indications of changes of
   speed and the use of tempo rubato and acceler-
   ando.

4. *Harmony*

   a) Romantic harmony is still tonal, but a much
   weaker sense of key center was to develop all
   through the nineteenth century. Almost all the

characteristics of harmony during this period show this gradual disintegration of the major-minor system

b) Tonality was weakened by the fusion of the major and minor modes, using chords typical of one mode in the other.

c) Harmony makes a greater use of chromaticism, nonharmonic tones, altered chords and extensive use of ninth and thirteenth chords. All these devices serve to build harmonic tension, but also weaken the sense of key-center (ex. 35).

Example 35   Wagner

d) Strong formal cadences were usually avoided with numerous deceptive cadences to give a harmonic sense of motion and tension.

e) Key-relationships are less formalized than in Baroque and Classic music. Modulation to distant keys and sudden moving in and out of keys for short periods of time also add to tension and to the weakening of a strong feeling for a particular key.

f) Modal harmonization of folk melodies, especially in nationalism, served to open new avenues of harmonic expressiveness.

5. *Texture*

a) The texture of Romantic music was generally a mixture of the vertical and horizontal elements. Polyphonic texture occurred more as a device than a style, with the lyric quality of the lied as a more dominant stylistic character.

b) The texture also can be described as *heavy* with an opaqueness of sound as opposed to the *lighter* and transparent quality of the Classic. Even in works for solo voice, the accompaniment provides a sonority of tonal fabric that serves to blend the voice with the instrument.

c) In orchestral works the greater number of instrumental parts gives a sense of a richer texture. In addition the texture is made even more sonorous by more subdivisions of instruments than before. For example, Wagner sometimes divides the first violin section into as many as four different parts.

6. *Media and tone color*

a) The piano became the most popular single instrument of the Romantic period because it could run the gamut of all ranges of sound and because it could be played by an individual. It became almost a musical symbol of Romanticism. Moreover, the piano was enlarged to give it a wider range and more tonal power. The instrument reached such heights of popularity that it became the favorite household instrument with every family that could afford it.

b) Tone color became an integral part of the melodic and harmonic texture. Melodies were created in terms of tonal coloring with their musical expressiveness identified with specific instruments. Harmonic texture was also influenced by the new orchestration that created new colorings by unusual combinations of instruments and the subdivision of the usual choirs of instruments. A new kind of sonority is possible by such combinations as the subdivision of the higher strings or an expanded brass section.

The orchestra grew to be the favorite large instrument of the century. It had the qualities of bigness, colorfulness, and sonority which could create Romantic expression. It had been expanded from the Classic orchestra by the addition of instruments such as the English horn and clarinet, and also by the addition of more brass and percussion. Moreover the virtuosity of the orchestra was increased by technical development of already existing instruments, especially brass and wood winds.

c) The solo song with piano accompaniment was also a favorite medium of Romantic expression. The voice is also a personalized instrument, for it combines with the literary elements of Romanticism to give an added intensity to the poetic text. Aside from the solo song and opera, vocal music was of minor importance in the period.

d) Opera is a major medium of expression in the Romantic era. Combining, as it does, drama, poetry and the visual experience of action, along with music, it is able to make a powerful impression on the emotions of an audience that was truly Romantic. Its popularity can be realized by noting the large number of Romantic operas that are still in the repertory of opera today.

The operetta, a light form of musical dramatic production makes its appearance in the nineteenth century as a development of the forms of comic opera of the eighteenth century. With its farcial or sentimental plot and its alternation of light songs and spoken dialogue, the operetta gives expression to romanticism in a popular form.

e) See Appendix A for a description of instruments.

IV. PRACTICE AND PERFORMANCE

Dynamics became more explicit than those of the Classic. Subtle shadings of coloring and minute gradations of loudness were indicated by a more definite terminology. Tempi were more accurately designated by the use of the metronome markings.

Due to the size and complexity of the orchestra, for the first time the orchestral conductor became a virtuoso. He became a performer whose instrument was gigantic and capable of every Romantic expression. The use of the baton by the conductor took him from the keyboard to the podium.

This was the era of massive festival performances. Because of the fondness for sonority and power, an enormous number of participants were often used. Sometimes, as in the case of Berlioz, the large orchestra and chorus were called for by the composer. At other times the usual number of performers were greatly augmented to suit the taste for massed effects. The large festival orchestra and chorus appeared in all countries and is still very popular. There have been many instances in which over a thousand performers have taken part in the performance of a single work.

The middle-class love for music-making led to the establishment of the choral society. Folk music, political songs and popular melodies provided the musical fare, but the artistic level was rather shallow. A few such societies made presentations of Handel and Haydn oratorios, but they had little effect on the Romantic quality of their own composers.

The art of improvisation was generally discarded in the practice of Romantic music, due to the complexity of its composition and the complete directions for performance. A few individuals, like Chopin and Liszt, continued to make brilliant use of it, but most of the cadenzas were written in a manner to give the effect of improvisation.

Because of the emphasis on individualism and the spectacular, it follows there would be a number of virtuoso performers during the Romantic. Beethoven, until deafness curtailed his performances, was a pianist of exceptional virtuosity. His early triumphs in Vienna were probably due to his pianistic artistry as much as to his compositions.

Franz Liszt was the most successful virtuoso pianist of the Romantic. His electric personality and theatrical effects coupled with his spectacular performance made him almost a legend in his own time. His virtuosity had a marked influence on piano performance for all time. Frederic Chopin was another pianist whose music and performance was so personal, refined, as well as brilliant, that he has become almost a symbol of the Romantic spirit. In addition both Carl Czerny and Anton Rubinstein were noted both as pianists and composers.

Niccolò Paganini developed the technic of the violin to its present state. His dazzling performances of double stops, harmonics, runs and trills are still a challenge to present day violinists. His fame as a performer was widespread and influenced many composers including Liszt and Berlioz. A later Romantic violinist, Joseph Joachim, also had a tremendous influence on the music of Brahms.

Because instrumental virtuosi were usually composers as well, their technical exploits were notated in their scores. This was not true, however, for operatic singers. Theirs was usually a spontaneous realization of the basic ideas of the composer, but hardly any two performers were alike. It was not until the development of the recording industry that we have reliable examples of a singer's technical skill.

Due to the fact that the orchestra was enlarged to become one of the more important media of Romantic expression, the orchestral conductor emerged as a virtuoso performer. Von Weber, Mendelssohn, Berlioz, Liszt, Wagner and Mahler were among the many who achieved fame as conductors, as well as, for their Romantic compositions. While they were not great composers, Hans von Bülow and Hans Richter became well known for their conducting skills.

V. INSTRUMENTAL COMPOSITIONS

A. Single Movement Forms and Structural Devices.

1. *Sonata-form.* The Romantic sonata-form is still based on the organizational principles of the Classic sonata-form. There was, however, a notable expansion of both the melodic and harmonic substance. Instead of two contrasting themes, composers often used groups of themes in the exposition. In this case each theme is usually given in a different, and often remote key, thus extending the harmonic range. In order to develop this melodic and harmonic material, the development is often much more lengthy than in the Classic. In order to reconcile the key changes and to re-establish the tonic, a long coda is sometimes added.

Ex: *Piano Sonata no. 23, Op. 57 (Appassionata),* Beethoven
First Movement, Symphony no. 3, E flat major, Op. 55 (Eroica),
Beethoven
First Movement, Symphony no. 3, F major, Op. 90, Brahms

2. *Two- and three-part song forms.* There was a wide assortment of descriptive titles attached to short forms which suggested moods or revealed the personal feelings of the composer. These were often referred to as *character pieces.* They are usually in two- or three-part forms, but sometimes are short enough to have but one section. Some of these forms were called nocturnes, preludes, caprices, serenades, bagatelles, impromptus, etc. A ballade is usually a longer work which suggests the possible moods of a story without actually defining a particular sequence of events. In addition, titles suggestive of personalities, scenes, or ideas were often applied to these shorter pieces. There is nothing except the mood and atmosphere to differentiate one from another in a formal manner.

Ex: *Nocturnes,* Chopin
Caprices for Violin, Paganini
Ballad no. 4, Chopin
Ballad, Op. 10 no. 1 Brahms

3. *Variations.* While the variation-form was sometimes used as a movement of a sonata or symphony, it also held a high place as an independent form for both orchestra and piano solo. Variations were created on a pre-existing theme, or on a specially composed melody. Occasionally each variation was made to suggest a particular mood or character of an idea suggested by the theme.

Ex: *Enigma Variations, Op. 36,* Elgar
Variations on a Theme by Handel, Op. 24, Brahms
Variations in D major, Op. 76, Beethoven

4. *Dance movements.* The nineteenth century saw the rise in importance of stylized dance movements for both the orchestra and solo instruments, especially the piano. Dances of a national character such as the Polonaise, Mazurka, Jota, were used by many composers. Moreover a more general type, Hungarian, Spanish, and Slavonic, was also the basis of many works. These are usually idealized concert versions which are expanded and are not functional for social dancing.

Sometimes dance movements which symbolized ideas or events such as the *Danse Macabre* and the *March to the Gallows* gave Romantic composers the opportunity to use realistic devices to intensify the mood or atmosphere.

Ex: *Polanaise Fantasie, Op. 61,* Chopin
Mephisto Waltz, Liszt
Danse Macabre, Saint-Saens

5. *Rhapsody.* Rhapsody was a term often used in Romantic music to designate a free fantasy on themes of a national or epic character. It is a single movement form with the usual contrasts and Romantic tensions. It appears in the literature for both orchestra and piano, sometimes for a combination of a solo instrument with the orchestra.

Ex: *Hungarian Rhapsody no. 2,* Liszt
Rhapsody in E flat major, no. 4, Op. 119, Brahms
Spanish Rhapsody, Op. 70, Albeniz

6. *Etudes.* A particular form for solo instruments was the etude. Originally it was a study piece designed for the perfection of technique, but was expanded as a concert work with emphasis on a display of virtuosity. Even when it became a concert piece, however, it never lost its function as a study piece. Each etude usually emphasized some particular technical problem. It is in a binary, or a three-part form with the usual tension of contrast and repetition.

Ex: *Etudes, Op. 25,* Chopin
Transcendental Etudes after Paganini for Piano, Liszt

7. *Concert overture.* The concert overture is a symphonic work in the manner of an overture that is not associated with an opera. In general, the concert overture does not attempt to tell a story, but creates a mood that can be associated with a literary theme, a place, or an event. Most works of this nature adhere closely to the principle of the sonata-form.

Ex: *Hebrides Overture,* Mendelssohn
Academic Festival Overture, Op. 80, Brahms

8. *Symphonic poem.*   One of the typical forms of orchestral program music is the symphonic poem. It was the invention of Franz Liszt and was sometimes called a tone-poem, especially when it was based on a poetic idea. The form is in a continuous movement and is based on the principle of variations on a theme, or contrasting themes, that are inspired by a program or a literary idea. It is a metamorphosis, or transformation of themes through various stages and forms in which the themes retain their identity.

Ex: *Les Préludes,* Liszt
Vltava (Moldau), Smetana
Till Eulenspiegel, Richard Strauss

B. Composite Forms

1. *Sonata and Symphony.*   The Romantic sonata and symphony, like the sonata-form itself, was based on the Classic pattern of sonata and symphony. Some composers, such as Beethoven and Schubert, adhered rather closely to the Classic, but others, including Berlioz, Mahler, Bruckner, and Tchaikovsky, made notable departures from it. During the early years in the Romantic era the piano sonata retained its popularity, along with sonatas for violin and piano and cello and piano. As the century progressed, however, the symphony became the most important composite instrumental form. To it composers could bring more and more sonority, as well as combining music with literary ideas because of its possibilities for realism. In general, themes of a Romantic symphony are more lyric and more contrasted than in the Classic. Modulations are more varied and often without the usual preparation. Because there is less emphasis on balance and logic, there is a more sectional scheme of organization. Unity between movements is often achieved by the cyclic principle of using the same themes, or portions of them in each movement. While the emphasis in the Classic sonata or symphony is on the first movement, the Romantic often places its

emphasis on the last movement. This is especially true when such works are cast in the cyclic form in which the climax, or culmination of the thematic material, takes place during the last movement. A number of composers include solo and choral vocal writing in their symphonies especially in the desire to emphasize the climax of the last movement. The minuet is usually replaced by the scherzo movement, a movement quicker in tempo that provides more contrast to the second and last movements. The variation-form is frequently used as either the second or last movement. Some composers used as many as five movements in their symphonies in contrast to the usual four movements in a Classic symphony.

Ex: *Sonata for Violin and Piano, c minor, Op. 30,* Beethoven
Sonata for Cello and Piano, F major, Op. 90, Brahms
Sonata no. 2, Op. 35, Chopin
Symphony no. 3, E flat major, Op. 55 (Eroica) Beethoven
Symphony no. 2 (Resurrection), Mahler
Symphony no. 5, e minor, Op. 64, Tchaikovsky
Symphonie Fantastique, Berlioz

2. *Concerto.*   The Romantic concerto became more symphonic than its eighteenth century counterpart; technical demands made the solo parts more spectacular. In addition the solo is much more dependent upon the orchestra for the musical development. The double exposition of the Classic concerto is usually abandoned. The Romantic predilection for continuous movement and cyclic form is also apparent in the solo concerto.

Ex: *Piano Concerto, a minor, Op. 54,* Schumann
Violin Concerto, D major, Op. 77, Brahms

3. *Chamber music.*   The forms of music for chamber ensembles generally followed the forms of the Romantic symphony and sonata. The instrumentation, however, remained much the same as in the Classic period. There was an increased emphasis on virtuosity which demanded a higher degree of professional skill for performance than in the chamber music of Haydn and Mozart.

Ex: *String Quartet, no. 16 in F major, Op. 135*, Beethoven
Piano Quintet in E flat major, Op. 44, Schumann
Clarinet Quintet in b minor, Op. 115, Brahms

4. *Ballet.* While the ballet had been a part of opera
in the seventeenth and eighteenth centuries, it
was not until the Romantic era that it achieved
consideration by composers as a unified dramatic
form independent of opera. Dramatic expression
is achieved by the music and a corresponding
dance pantomime, both solo and ensemble, that
serves the same purpose as the vocal solo and
chorus in opera.

Ex: *Creatures of Prometheus*, Beethoven
Swan Lake, Tchaikovsky

5. *Symphonic suite.* The Baroque idea of the suite
was revived about the middle of the nineteenth
century. However, instead of the traditional
scheme of dances, it presents a free succession of
contrasting movements, usually national dances
or ballet movements. It is sometimes a series of
extracts from a ballet, or incidental music to a play
and often suggests a series of scenes, of even a
story, as in a suite of symphonic poems. It was
usually written for orchestra, but also appeared
in the literature for piano.

Ex: *Nutcracker Suite, Op. 71A*, Tchaikovsky
Peer Gynt Suite no. 1, Op. 46, Grieg

VI. VOCAL COMPOSITIONS

A. Single Movement Forms and Structural Devices

1. *Art Song (Lied.)* The solo song occupied an important place in Romantic music. Romantic poetry was combined with the voice and piano in a
highly personal and subjective musical expression. There were two basic types of formal organization used in these works: (1) strophic plan
and (2) through-composed. The latter has more
possibilities for Romantic expression because

every poetic idea can have its own musical counterpart. The piano created and sustained the mood of each poem and is more of an equal partner than merely an accompaniment to supply rhythm and harmony for the vocal line. German composers set poems by such writers as Heine, Schiller, and Goethe, poets who epitomized the Romantic spirit. The song cycle is a series of songs to poems by a single poet which are related by a central idea, or theme. Schubert, Schumann, Brahms, and Hugo Wolf were the most important composers of the German lied. While the German lied holds the prominent place in song literature, both the French and the Russians also fostered an art song literature of high quality. The French especially were helped by the French Romantic poets to create songs of exceptional lyric beauty.

Ex: *Dichterliebe,* Schumann
Winterreise, Schubert
Without Sun, Songs and Dances of Earth, Mussorgsky
Five Poems of Charles Baudelaire, Debussy

2. *Choral music (sacred and secular).*   There was very little music written for liturgical purposes in the Romantic period. However, composers wrote Te Deums, Requiems, Beatitudes, for voices and instruments. Again the emphasis was usually on the symphonic ideal rather than on the vocal qualities. These are heard most often in the concert hall, but could be used in the Church for special occasions.

Ex: *Te Deum,* Verdi
German Requiem, Brahms
Mass in F major, Bruckner

While there was a great wealth of secular choral music written in the nineteenth century, only a few important works have survived and most of these are for voices and orchestra. Some composers, Beethoven, Liszt, and Mahler, used the chorus as a part of the symphonic form.

Ex: *Symphony no. 9, d minor, Op. 125, (choral)* Beethoven
Song of Destiny, Brahms

B. **Composite Forms**

1. *Opera.*   Opera provided the best opportunities for all aspects of Romantic music to be combined into a single form. All Romantic opera can be described as an extravagant spectacle with a tendency toward heroic and epic subjects, supernaturalism, mystery, and passion. Eighteenth century opera was dominated by the Italian style with its multiplicity of closed forms, but in the nineteenth century, Italy, France, and Germany each maintained their own styles with special qualities that were indigenous to each. Therefore, it becomes necessary to describe briefly the form of opera in each of these countries.

   a) *Italian opera.*   Early Romantic opera in Italy retained the Neapolitan style with a series of recitatives, arias, duets, and choruses without much continuity of dramatic action. Later in the century, mainly under the influence of Verdi, it showed a greater dramatic unity and characterization of personages and events. Plots are often quasi-dramatic, but there is a general improvement in quality. The recitative and aria are still the principal closed forms with melody in the popular belcanto style and an emphasis on virtuosity. There is also more balance between voice and instruments, but the orchestra still serves as an accompaniment, not as an equal partner.

   Another facet of Italian Romantic opera is the movement known as *verismo,* or realism. Realism was not limited to music, but was also shown in the choice of libretti that presented subjects from everyday life and depicted people in familiar situations.

Ex: *Lucia di Lammermoor,* Donizetti
      La Traviata, Verdi
      Tosca, Puccini
      Pagliacci, Leoncavallo

b) *French opera.*   Opera in nineteenth century France showed some characteristics that were different from the Italian. During the early part of the century there was a marked distinction between Grand Opera and Opéra Comique, but as Romanticism matured the two styles merged into one. Opéra Comique is generally distinguished from Grand Opera by use of some spoken dialogue instead of a continuous musical texture. Generally it was simpler in musical expressiveness and used fewer characters with very little chorus. These two styles were compromised in the French Lyric opera. The theatrical aspect and the simpler forms of Opéra Comique were combined with the virtuosity and drama of the Grand Opera. A particular trait in all French opera was the ballet and it became even more important during the Romantic era. There is a unity of dramatic action with the music that is seldom found in the Italian style. There is also less virtuosity with more emphasis on the lyric quality of melody. Moreover, French Romantic opera rarely displays the intensity and passion of either the Italian or the German but is more moderate in its music and in its dramatic qualities.

Ex: *The Hugenots,* Meyerbeer
Carmen, Bizet
Pelléas et Mélisande, Debussy

c) *German Opera.*   Opera in Germany presents two significant styles: (1) German Romantic opera and (2) music-drama, the latter conceived and developed by Richard Wagner. In the Romantic opera the stories were often based on German legends and folklore with the mystery of nature and supernatural forces serving to intensify dramatic expression. Recitatives and arias are still closed forms and are often based on folk-song or folk-style melodies. Melodrama, orchestrally accompanied speech, is sometimes used for special effects. The orchestra becomes a powerful instrument in creating atmosphere, moods and even bits of realism. There is also a type of leit-motif in which particular instruments and melodies are used to identify and characterize individuals.

Ex: *Der Freischutz*, Weber

The ideal of music-drama, or the art of the future as it was called by Wagner, was that of an art form in which all the arts would be woven into one cohesive and continuous line of dramatic expression. Wagner continued the German tradition but wrote his own stories, drawing heavily upon German myths and folklore. His libretti are filled with romantic mysticism and supernaturalism, and almost all are concerned with the concept of redemption through love. There are few closed forms, such as recitative and aria. The vocal line is a continuous melody arising out of an orchestral fabric that is also continuous, without usual cadences. The leitmotif became a unifying device in the sonorous and tension-filled musical texture. The Wagnerian leitmotif is a musical figure that is associated with a particular idea, person, object, mood or situation. Because Wagner uses the orchestra as the main source of dramatic expression, his operas are symphonic in nature. Consequently, it has been possible to have successful concert performances of much of his music without staging and even without the vocal part.

Ex: *Tristan and Isolde*, Wagner
       Parsifal, Wagner

d) *Nationalistic opera.* In addition to the Italian, French and German operas, there were operatic developments in those countries where nationalism was strong, expecially in

Russia and Bohemia. These operas were also based on folklore or upon events of national significance with nationally important personages. Composers such as Mussorgsky in Russia created works that are highly original with great dramatic power without using the closed forms of the Italian and without imitating Wagner.

Ex: *Boris Godunov,* Mussorgsky
       Bartered Bride, Smetana

2. *Oratorio.* The Romantic oratorio followed the choral tradition of Handel in the works of Mendelssohn, who added the melodic, harmonic, and tonal qualities of the Romantic style. While there were very few who wrote in the Protestant tradition, there were many composers who set quasi-religious stories that were full of mysticism and Catholic symbolism to music in the manner of the oratorio. These were sometimes referred to as hybrid forms, for they are not opera, oratorios or cantatas. The orchestra generally plays a more important role, with the chorus and soloists becoming only a musical device in a symphonically conceived work. Both Liszt and Berlioz wrote a number of compositions in this fashion for performance in the concert hall.

Ex: *Elijah,* Mendelssohn
       L'Enfance du Christ, Berlioz
       La Damoiselle élue, Debussy

VII IMPORTANT COMPOSERS

1. *Ludwig van Beethoven* (1770–1827) has been listed among the composers of the Classic style, but it is as a Romanticist that his greatest compositions were conceived. Born in Bonn, Germany, Beethoven displayed strong musical gifts as a child. He suffered at the hands of his father who hoped he could mold the young talent into a prodigy like Mozart. The incompetence of his father as a manager and as the head of the family finally

caused Beethoven to become the sole support of his family. His gifts as a pianist, organist, violinist, and composer won him an official position at the Bonn Court where he remained until 1792 when he left for Vienna, where he was to live the rest of his life. While he was first known in Vienna as a brilliant pianist a slowly developing deafness caused him to abandon performance for composition. He was the first composer in music history to live independent of the exclusive patronage of the aristocracy and to make a comfortable living from the sale of his compositions.

His life is generally divided into three periods. The first, as a pianist composer ends about 1802. Compositions from this period hold the seeds of Romanticism, but are still cast in the molds of the Classic tradition of Mozart and Haydn. The second period of maturity ends about 1814 and reveals his development as a complete Romanticist. The third and last period is somewhat of an enigma. Here Beethoven seemed to be breaking the bounds, even of Romanticism, by becoming more introspective, more profoundly spiritual, more improvisational and even recalling the contrapuntal style of the Baroque.

Beethoven was largely responsible for freeing music from the restraints of Classicism and for leading the way to individualism and subjective feeling in music. He made important contributions to the literature of every media of musical expression, especially the symphony and the string quartet. His works became models for his contemporaries as well as the later composers. Almost all of the Romanticists found justification in Beethoven for their own individualism of style. His main contributions can be summed up as follows: (1) He showed a remarkable economy of material in the sonata form that led the way to the cyclic type of multiple forms. (2) His themes were often constructed from short motives that were gradually built up and expanded into full length lyric melodies. (3) He raised the piano to a high level of use and Romantic expression.

(4) He showed a polyphonic grasp of thematic development. (5) Dissonance became a functional part of his harmonic structure. (6) He achieved a new fluency in modulation that opened new possibilities of harmonic contrast and interest. (7) He changed and expanded the traditional forms of the sonata and symphony to accommodate his thematic material and expressive purpose, rather than making his material fit the forms.

Beethoven's works include nine symphonies, numerous overtures, five piano concertos, one violin concerto, thirty-two piano sonatas, twenty-one sets of variations for piano, ten violin sonatas, sixteen string quartets, nine piano trios, an opera, *Fidelio*, an oratorio, *Christ on the Mount of Olives*, and the great *Missa Solemnis*. In addition to the foregoing major works there are a number of songs, miscellaneous chamber music and a number of compositions for various solo instruments. If one were to select a few works that stand out more firmly as monuments to his creative genius, the following would certainly be included: *Symphonies no. 3, Op. 55 in E flat major (Eroica); no. 5, Op. 67 in c minor, no. 9, Op. 125 in d minor (Choral); String Quartets. Op. 95 in f minor and Op. 127 in E Flat major; The Emperor Concerto* for Piano and Orchestra, *Op. 73 in E flat major; Piano Sonatas Op. 13 in c minor (Pathetique)* and *Op. 57 in f minor (Appassionata); The Missa Solemnis, Op. 123 in d minor;* the opera *Fidelio.*

2. *Niccolò Paganini* (1782–1840) was the first of the great instrumental virtuosi of the nineteenth century. An Italian violinist, he developed a spectacular technique that enabled him to dazzle his audiences. In addition, his innate showmanship gave him an almost hypnotic power over his listeners. His compositions consist mainly of virtuoso etudes for violin and a brilliant violin concerto. He had a profound effect on many Romantic composers, especially Schumann and Liszt who tried to adapt Paganini's concepts of virtuosity to the piano.

3. *Carl Maria (von) Weber* (1786–1826) was the founder of the German Romantic school of opera. His
   father was an amateur musician and also the director of a traveling theatrical group. No doubt
   this environment helped to stimulate young Weber's imagination as a dramatic composer. He was
   something of a child prodigy, learning the piano
   and violin at an early age and also having his first
   piano works published at the age of 12. His important posts as a mature musician were as Ca-
   pellmeister at Prague and as Director of the Opera
   at Dresden. In addition to his fame as a composer,
   he was well-known as a brilliant pianist and conductor, the first to use a baton and become a performer on the orchestra. While he composed in
   almost every media, his best works are for piano
   and the stage. The piano works are brilliant concert pieces with emphasis on virtuosity and, with
   the exception of the *Invitation to the Dance*, are seldom performed today. His opera *Der Freischütz* is
   based on a German folk tale that dwells on supernatural phenomenon, and reveals the sentimentality of middle class personages. While
   Weber broke with the Italian operatic tradition,
   he still used arias in the Italian manner. It was
   the chorus effects, the orchestral tonal coloring,
   and the stories that made the operas typically
   German. He suggests the later leitmotif of Wagner in identifying moods and ideas in a musical
   manner. The overture became a collection of the
   most important melodies of the opera, serving as
   a sort of preview of what was to come. His most
   important operas are *Der Freischütz, Euryanthe,* and
   Oberon. The latter was first produced in England
   a few months before his death in 1826.
4. *Gioacchino Rossini* (1792–1868) was one of the most
   brilliant of the early Italian Romantic opera composers. He exhibited a remarkable flow of melody in the bel canto tradition. This combined with
   brilliant orchestration, dynamic rhythms and
   clear-cut phrases made his operas popular all
   through Europe. One of his notable devices of orchestration was the use of crescendo by means of

numerous repetitions of a phrase, adding instruments and increasing the degree of loudness with each repetition. Rossini was at his best in opera buffa and his principal works in this form are *La Gazza Ladra*, *L'Italiana in Algeri* and *Il Barbiere di Siviglia*. The latter became his most popular opera and was produced in almost every opera house of Europe.

5. *Franz Schubert* (1797–1828) was the only Viennese composer to claim that city as his birthplace. His early musical training was as a member of the Vienna Court singers and as a student in the *Convict*, a training school for the singers. Here he learned to play the violin and studied theory, as well as singing. When his voice changed he had to leave the school. For a time he held a post as an elementary school teacher, but gave it up after three years. After this brief period of teaching, Schubert's life was illustrative of a kind of Bohemianism often associated with the Romantic spirit. He was one of the few composers to live in poverty. He never held a position as a musician in either an institution or in an aristocratic household. Moreover, he did not even have the security of a benevolent patronage nor a steady income from the sale of his works. He eked out a precarious existence as a private tutor, sold a few compositions to publishers and had a few commissions for works. The greatest portion of his works can be ascribed to art for art's sake. His early death at the age of 31 was unquestionably hastened by actual poverty. While Schubert's piano, chamber and orchestral workds are significant contributions to the literature of music, it is in the art songs that his expression of Romanticism reaches its height. The outstanding qualities of his music are his lyric melodies and harmonic coloring. Moreover, in his lieder there is a musical sensitivity to the poetic expression that makes Schubert's songs among the finest in all vocal literature. His piano works, chamber music, and orchestral works are generally classic

in their formal organization. The Romantic element lies in the substance of melody and harmony.

Schubert composed over 600 songs, nine symphonies, twenty-two piano sonatas, seventeen operas, six masses, about thirty-five chamber music works and numerous occasional pieces for orchestra and solo instruments. It is only Schubert's operas that have failed to gain recognition. Some of his best songs can be found in the two song cycles, *Die Schöne Müllerin* and *Die Winterreise*. Of his symphonies the *Unfinished, no. 8 in b minor* and *no. 9 in C major*, are the best-known. The *Quartet in d minor (Death and the Maiden)*, the *Quintet in A major, Op. 144*, and the *Piano Trio in B flat major, Op. 99* hold a high place in the literature for chamber music. The *Piano Sonatas in c minor and B flat major* are his finest works for this instrument.

6. *Gaetano Donizetti* (1797–1848) was one of the most prolific of the Italian opera composers. Donizetti's music is notable for its remarkable melodies, by means of which he could express the whole gamut of emotions. Actually his harmony, rhythm and orchestration are at times repetitive, but it is his talent for melody and stagecraft that caught the public's favor and served to keep many of his works popular to this day. While he wrote a vast amount of instrumental music, cantatas, and church music, his operas are all that have survived. The best of these are *Lucia di Lammermoor* and the comic operas *La Fille du Regiment* (The Daughter of the Regiment) and *Don Pasquale*.

7. *Vincenzo Bellini* (1801–1835) is remembered for his gift of melody like all Italian opera composers. More reserved in range of expression than Donizetti, Bellini was exceedingly adept in psychological characterization. The Romantic element lies mainly in his sentimental melodies rather than in the tension of harmony and sonority of sound. All of his operas were of a serious nature

and the more important works are *Norma, La Sonnambula* (The Sleepwalker), and *I Puritania* (The Puritan).

8. *Hector Berlioz* (1803–1869) was one of the first of the recognized composers who did not come from a musical family, or at least a strong musical background. His father was a doctor and young Berlioz was also destined for a medical career. However, his interest in music gained the upper hand and he deserted medical studies in Paris in favor of composition. Berlioz never became a proficient performer on any instrument, nor was he a practicing musician in the professional sense. His only musical post was a music librarian at the Paris Conservatory. In effect he was a free-lance composer-conductor, writing music and then arranging concerts for its performance. He wrote only in the larger forms of the overture, symphony and opera, composing virtually nothing for solo instruments or chamber music.

Berlioz was a pioneer in the area of symphonic program music. He developed the *idée fixe,* a recurring melody or theme that identifies programmatic ideas and persons in a purely musical manner. His most famous programmatic symphony is the *Symphonie Fantastique.* Berlioz was a master of orchestration, bringing new orchestral colors and even new sounds into the orchestral fabric. He also enlarged his orchestra to almost gigantic proportions, even planning a work for an orchestra of 465 performers. His technic of orchestration and instrumentation was set forth in his *Treatise of Instrumentation and Orchestration* published in 1844, a book which served as a dictionary of orchestration until well into the twentieth century. Berlioz was also a musical journalist, a career that enabled him to actively campaign in behalf of the Romantic ideals in opposition to the conservatism of Classicism.

His important works, in addition to the *Symphonie Fantastique* are: *Harold in Italy,* for solo viola and orchestra; *Romeo and Juliet,* for solo voices, chorus and orchestra; *The Damnation of Faust*, a concert opera; *A Requiem Mass*, the *Childhood of Christ* for solo voice, chorus and orchestra, and the opera *Les Troyens*. In addition he wrote a number of concert overtures, of which the *Roman Carnival* and *Benvenuto Cellini* are still frequently performed.

9. *Felix Mendelssohn-Bartholdy* (1809–1847) was the son of a wealthy banker and the grandson of a famous philosopher. He was also fortunate in being surrounded with the finest opportunities for becoming a musician, for he had the wealth for unlimited study and a highly cultivated cultural and social background. He became a proficient concert pianist as well as a competent composer. His most important position was as Director of the Royal Conservatory in Leipzig, which he founded, and as Conductor of the Gewandhaus Orchestra, also in Leipzig. He was widely traveled and his music became very popular in many countries, especially in England. Among his other accomplishments, Mendelssohn was largely responsible for the Romantic revival of interest in the works of J. S. Bach. Mendelssohn's music is closely allied to the Classic traditions in form, the Romantic element showing in his melodies and imagination of orchestral coloring. His music has little of the passion and violence of Romanticism, but almost always expresses a serenity and a sentimentality that had a wide audience appeal.

Mendelssohn wrote a great deal of music in his short life, but his fame rests largely on his works for piano, orchestra, and two oratorios, *Elijah* and *St. Paul*. Among the orchestral works the music to *Midsummer Night's Dream*, *The Hebrides Overture*, *The Scottish*, and *Italian Symphonies* are the most often performed. His *Violin Concerto in e minor* has remained a classic in violin literature. His finest large work for piano is the *Variations Serieuses*, *Op. 54*. Other popular Romantic piano pieces are the *48 Songs Without Words*. The oratorio *Elijah* is perhaps the finest Romantic oratorio and was written especially for performance in England.

10. *Frederic Chopin* (1810–1849) was born in Warsaw, Poland, but left his native land at the age of twenty and spent the rest of his short but creative life in Paris. He composed almost exclusively for the piano and was most successful in the shorter forms of occasional pieces such as the etude, nocturne, impromptu, mazurka, and polonaise. He exploited the melodic and harmonic possibilities of the piano to a greater degree than any other composer. He concentrated on melody which he decorated with delicate and graceful passages of coloratura. He also made daring harmonic innovations with enharmonic modulations and new dissonances which often prolonged harmonic tension far beyond that of his contemporaries. Moreover, Chopin enhanced the harmonic texture of piano music by a skillful use of the pedal to increase the number of tones in a chord. He was also responsible for the development of the left-hand figuration based upon tenths rather than the fifth and octave of the Alberti bass.

Chopin's music is often associated with Polish nationalism. The *Polonaise* and *Mazurka* represent this facet of his creative output. Setting aside the larger forms as being of lesser importance, it is the 24 *Preludes*, the *Impromptus*, the *Waltzes*, and the *Ballads* that hold the interest of present-day pianists and their audiences.

11. *Robert Schumann* (1810–1856) was the son of a book-seller, a circumstance that brought him into close contact with the writings of the new Romantic movement during his formative years. After a period of law study and an unsuccessful attempt to become a concert pianist he turned his efforts toward composition and musical journalism. He founded and became editor of the *Neue Zeitschrift für Musik,* a journal devoted to musical criticism. He also taught for a time at the Leipzig

Conservatory and was Musical Director at Düs-
seldorf. However, organized musical activity was
not congenial to his nature and he devoted most
of his time to writing, composing and to concert
tours with his wife, Clara Wieck, who was the first
prominent woman concert pianist. Schumann
suffered from a mental disorder and, after attempting suicide, was confined to an asylum
where he died in 1856.

Schumann, more than any other composer, became the spokesman for the revolt against Classicism and the champion for revolutionary
tendencies in music. In addition, he became the
ardent supporter of such men as Chopin and
Brahms and it was through his writing that much
of their music became known to the concert
world. His compositional efforts cover the range
of music from opera through piano works and
solo song. It is in the smaller forms that he is most
successful. While the symphonies, piano concerto, and some chamber works are still retained
in the repertory, it is generally recognized that
Schumann did not have the craftsmanship to
mold the larger forms successfully. Schumann's
music can be characterized by its lyric melody, its
vague and imaginative formal structure and its
remarkable range of expression from the most
tender to the heights of passion. He showed his
interest in Bach by using contrapuntal devices
within the framework of Romantic harmony. His
piano music is very idiomatic, making full use of
the harmonic and tonal possibilities of the instrument. He had a Romantic predilection for
suggesting poetic titles for many of his piano and
orchestral works, but admitted that the music was
always composed before the title was attached. In
the lieder he is second only to Schubert. The
piano plays an almost equal role with the voice
in the songs, since he often used the piano as a
commentary on the vocal melody to suggest and
sustain the mood of the poem in a kind of musical prologue and epilogue. His major works include a large number of songs of which the love

songs are perhaps the best. The cycle *Dichterliebe* on poems by Heine represents the finest of these. The piano music includes the *Concerto in a minor, Carnival, Kreisleriana, Papillons,* the *Symphonic Etudes* and many other short forms. Also important are the four symphonies and numerous chamber music works.

12. *Franz Liszt* (1811–1886) was one of the most fascinating of the Romantic personalities. As a virtuoso pianist-composer he left the imprint of his virtuosity and sentimental Romanticism on almost all subsequent pianists. Born in Hungary, he studied in Vienna and then in Paris where he became known as a concert pianist. He later settled in Weimar, Germany, where he devoted the major portion of his energies to composing and teaching with only an occasional concert tour. Liszt was deeply impressed by the virtuosity of the great Italian violinist Paganini and tried to do for piano technic what Paganini had done for the violin. In addition, he inaugurated the recital as a popular form of musical presentation. Liszt was also a popularizer of music and made innumerable transcriptions for the piano of all sorts of music from Beethoven symphonies to Schubert lieder. As a Romantic realist, Liszt was a champion of program music and was responsible for the invention of the symphonic poem. His orchestral music gives the effect of an extravagant theatrical style with a wide range of emotion from tender sentimentality to intense passion. To gain these effects he used a large orchestra and followed the lead of Berlioz in colorful orchestration.

Liszt's piano music contains brilliant technical passages, chromaticisms, sentimental melodies, and a vague sense of organization. The outstanding piano works by Liszt are *The Concerto in E flat major, The Sonata in b minor, The Hungarian Rhapsodies, Mephisto Waltz, The Transcendental Etudes,* and numerous short virtuoso pieces. While Liszt's orchestral music has less appeal today than in the nineteenth century, the Symphonic Poems, *Les Préludes* and *Mazeppa* are the most often programmed by present-day orchestras.

13. *Giuseppe Verdi* (1813–1901) is the greatest figure in the history of Italian opera. He was no revolutionist like Wagner, for he never departed completely from the traditions of the closed forms of recitative and aria. He enriched the long established forms with superb melodies, dramatic scenes, and an instinctive sensitivity for the theater. Some of his earlier works were tinged with nationalism and succeeded in stirring up the patriotism of Italians for their own freedom and unity as a nation. Verdi's position as a nationalist was further enhanced by a brief period as an elected member of the Italian Parliament. His operas cover a wide range of subjects from the Egyptian story of *Aida* through the dramas of Shakespeare. With the exception of the *Requiem*, his non-theatrical works are of lesser importance. Verdi's more important operas are *Macbeth, Rigoletto, Il Trovatore, La Traviata, Un Ballo in Maschera* (A Masked Ball), *La Forza del Destino* (Force of Destiny), *Don Carlos, Aida, Otello,* and *Falstaff.* All of these works are still prominent in the repertory of opera companies.

14. *Richard Wagner* (1813–1883), one of the most controversial figures in music history, was the arch-Romanticist of the nineteenth century. Raised in a theatrical atmosphere by his stepfather who was an actor and playwright, young Wagner's musical training was rather desultory. However, his ambition to be a conductor and a theatrical composer finally brought him conducting posts with provincial orchestras. Filled with ambition, he went to Paris where he hoped to rival the success of Meyerbeer. After a disastrous three years in Paris he finally returned to Germany. The Paris years, however, saw the completion of the operas *Rienzi* and the *Flying Dutchman*, both of which were finally produced in Dresden, but Wagner

became embroiled in the revolutionary movements of the time and was forced to flee Germany.

He was to spend the next twelve years in exile during which time he wrote *Tannhäuser* and *Lohengrin*. It was during these years that he formulated his theories about the opera, writing a number of essays on aesthetics, the most important of which was *Oper und Drama*. It was in this essay that he set forth the idea that the ideal artform would be equal portions of music, drama, poetry, and stagecraft. He called this art form the music-drama (the art of the future). One of the important results of his new theories was the beginning of the *Ring of the Nibelungen*, a gigantic saga of four operas to be given on successive nights: *Das Rheingold, Die Valküre, Siegfried*, and *Gotterdämmerung*. Drawing heavily on German and Norse mythology and based on the idea of redemption through love, the *Ring* is the longest and most complicated dramatic work ever to be successfully staged. The whole cycle was to take more than twenty years to complete.

In 1864 Wagner was invited to Munich by the young King Ludwig II of Bavaria and it was here that *Tristan and Isolde* was first produced. Because of Wagner's expensive tastes, the drain on the Bavarian treasury was too great and he was forced to leave the country. He then moved to Lucerne, Switzerland, where he wrote *Die Meistersinger*. The *Ring* was finished in 1874. Wagner had long dreamed of a theater especially constructed for his own works and finally in Bayreuth, in Northern Bavaria, such a theater was built with revolving stage, sunken orchestra pit and every device of stage mechanics possible at that time. In 1876 the first performance of the *Ring* took place in this theater, which has since become a mecca for lovers of Wagnerian opera. His last opera was *Parsifal*, a quasi-religious drama based on the story of the Holy Grail. He died in Venice in 1883.

Critics of Wagner were usually either violently opposed to his theories and music or were ardent partisans in his struggle for recognition. As a man, he was a supreme egotist. As one writer has put it: "Wagner thought of himself as the world's greatest composer, poet, dramatist, philosopher, and politician, and remarkably, he was very nearly all of these."

Wagner's musical style reveals the Romantic ideal at its greatest intensity. A few of the most important devices he used to achieve his Romantic expressiveness follow. (1) He used the leitmotif to identify people, objects, ideas, and emotions in his music-dramas. In addition to serving as a unifying device, it also convinces the listener of the reality of his Romantic illusions. (2) Wagner's music-dramas were through-composed, rather than being made up of closed forms of recitatives and arias. (3) He carried the dissolution of tonality to the very edge of atonality by the use of chromatic harmonies and vague cadences. This tendency is especially prevalent in *Tristan and Isolde*, in which he achieved climaxes of great power and tension. (4) The orchestra carries the burden of dramatic expression, thus making his operas predominately symphonic in nature. (5) Consequently, he enlarged the orchestra by adding instruments and subdividing the normal sections. This gave him a new range of tonal coloring that made it possible to reach new heights of orchestral tensions.

15. *Charles Gounod* (1818–1893) was a French composer who is best known for his operas and for his Romantic sacred music in the Catholic tradition. His most famous works are the operas *Faust* and *Romeo and Juliette*. Both of these remain in the opera repertory of today. *Faust* was first composed as a lyric opera with spoken dialogue and was later reworked in its present form with recitatives and arias. Gounod's music is filled with sentimental lyricism and a type of mild Romanticism that was imitated by many lesser talents of his time.

16. *César Franck* (1822–1880) was a Belgian organist and composer whose musical style is that of French Romanticism. He lived in Paris where he was an organist, choirmaster, and teacher of such composers as d'Indy and Chausson. His music reveals a polyphonic treatment of Romantic melody and a harmonic substance comparable to that of Wagner. There is an air of Romantic mysticism in almost all of his works. He was one of the few Romantics to write extensively for the organ, but his religious music is climaxed by the oratorio, *Les Beatitudes.* He is best known for the *Symphony in d minor, String Quartet,* and a *Violin Sonata in A major.* He also wrote a number of works for piano, including the *Symphonic Variations for Piano and Orchestra.*

17. *(Friedrich) Bedřich Smetana* (1824–1884) is considered the father of Czech music. An ardent nationalist, he wrote a long orchestral work called *My Fatherland,* consisting of six symphonic poems depicting scenes from the life and history of Bohemia. The *Vltava* is the most successful of this cycle. Smetana was a disciple of Liszt and his symphonic poems are modeled after those of Liszt. A *Quartet in e minor* (From my Life) and an opera, the *Bartered Bride,* are his best known works in each of these media.

18. *Anton Bruckner* (1824–1896) was an Austrian composer whose symphonic style, serious and profound, permeates everything he wrote. An organist and a deeply religious man, Bruckner wrote a number of religious works for the Catholic church, including a *Te Deum* and three *Masses.* His nine symphonies make up his major works and are marked by their great length and a rather massive tonal structure. There is also a kind of religious mysticism about all of his works, especially in the slow movements. He used song-like themes as a basis for the symphonic forms and achieved great climaxes by using them in a choral-like manner with instrumentations that suggest a full organ sound. Bruckner is looked upon as a nationalist in his native Austria.

19. *Alexander Borodin* (1833–1887) was a member of
the Russian *Five,* a group which was dedicated to
the development of an indigenous Russian style
in music. Other members of the *Five* included
Mily Balakirev, César Cui, Modest Mussorgsky,
and Nikolai Rimsky-Korsakov. While profes-
sionally Borodin was a teacher of chemistry, his
intense interest in music brought forth a number
of notable compositions. His music reveals a kind
of Russian orientalism that was based on Cauca-
sian and central Asian coloring. His main works
are an opera, *Prince Igor;* a symphonic poem, *In
the Steppes of Central Asia,* three symphonies, two
string quartets, and numerous smaller works.

20. *Johannes Brahms* (1833–1897) was born in Hamburg, Germany, and began the study of the piano
at the age of eight. By the time he was thirteen
he was playing the piano in taverns to help supplement the meager income of his family. After
a period of teaching and concertizing he moved
to Vienna in 1863, where he was to remain until
his death in 1897. While he held minor positions
as director of various choral societies, he was
never interested in a permanent position, but
preferred to remain as an independent free-lance
composer.

It was Schumann who called attention to Brahms'
genius as a composer in an essay in the *Neue Zeitschrift für Musik.* Stylistically, Brahms is Romantic
in his emotional expressiveness, but more Classic
in his formal organization. He is sometimes referred to as a Neo-Classicist because of his de-
votion to the principles of the Classic sonata and
the polyphonic treatment of his musical materials. He was an absolutist, writing no program
music in the Romantic sense of the term. Brahms
often used a motif as a basis for an entire movement, or even a complete symphony. His orchestration is always full, giving a massive kind
of musical sound. Rhythmically, Brahms is exceedingly complex, using cross-rhythms with

numerous shifting of accents and metric patterns. He is best known for his four symphonies: *no. 1 in c minor, Op. 68, no. 2 in D major, Op. 73, no. 3 in F major, Op. 90, and no. 4 in e minor, Op. 98*. Other important works are the *Violin Concerto in D major, Op. 77*, the *Piano Concerto in B flat major, Op. 83*, a substantial amount of chamber music, and the *German Requiem, Op. 45*. In addition he wrote a number of songs, *The Song of Destiny, Op. 54*, the *Alto Rhapsody, Op. 53* for chorus and orchestra.

21. *Georges Bizet* (1838–1875) was one of the first French composers to be influenced by Wagner. Perhaps this influence was responsible for the failure of his earlier works, for the French gnerally were not sympathetic towards the Wagnerian style. Bizet's fame rests almost solely on *Carmen* which was a failure when it was first performed in 1875. In *Carmen* Bizet introduced realism into French opera. Wagnerian influences are apparent in such devices as the *death motive*, but Bizet was also original in the vivacity of the music and the psychological characterizations. *Carmen* has become the most popular opera of all times. Bizet also achieved some success with incidental music to *L'Arlésienne*, a play by Daudet, but most of his music gained popularity only after his death.

22. *Modest Mussorgsky* (1839–1881) was an ardent Russian nationalist and probably the most talented and important member of the *Five*. Mussorgsky was untutored in the basic theory of music, but possessed a great genius for creative expression. He never held a musical post, but spent most of his life as a government clerk and his early death was probably hastened by malnutrition and excessive use of alcohol. His greatest works are in the medium of song and opera, although his *Pictures at an Exhibition* for piano, and *A Night on the Bald Mountain*, a programmatic work for orchestra, have retained their popularity. His greatest gift was his ability to translate the inflection of speech into dramatic, passionate, and

poetic melody. His most famous opera is *Boris Godunov* in which he created a nationalistic music-drama. Divorced from the Italian operatic tradition and yet not imitative of Wagner, *Boris Godunov* is truly an original work that had great influence on many non-Russian composers. Because Mussorgsky was unskilled as an orchestrator, his operas and orchestral music were revised and orchestrated by Rimsky-Korsakov and it was in this version that they were first introduced to the European audiences.

23. *Piotor (Peter) Ilyitch Tchaikovsky* (1840–1893) embarked on a course of law study and entered government service, but gave it up at the age of twenty-three and turned to music. After only two years of intensive study he was appointed professor of composition at the Moscow Conservatory. While Tchaikovsky is associated with the Russian spirit in music, and emotionally was a nationalist, he was not a member of the *Five* because he also wrote in the style of Schumann and Berlioz. His melodies are lyric with a tinge of the Slavic modal harmonies that identify them with Russian folk song. His music is sentimental and sometimes even trivial. Nevertheless, it has a directness and a range of emotional expression that has a wide appeal to all audiences. He is best known for the *Fourth, Fifth,* and *Sixth (Pathétique) Symphonies,* The Overture, *Romeo and Juliet,* the *Nutcracker Suite,* the *First Piano Concerto in b flat minor,* and the ballet, *Swan Lake. Eugene Onegin,* one of two operas, is still in the operatic repertory.

24. *Antonin Dvořák* (1841–1904) was another Czech nationalist. He first gained recognition through his Slavonic orchestral dances and later turned to symphonies and chamber music. His style is closer to that of Brahms, although there are suggestions of Wagnerian harmonies in his music. His best known work is the *Symphony no. 9 in e minor,* better known as the *New World Symphony,* written during a sojourn in the United States

where he had come to be the Artistic Director of the National Conservatory in New York. The *New World* is based on themes that suggest Negro and Indian folk tunes, although Dvořák denied any conscious use of such material. Other works that remain alive in music literature are an overture, *Carnival, Concerto for Cello, American String Quartet, Stabat Mater,* and a number of songs.

25. *Edvard Grieg* (1843–1907) was a Norwegian nationalist who wrote in the traditional style of the German Romantics inasmuch as he was trained under the influence of Mendelssohn and Schumann. However, he was successful in adapting the German style to the modal melodies and harmonies of Norwegian folk song and dances. The result was a literature of lyricism with freshness and charm. Grieg's important large works include the incidental music to *Peer Gynt* and the famous *Piano Concerto in a minor.* The special charm of his music, however, is found in the shorter works—songs, dances, and the many *Lyric Pieces* for the Piano.

26. *Nikolay Rimsky-Korsakov* (1844–1908) was a member of the Russian *Five* and has been credited with writing the first Russian Symphony. He was a naval officer and a self-taught musician. In spite of his lack of formal training he was appointed Professor of Instrumentation and Composition at the St. Petersburg Conservatory, a position which he held until his death. His music utilizes the true Russian folk-idiom and oriental melodic patterns. His musical output is not large, mainly because he gave a great deal of his time to revising and orchestrating the works of his friends, especially Mussorgsky. Rimsky-Korsakov's best operas are *Pskovityanka* (The Maid of Pskov), *Sniegurotchka* (Snow Maiden), and *Le Coq d'or* (The Golden Cockerel). His orchestral works include *Scheherazade* and *Sadko*. The latter is the first Russian tone poem. Rimsky-Korsakov is also author of a textbook on orchestration, *Foundations of Orchestration,* and an autobiography, *The Chronicle of My Musical Life.*

27. *Gabriel Fauré* (1845–1924) was one of the later Romantic composers who remained outside the influence of Wagner and Brahms. He developed an almost impressionistic, melodic, and harmonic substance that evolved from the use of modal scales and transient harmonies. He is best known for his songs, but his *Requiem, Violin Sonata in A major,* and the *First Piano Quintet, Op. 15* have remained popular.

28. *Giacomo Puccini* (1858–1924) was the most famous and successful Italian opera composer after Verdi. He was a notable representative of the so-called *verismo style,* a style which dealt with realistic subjects from everyday life and used a kind of melodramatic recitative with less emphasis on traditional subjects and forms. He was skillful in the technique of the theater and his operas contain a kind of Romantic sentimentality that caused them to rival Verdi's in popularity. Puccini's most successful operas are *Manon Lescaut, La Bohème, Tosca, Madame Butterfly,* and *Turandot.*

29. *Hugo Wolf* (1860–1903) was an Austrian composer who represents the Wagnerian influence on the lied. His complex contrapuntal texture and chromatic harmony give his songs a tension and expressiveness not unlike the music of *Tristan and Isolde.* Moreover, Wolf had the capacity for a deep insight into the poetic spirit of the text. On hearing his lieder, one feels the text to be the dominant element, with melody and harmony subordinate. He uses the piano to intensify the dramatic element and not as a mere accompaniment. While he also wrote an opera and some instrumental works, it is for his more than 300 lieder that he is remembered. Many of his lieder were published posthumously and some still are unpublished.

30. *Gustav Mahler* (1860–1911) was an Austrian and the last great composer of the Viennese Romantic style. He held various positions as a conductor, including the directorship of the Vienna Court Opera, the Metropolitan Opera and the New York

Philharmonic Society. Mahler's symphonies (he completed nine) are dramatically conceived, colossal tone-paintings. His scores call for enormous orchestral resources comparable to those used by Berlioz. Mahler was also a skillful and imaginative orchestrator, devising new sounds and even special tunings for strings to achieve dramatic effects. Using song as melodic material with solo voice and choral groups, his symphonies were sometimes expanded into choral works symphonically conceived. He frequently attached programmatic notes, or poetic quotations to his scores to suggest a feeling or a mood. Mahler's most important works are *Symphony no. 1 in D major; Symphony no. 2 in c minor; Symphony no. 8 in E flat major*, called the *Symphony of a Thousand* because of its great number of participants; *Lied von der Erde* (Song of the Earth) for tenor, contralto, and orchestra, and *Des Knaben Wunderhorn* (The Youth's Magic Horn) a cycle of ten songs with orchestra.

31. *Claude Debussy* (1862–1918) a French composer, was the leading figure of the impressionistic movement in music, the most influential development of nineteenth century French music. Impressionism was an antirealistic movement that originated first in the fields of painting and poetry. In addition to being antirealistic, it was anticlassical; even its Romantic qualities were milder, and avoided the violence and passion of the earlier Romanticists. It was concerned with vague and transitory suggestions to evoke moods and atmosphere. Debussy was one whose music was directly influenced by painting and literature, for he was greatly stimulated by the paintings of Monet and the poetry of Verlaine and Mallarmé. He tried to suggest the same kind of feeling as his colleagues in painting and poetry. He sought to express the shimmering effects of light and shade in painting by tone-color and chordal structure in music, sacrificing lyric melody, traditional forms, and polyphonic complexities for suggestive harmonic progressions. In

The Kiss—Rodin (1886). Rodin has used the play of light and shadow over the surface of the entwined figures to make them almost abstract. Composers of the late Romantic era, such as Debussy and Ravel, achieved a parallel effect in music by tonal coloring and subtle harmonies. This music is called Impressionistic. (Art Resource, NY)

order to achieve a more luminous tonal coloring he destroyed the traditional function of the successive scale steps by the use of the whole tone scale where each note has a subtle persuasion all its own. Debussy also added to musical vagueness by weakening his cadences with parallel chordal progressions and unresolved dissonances.

Debussy's untraditional practices aroused much controversy, even in his early works such as the *Prelude a l'aprèsmidi d'un faun* (An afternoon of a faun), the *Nocturnes*, and *La mer*. An opera, *Pelléas et Mélisande* is almost a music drama with a restrained music expression that creates the emotional atmosphere of Maeterlinck's drama. A string quartet and a number of pieces for piano including the *Twenty Four Preludes*, are among the list of works before 1910. The very late compositions written during the last years of his life, the violin and cello sonatas, the two books of etudes, place Debussy in the forefront as an innovative composer, bridging the romanticism of the nineteenth century to the twentieth.

32. *Richard Strauss* (1864–1949) was one of the last of the Romantic realists. Like a number of the late nineteenth century composers, he was also distinguished as a conductor, both in opera and in the concert hall. It is as a composer, however, that he made his greatest musical impact for he was one of the virtuosi of orchestral writing. Strauss was a disciple of Liszt, Berlioz, and Wagner, adapting their realistic methods and devices to his own uses. After a few early works in the forms of the sonata, quartet, and symphony, he turned to program music for his expression. His realism is sometimes subjective in that he attached ideas and states of feeling to melodic and harmonic ideas as in the symphonic poem, *Tod und Verklärung* (Death and Transfiguration) for which he had the poet Ritter compose a poem to illustrate the music. On the other hand he used realism in a descriptive manner by suggesting scenes,

movements and actual sounds of life and nature, as in the *Alpine Symphony* where he employs a wind machine and a thunder machine to portray a storm scene. Strauss' realism covers a wide range of subjects from the humorous to the hysteric.

His music is brilliantly orchestrated with dramatic and sweeping sonorities that are marked by strong harmonic dissonances and sharp contrasts in tonal coloring. He makes use of parallel chord progressions and arbitrary dissonances that obscure tonality but do not deny it. Moreover, he uses a contrapuntal fabric that ignored the traditional intervallic relationships between the moving parts that are pushed relentlessly to their climactic conclusions.

While Strauss' earlier works were mainly symphonic poems, he also made an imposing contribution to opera. His first opera of note was *Salome*, based on the text of Oscar Wilde, an opera that shocked the public of the 1900s more by its subject than its music. *Electra*, on the other hand, used sharp dissonances and strong tonal color to characterize the decadent story of hate and sordid revenge. *Der Rosenkavalier*, a comic opera written in 1911, is more Classic in its form, but is still infused with the lyric sentimentality of Romanticism. While he lived almost to the middle of the twentieth century, his period of creative greatness seemed to end with *Der Rosenkavalier*. The best of his symphonic poems are *Don Juan, Till Eulenspiegel's lustige Streiche, Tod und Verklärung, Ein Heldenleben* (A Hero's Life), *Also Sprach Zarathustra* and *Don Quixote* (a variation for cello and orchestra). In spite of Strauss' seeming preoccupation with the larger forms of program music, a number of fine songs comprise a distinct contribution to song literature.

33. *Jean Sibelius* (1865–1957) was the most important Finnish composer of the late nineteenth and early twentieth century. His style remained deeply rooted in the nineteenth century Romantic tradition. He consciously carried out a program of

nationalistic musical expression, basing much of his thematic material on Finnish folk song idiom though never employing the folk melodies literally. The great preponderance of his works are for orchestra. Besides seven symphonies in the classic-romantic tradition, his most typical nationalistic orchestral compositions are the tone-poems based on Finnish legend, history and landscape. Among his best known works in this genre are *Finlandia, En Saga,* and *Pohjala's Daughter.*

VIII. OTHER COMPOSERS

A. Austria
1. *Johann Hummel (1778–1837)*
2. *Carl Czerny (1791–1857)*
3. *Johann Strauss (Sr.) (1804–1849)*
4. *Johann Strauss (Jr.) (1825–1899)*

B. England
1. *John Field (1782–1837)*
2. *Sir Arthur Sullivan (1842–1900)*
3. *Sir Edward Elgar (1857–1934)*
4. *Samuel Coleridge-Taylor (1875–1912)*

C. France
1. *François-Ardrien Boieldieu (1775–1834)*
2. *Daniel-François-Esprit Auber (1782–1871)*
3. *Jacques Offenbach (1819–1880)*
4. *Henri Vieuxtemps (1820–1881)*
5. *Edouard Lalo (1823–1892)*
6. *Camille Saint-Saëns (1835–1921)*
7. *Leo Delibes (1836–1891)*
8. *Emmanuel Chabrier (1841–1894)*
9. *Jules Massenet (1842–1912)*
10. *Vincent d'Indy (1851–1931)*
11. *Ernest Chausson (1855–1899)*
12. *Gustave Charpentier (1860–1956)*
13. *Paul Dukas (1865–1935)*

D. Germany
1. *E. T. A. Hoffman (1776–1822)*
2. *Ludwig Spohr (1784–1859)*
3. *Giacomo Meyerbeer (1791–1864)*

4. *Heinrich Marschner* (1795–1861)
5. *Karl Loewe* (1796–1869)
6. *Albert Lortzing* (1801–1851)
7. *Otto Nicolai* (1810–1849)
8. *Robert Franz* (1815–1892)
9. *Engelbert Humperdinck* (1854–1921)
10. *Max Reger* (1873–1916)

E. **Italy**
   1. *Muzio Clementi* (1752–1832)
   2. *Gasparo Spontini* (1774–1851)
   3. *Arrigo Boito* (1842–1918)
   4. *Ruggiero Leoncavallo* (1858–1919)
   5. *Pietro Mascagni* (1863–1945)
   6. *Ferrucio Busoni* (1866–1924)
   7. *Ermanno Wolf-Ferrari* (1876–1948)

F. **Poland**
   1. *Henri Wieniawski* (1835–1880)
   2. *Ignace Paderewski* (1860–1941)

G. **Russia**
   1. *Mikhail Glinka* (1804–1857)
   2. *Anton Rubinstein* (1829–1894)
   3. *César Cui* (1835–1918)
   4. *Mily Balakirev* (1837–1910)
   5. *Alexander Scriabin* (1872–1915)
   6. *Sergey Rachmaninoff* (1873–1943)

H. **Spain**
   1. *Isaac Albeniz* (1860–1909)

I. **Sweden**
   1. *Franz Berwald* (1796–1868)

J. **United States**
   1. *Louis Gottschalk* (1829–1869)
   2. *Arthur Foote* (1853–1937)
   3. *George Chadwick* (1854–1931)
   4. *John Knowles Paine* (1839–1906)
   5. *Edgar Stillman Kelley* (1857–1944)
   6. *Edward MacDowell* (1861–1908)
   7. *Daniel Gregory Mason* (1873–1953)

IX. IMPORTANT WRITERS ON MUSIC

There was a wide variety of writings on musical subjects in the nineteenth century that can be placed in the following categories: (1) music theory, (2) criticism, (3) history and biography, and (4) aesthetics.

The teaching of music outgrew the old apprenticeship method, partly because of the large number of nonprofessionals who became interested in the processes and techniques of musical composition. Moreover, it was in conservatory and university classes that much of the music theory was taught. To meet the growing demand for a systematic approach to theory, manuals of harmony, counterpoint, form, composition and orchestration were written.

The art of musical criticism won the attention of many writers including the composers themselves. With a less sophisticated audience than in the eighteenth century there was an interest in, and a need for, interpretations and evaluations of musical works and their performances. Evaluations of music were made not only of the contemporary but also of the older composers. In addition the rise of the virtuoso performer made his performance noteworthy and reviews of his performance had a profound effect on his box-office appeal.

The most famous journals that served as sounding boards for critical writings were the *Allgemeine Musikalische Zeitung* published in Leipzig, the *Neue Zeitschrift für Musik* founded by Schumann in 1834 in Leipzig, and the *Gazette Musicale* published in Paris.

With history becoming a science and with the romantic cult of personality, both history and biography became important areas of literary efforts. The science of musicology was systematized in the late nineteenth century, a science that led to authoritative editions of older composers and definitive biographies of composers and performers.

The Romantic period, as we have seen, was a time of conflicting theories and ideas about what music could and should express. Writers on aesthetics argued the pros and cons of the various opinions regarding music. This was especially true of the conflict between program and absolute music and the new theories of opera.

1. *Ernst Theodore Amadeus Hoffman* (1776–1822) was a German writer and composer. He espoused the romantic ideal of the union of the arts and wrote poetic and romantic appraisals of such composers as Mozart and Beethoven. He used the pen name of Johannes Kreisler (made famous by Schumann's *Kreisleriana*). His critical writings were published in the *Allgemeine Musikalische Zeitung*.

2. *François Fétis* (1784–1871) was a Belgian music theorist and historian. While he wrote a number of theoretical treatises, his most famous work is the monumental *Biographie universelle des musiciens et bibliographie générale de la musique* in eight volumes, Paris 1833–1844. This was the first fairly complete dictionary of musicians and still serves as a prime source for some composers.

3. *Hector Berlioz* (1803–1869) wrote the first important treatise on orchestration, *Traité d' instrumentation et orchestration modernes*, Paris 1844. (Treatise on instrumentation and orchestration, New York 1948.) This work remained a standard textbook on the subject until fairly recent times. In addition Berlioz made frequent contributions of critical essays to the *Gazette Musicale* and published a book of essays on orchestral music, *Les Soirées de l' orchestre* (Evenings in the orchestra, Paris 1853; New York 1956).

4. *Charles-Edmond-Henri de Coussemaker* (1805–1876) was a French music historian who wrote a number of important works on early music. His interest in ancient documents led to a number of valuable collections of early music. His major work is *Scriptorum de musica medii*, (Writings of Medieval Music) Paris 1864–1876.

5. *Robert Schumann* (1810–1856) was the founder and editor of the *Neue Zeitschrift für Musik*, published in Leipzig. His writings were militant essays propagandizing the new Romantic ideals. In the imaginary *Davidsbündler* (Society of David) the different facets of his own romantic personality were represented by the characters of Florestan and Eusebius, names he often used in signing his essays. Schumann was also the first composer to recognize the genius of Chopin

and Brahms, writing enthusiastic criticisms of their music.

6. *Franz Liszt* (1811–1866) also made numerous contributions to the literature about music as a critic, as a commentator on the current musical scene, and as a champion of the *modern* style of his day. He wrote a series of articles *On the Position of Artists* in which he discussed the social consciousness of composers and performers. He also wrote on church music, calling for a return to the function of music as a spiritual force.

7. *Richard Wagner* (1813–1883) was the most prolific writer on music of all the Romantic composers, both in the area of aesthetics and criticism. In addition to being the author of libretti for his own operas, Wagner wrote essays and pamphlets on a variety of musical subjects. Of special significance were his writings on the problems of opera. *Oper und Drama*, Leipzig 1851, outlined his theories of the *artwork-of-the-future*. His autobiography set forth his ideas on the union of the arts and his own thoughts on almost everything from music to politics. He also wrote an important essay, *Religion and Art*, that was a counterpart of his opera *Parsifal*.

8. *August Wilhelm Ambros* (1816–1876) was an eminent German historian and musicologist. His *Geschichte der Musik*, Leipzig, 1862, was one of the first music histories that tried to draw a parallel between developments in music and the developments in the visual arts.

9. *Sir George Grove* (1820–1900) was an English historian and musicologist. His chief claim to fame as a writer on music was in the *Dictionary of Music and Musicians* in four volumes, London 1879–1889, a work that has gone through many editions and revisions, the latest in 1980 expanded to twenty volumes.

10. *Herman von Helmholz* (1821–1894) was a German scientist and an expert on acoustics. His *Lehre von den Tonempfindungen als physiologische Grundlage für die Theorie der Musik* (On the Sensations of Tone as a Physiological Basis for the Theory of Music, New

York, 1948) Brunswick 1863, laid the foundation for modern research in the physical and physiological aspects of musical sound and hearing. He based his work on experimentation, but drew heavily upon the researches of Rameau and Tartini.

11. *Eduard Hanslick* (1825–1904) was the most famous of the romantic critics and aestheticians in the field of music. While he was born in Prague, he lived most of his life in Vienna. Hanslick was a champion of absolutism in music and his book *Vom Musikalischen Schönen: ein Beitrage zur Revision der Aesthetik der Tonkunst* (On the Beautiful in Music; a Contribution to the Revision of Musical Aesthetics, New York 1957) Leipzig 1854, is his most notable work. It has been translated into many languages including English. In this work Hanslick argued that the beauty of a musical composition lay wholly in the music itself, without extramusical ideas. His opposition to the new school of Romantic realism led to his criticism of Wagner, Liszt, Berlioz, and the other programmatic composers. In retaliation Wagner caricatured Hanslick in the character of Beckmesser in *Die Meistersinger*, a distinction that led to an undeserved lack of appreciation of Hanslick's writings. While he opposed the Wagnerian group, he wrote glowing accounts of Schumann and Brahms who represented the more classic facets of Romanticism.

12. *Karl Franz Chrysander* (1826–1901) was a German music historian and critic. He shared in the editing of the monumental collection of music, *Denkmäler der Tonkunst*, five volumes, Leipzig 1869–1871. Chrysander is best known, however, for his writings on the life and works of Handel. He started the *Deutsche Handelgesellschaft* (German Handel Society) and wrote a definitive biography of Handel published in Leipzig in 1858–1867.

13. *Ebenezer Prout* (1835–1909) was an English theorist and teacher. He was the author of numerous textbooks on theory including harmony, counterpoint, fugue, and musical form. His text on orchestration went through many editions and has been used as a handbook of instrumentation until well into the twentieth century.

14. *Hugo Riemann* (1849–1919) was a German musicologist who is generally credited with systematizing the science of musicology. He led the way in a stylistic study of types and periods of music, a specialization that has resulted in a wealth of authoritative studies by present day musicology. The list of Riemann's writings is long, but most significant is the *Musiklexikon*, Leipzig 1882, a work that is recognized as a standard reference in music. It has gone through many editions, the latest in 1959.

15. *Vincent d'Indy* (1851–1931) was one of the few successful composers to write a text on the art of musical composition, *Cours de Composition Musicales* (Course of Musical Composition), Paris 1903–1933. A student of César Franck, d'Indy also wrote an authoritative biography of the Belgian master.

Supplementary Readings

Austin	pp. 1–177
Borroff	pp. 453–566
Cannon-Johnson-Waite	pp. 341–418
Crocker	pp. 355–480
Einstein, *Music in the Romantic Era*	
Grout	pp. 520–681
Lang	pp. 734–989
Schirmer	Part Five ch. 23–28, 30, 39
Wold-Cykler	chs. 10–13

Further References

Abraham, Gerald. *A Hundred Years of Music.* New York: Knopf, 1938.

Barzun, Jacques. *Berlioz and the Romantic Century.* New York: Little, Brown, 1950. (2 vols.).

Chase, Gilbert. *America's Music.* New York: McGraw-Hill, 1955.

Courcy, G. I. C. de *Paganini.* Norman: University of Oklahoma Press, 1957.

Grout, D. J. *A Short History of Opera.* New York: Columbia University Press, 1947.

Locke, Arthur, W. *Music and the Romantic Movement in France.* New York: E. P. Dutton, 1920.

Longyear, Rey M. *Nineteenth-Century Romanticism in Music.* Englewood Cliffs: Prentice-Hall 2nd ed., 1973.

Newman, Ernest. *The Wagner Operas.* New York: Knopf, 1949.

Praz, Mario. *The Romantic Agony.* New York: Oxford, 1951.

Rolland, Romain. *Jean Cristophe.* New York: Modern Library Ed. 1938.

Soloman, Maynard. *Beethoven.* New York: Schirmer, 1977.

Thayer, A. W. *Life of Ludwig van Beethoven.* Princeton: Princeton University Press, 1964.

Wagner, Richard. *Prose Works.* Translated by W. W. Ellis, London: 1892–1899. (8 vols.).

Zetlin, Mikhail O. *The Five, the Revolution of the Russian School of Music.* New York: International Universities Press, 1959.

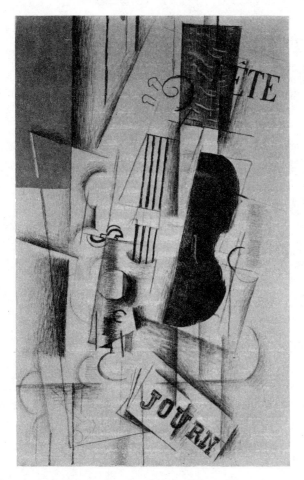

Musical Forms—Braque (1913). This painting reveals the abstract character of recognizable objects by fragmenting three dimensional forms. Much of the twentieth century music, with its fragmented melodies, indescisive harmonies and rhythmic complexities only suggest the traditional melodies, harmonies and rhythms. (Philadelphia Museum of Art)

8

Chronology
of the Twentieth Century

1856	Sigmund Freud (1856-1939)	1875	Maurice Ravel (1875-1937)

1856   Sigmund Freud
        (1856-1939)
1864   Leos Janáček
        (1864-1928)
1866   Vasily Kandinsky
        (1866-1944)
        Erik Satie (1866-1925)
1868   Scott Joplin
        (1868-1917)
        Edmond Rostand
        (1868-1918)
1869   Frank Lloyd Wright
        (1869-1959)
1871   Georges Rouault
        (1871-1958)
1872   Bertrand Russell
        (1872-1970)
        Ralph Vaughn
        Williams
        (1872-1958)
1873   W. C. Handy
        (1873-1958)
1874   Winston Churchill
        (1874-1965)
        Arnold Schoenberg
        (1874-1950)
        Charles Ives
        (1874-1954)

1875   Maurice Ravel
        (1875-1937)
        Thomas Mann
        (1875-1955)
1876   Constantin Brancusi
        (1876-1957)
        Manuel de Falla
        (1876-1946)
1877   Piet Mondrian
        (1877-1944)
1879   Raoul Dufy
        (1879-1953)
        Albert Einstein
        (1879-1955)
        Paul Klee (1879-1940)
        Josef Stalin
        (1879-1953)
1880   Ernest Bloch
        (1880-1959)
1881   Pablo Picasso
        (1881-1973)
        Wilhelm Lehmbruck
        (1881-1919)
        Béla Bartók
        (1881-1945)
1882   Igor Stravinsky
        (1882-1971)
        James Joyce
        (1882-1941)

1883	Walter Gropius (1883–1969)	1899	"Duke" Ellington (1899–1974)
	Anton Webern (1883–1945)	1900	Aaron Copland (1900–)
1884	Franklin D. Roosevelt (1884–1945)		Ernst Krenek (1900–)
1885	Alban Berg (1885–1935)	1901	Alberto Giacometti (1901–)
	Edgar Varèse (1885–1965)	1903	Wright brothers first airplane flight
1887	Charles-Eduard Jeaneret (Le Corbusièr) (1887–1965)	1904	Salvador Dali (1904–) Willem de Kooning (1904–)
	Heitor Villa-Lobos (1887–1959)		Luigi Dallapicolla (1904–1975)
1888	Jean Arp (1888–1966) T. S. Eliot (1888–1965)	1906	Peter Blume (1906–)
1889	Adolf Hitler (1889–1945)		Dmitri Shostakovitch (1906–1975)
1890	Naum Gabo (1890–1977)	1908	Elliott Carter (1908–)
1892	Arthur Honneger (1892–1955)		Oliver Messaien (1908–)
	Darius Milhaud (1892–1974)	1909	Peary discovers the North Pole
1893	Joan Miró (1893–1983)	1911	Amundsen discovers
1895	Paul Hindemith (1895–1963)		the South Pole
	Carl Orff (1895–1982)	1912	Jackson Pollock (1912–1956)
1896	Roger Sessions (1896–)		John Cage (1912–)
1897	Ragtime from c.1897–1915	1913	Benjamin Britten (1913–1976)
1898	Alexander Calder (1898–1976)		Witold Lutaslawski (1913–)
	Bertold Brecht (1898–1956)	1914	Beginning of the First World War
	George Gershwin (1898–1937)		Griffith films first great epic, *Birth of a Nation*
	Ernest Hemingway (1898–1961)	1915	Panama Canal opened
		1917	First printed use of the term "Jazz" Russian Revolution

1918	First World War ends	1934	Peter Maxwell Davies
	Leonard Bernstein		(1934–)
	(1918–)	1938	Nuclear fission
	Leon Kirchner		discovered
	(1919–)	1939	Second World War
	George Rochberg		begins
	(1918–)	1939–50	Television developed.
1920	First commercial radio	1945	Atomic bomb destroys
	broadcast		Hiroshima and
1922	Yannic Xenakis		Nagasaki
	(1922–)		Second World War
1923	György Ligeti		ends
	(1923–)	1946	First assembly of the
1925	Luciano Berio		United Nations
	(1925–)	1950	Pop and Op art (c.1950)
	Pierre Boulez		Chinese Revolution
	(1925–)	1957	First satellite (sputnik)
	Gunther Schuller		launched by Russia
	(1925–)	1960	Rock and roll (c.1960)
1926	Hans Werner Henze	1963	President John F.
	(1926–)		Kennedy assassinated
1928	Karlheinz Stockhausen	1967	Heart transplant
	(1928–)	1969	United States lands
1929	George Crumb		first man on the moon
	(1929–)	1980–82	Unmanned satellite
1933	Krzysztof Penderecki		lands on Mars
	(1933–)		Satellite explores and
			collects data on Jupiter

8

Twentieth Century

Historical Perspective

History is generally defined as that branch of knowledge that relates and analyzes past events. Music history, as evidenced in the many texts on the subject, deals preponderently with the description and analysis of past musical creativity; often to the utter disregard of more recent and contemporary events. This is not a criticism of historical reporting. It is rather the recognition of the fact that there is a need for perspective in assessing the importance of events, which ones deserve relating, what should be analyzed and to what purpose.

For example, in the first half of the eighteenth century J. S. Bach was little known beyond his immediate sphere of activity, while George Phillip Telemann was widely recognized as an international figure. Until almost one hundred years after his death Bach's music was practically unknown. With very few exceptions none of it was even available in published form until the nineteenth century. In the eyes (and ears) of contemporaries, Telemann was by far the more widely acclaimed. Bach was third choice for the post of cantor at St. Thomas Church in Leipzig after Telemann and Graupner. But what has historic study revealed as to the relative importance of these very able composers? A glance at the space allotted to these men in any text on music history will give the answer.

Music history reveals countless discrepancies between the views of past scholars and public concerning their contemporaries and the views of later scholars and public who view the past in perspective. With this thought in mind, the authors of *An Outline History of Music* have added a section (Some Recent Developments" under several of the headings of Chapter Eight.

Their inclusion makes no claim to completeness nor to relative values. The authors have merely tried to indicate some of the tendencies in music since the middle of the twentieth century, which are evident at the time of this present revision.

Again it must be noted that the speed of communication and change is so great that any attempt to cover all trends is doomed to failure. What may have looked important and permanent in the seventies may already be fading into oblivion in the eighties. We hope that our endeavor, however, will encourage the reader to be aware of the present, and yet to recognize that without perspective it is impossible to make any real judgment concerning musical events of today beyond personal likes and dislikes. One of the twentieth century's most influential composers, Arnold Schoenberg, stated," Contemporaries are not the final judges, but are generally overruled by history."[1]

I. SOCIOCULTURAL INFLUENCES ON MUSIC

A. General Considerations

The transition from nineteenth century Romanticism to twentieth century "modernism" is, perhaps, as violent an upheaval in musical thought as was the transition from the ars antiqua to the ars nova, or from the Renaissance to the Baroque. As in the earlier revolutions, the seeds of the new are already to be found in the dissolution of the old. The audible results of this musical revolution show as wide a difference with nineteenth century and earlier musical ideas as the technological phenomena of the nuclear age differ from those of the nineteenth century. The attainment of these results has been an orderly and evolutionary one.

Because the speed of twentieth century attainments in all areas has been so accelerated, music, subjected to this same acceleration, has moved from one new idea to another with such rapidity that no previous era can be compared with the diversity and extremes of its expressions. The search for originality on the part of every composer has led to a great variety of

1. Arnold Schoenberg "Composition with Twelve Tones" in *Style and Idea* (1941) p. 103.

expression, reversion to past historical styles, neo-Classicism, neo-Romanticism, serial composition, electronic music, microtonal music, music concrete, even post serial and aleatory music. The insistence on originality is so compelling that its end results often appear questionable.

The sociocultural influences which affect music are many and varied, but the annihilation of space through the application of the technological results of scientific discovery is probably the basic influence on musical creativity and production.

The basic scientific research already begun in the nineteenth was continued in the twentieth century, and led to a number of discoveries and inventions that influenced man's relationships beyond all previous imagination. The invention of rapid sound communication, such as the telephone and telegraph in the nineteenth century, led to the further development of sound transmission and resulted in the invention of the phonograph and radio. By the middle of the twentieth century radio and phonograph recordings had made music available to an enormous number of the world's civilized societies.

Two great political revolutions, communism and fascism, made deep impressions on musical composition in the twentieth century. Fascism in Italy and its Nazi counterpart in Germany were comparatively short lived. In their most virulent forms nazism and fascism damned all nontraditional creativity as decadent and typical of the weaknesses of western democratic society. For almost twenty years the healthy creativity of Germany and Italy was carried on only by exiled composers who fled their native lands, mainly to the United States. Since the end of the Second World War there has been a very active resurgence of creative life in these countries.

In the first years of the Soviet Union, following the First World War, there was a brief period in which the most advanced of contemporary musical expression found performance and creative encouragement. This ended in the late 20s with the advent of Stalin as a dominant figure, and until after his death in the 50s Russia was cut off from participation in the mainstream of twentieth century musical creativity and performance. A strong emphasis on traditional nationalistic trends of the nineteenth century prevailed for the most part.

The other states of Europe had scarcely recovered their economic and artistic equilibrium after the First World War before the impending cataclysm of the great economic depression of the 30s and the disaster of the Second World War overtook them.

B. **Some Recent Developments**

The general sociocultural influences of the first part of the twentieth century were continued in the second half of the century. The development of scientific research due to the second world war was turned to commercial and social uses with great vigor. Not only was the speed of communication in all its aspects increased, but all phases of communication were made universally available. Some of the post 1950 developments include television, solid-state physics (transistors), rocket propulsion (space satellites, interstellar exploration) laser beams, computers, etc. Each of these contributed more or less to the musical scene of the late twentieth century.

Development of the phonograph and recording have led to long-play records which enable the complete performance of large works. The portable radio and cassette recorders and other inexpensive and readily available instruments now permit almost every human being in the world to listen to all kinds of music. It is now possible to have musical performance at every social event. Music from the banal to the most esoteric from all periods of history, music performed by all kinds of performers and all types of instruments is at the command of almost any individual through one of the modern means of transmission. Such a plethora of musical experience was never at the disposal of the wealthiest patron, secular or religious, in the past. At the present moment it is even possible to record not only live performances of radio for future reproduction, but television programs are capable of being recorded on tape and replayed at the convenience of the listener and viewer.

In addition to these advances in technology that have made music available to a widely diversified audience, there have been other major discoveries which have influenced music directly and indirectly. Nuclear physics, space travel and the laser beam, to name a few, have all had their impact on composers. They have served to widen the imagination and sensitivity of the creative artist. A good example of this is Penderecki's *Threnody for the Victims of Hiroshima*, which was directly influenced by the consequences of nuclear physics and the atom bomb.

The invention of electric instruments for musical reproduction has also led to the invention of electronic sound producing instruments. Such instruments since 1950 have engaged a number of composers in experimentation with, not only an entirely new field of sound complexes, but also new possibilities of composing these sounds. Rhythmic complexities completely beyond the possibility of human realization are comparatively easy to achieve on electronic instruments. Sound generators and synthesizers are the most commonly used electronic devices in musical composition. They have opened up entirely new vistas of tonal color. In addition to these instruments directly manipulated by composers are the electronic computers, which invite the possibility of automatic musical composition. Programmed computers have already been used in more recent times to compose music.

This continued incursion of electronic devices has led to a great variety of experiments, both in the area of composition and performance. A continual urge to achieve uniqueness has led to multimedia experiments with music, dance, lights and other effects. They often become spontaneous "happenings" that cannot be duplicated.

A somewhat subtle environmental factor of the twentieth century has also made its influence felt on musical composition. It is obvious that modern man lives in an environment which is much more acoustically disturbing than that of any past era. The noise of modern life has increased many-fold even during this century. Automobiles, tractors, airplanes, mechanical construction machines, office machinery, factory machinery have brought about a high level of nervous tension which expects and demands a high level of acoustical stimulus in all forms of communication. Whereas speakers less than fifty years ago addressed large audiences without the aid of public address systems, present day speakers find it necessary to address an even limited audience in acoustically adequate halls through loud speaker systems. This raising of the sound level has affected music as well. While orchestras and ensembles are not necessarily larger, the tone level of the individual instruments, and the quality of tone called for, often tend to be strident, piercing and in many respects like that delivered over electric reproducing machines. Composers today are not unmindful of the fact that it is through the medium of recorded sound that they have the greatest opportunity to reach their audience. Consequently, they compose with recording in mind. This leads to the manipulation of the recording devices which control and change the original sound to meet the needs of present day acoustical levels.

A corollary of the previous phenomenon is the fact that to many listeners recorded music is much more acoustically satisfactory than that of most large concert halls. Moreover recorded music makes it unnecessary for the listener to discommode himself in attending a concert or opera. As a result there are many avid music lovers who rarely hear music "in the flesh." Recordings are capable of almost perfect technical performance since all mistakes can be erased and repaired through editing, cutting, and splicing of the original tape. What this means to the human factor in music remains to be seen. It undoubtedly leads the composer to expect a perfect performance despite all difficulties in the composition.

The possession of a high degree of technical proficiency by the performing artist is also the common expectation of both the composer and listener. Since the number of needed performers has declined so drastically in the last thirty years it is to be expected that only the most technically proficient will survive. Performance skill has reached such a high level that composers have no hesitation in writing what seems to be music exclusively for the virtuoso.

The political ferment of the post World War I period finally led to the Second World War and its aftermath of social, scientific and political upheavals. Among these were the persecution of the Jews, the Civil Rights Movement, Women's Liberation and Environmentalism. While these concerns were especially felt in the United States of America, they were indeed world-wide phenomena and contributed to the creative artists' insight into social and moral problems of humanity. Creative persons often try to express their own personal concern and feelings in terms of their art.

Those countries that joined the Communist Bloc at the end of World War II such as Poland, Czechoslovakia, Hungary, Bulgaria, Rumania and East Germany were also cut off from the avant garde trends of the second half of the century. This continued until the death of Stalin freed them in part from the restrictions on artistic creativity. Since the middle of the 50s there has been a very decided break in the traditional nationalistic trends in the musical works of the composers of the eastern European states. Cultural exchange between the communist countries and the rest of the world has been one of the first communication "breakthroughs" in the 50s and 60s. The music of the west, avant garde and popular, has not only been introduced to the east, but it is being widely performed by east European artists. The composers of these countries, notably Poland, Rumania and Czechoslovakia are as representative of the late twentieth century trends as composers of the west.

Another political change that has had an effect on music has been the dissolution of great overseas empires in recent years especially the British, Dutch and the French. The emergence of new nations have been the result of this movement and have led to new nationalisms in these underprivileged nations. Consequently, indigenous music and art, both popular and serious, especially from Africa and Asia, have spread worldwide and have been an influence on composers in both Western and Non-Western countries.

The internationalism of all music cultures has also resulted in a revival of many exotic musical practices and a resurgence of interest in heretofore obsolete musical instruments, especially those of the Renaissance and Eastern cultures.

The revolt of youth, like other great political and social upheavals of the twentieth century, has given rise to a phenomenon in which music and text have often collaborated in past times, the songs and music of protest. There are, however, instances of creativity of deep musical significance in all forms of composition, whose themes are those of protest of man's inhumanity to man: socially, politically, economically, and religiously. Such work as Kraft's *Contextures: Riots-Decade 60* and Penderecki's *Threnody* represent the effect of such movements on musical creativity. Like much composition of the past, depth of musical and aesthetic value will determine their ultimate artistic fate.

Commercial exploitation of music through recorded media and through management of performers has had a marked influence on the course of musical composition. Because of the lag in understanding between composers and the general public as patron, the overwhelming mass of music published and distributed via the concert stage tends to emphasize the music of the past three hundred years. As a consequence there is a very limited audience for the contemporary composer who deviates from the tradition of the last three centuries and whose music is not likely to be "immediately acceptable." In fact, such a limited audience is probably made up primarily of

other musicians or those who through special training are capable of some understanding of the new
music. As a result modern composers are often ac-
cused of writing only for the musical elite.

Since the 1950s there has been a world-wide emphasis on the teaching of music in the public schools and
institutions of higher education. Both creative and
performing musicians have found appointments on
the faculties of music schools and universities along
with the musical research scholar where students and
highly competent performing colleagues have made
the performance of contemporary works possible.
Such institutions have in a way offered the creative
artist and performer the patronage which musicians
in the seventeenth and eighteenth centuries enjoyed
at the hands of aristocracy.

The secondary schools have been generally more active in their offerings of music instruction than the
elementary schools. In America this is generally represented by an emphasis on peformance, while in the
schools of other countries there is a tendency to teach
music on an academic basis. The teaching of music in
the elementary schools is probably the weakest link
in the chain of music education in all countries.

II. FUNCTION OF MUSIC

A. General Considerations

The commercial aspects of music distribution along
with new media of musical communication have led
to great changes in the function of music in the twentieth century.

The organized concert series in large and small urban
centers is a purely twentieth century phenomenon.
The availability of any and all performing artists in
comparatively remote areas encourages large audiences for a season of *star* performances. The composer is more and more at the mercy of a shrinking
number of performers who through managerial pressure feel the necessity of emphasizing the traditional
works to satisfy a large but often undiscriminating

audience. Such concerts have their positive value in that they undoubtedly have raised the musical taste of the general public from that of the past century. Programs are likely to contain a great preponderance of highly valuable standard literature. It remains to be seen whether this raising of taste will eventually bring about a desire to hear the compositions of living composers.

Music for the twentieth century phenomena, the motion picture and television, are outlets for living composers. Nowhere, however, is the effect of the mass audience more clearly discernible than in this function. After almost seventy years of motion picture music, fifty of which have been in the form of recorded performance, there have been very few pieces of music that might be said to be distinguished as artistically noteworthy. Neither incidental motion picture music nor that which is written for a musical picture has distinguished itself. Even those films which have won distinction as highly artistic works, and for which competent composers have written very successful scores, indicate that writing music for films is really a task of incidental character. Most audiences, however, are being introduced to a variety of contemporary musical styles through the media of motion pictures and television. In one sense the ideal of Wagner's thesis that music and drama should be a synthesis is more nearly achieved in the best of motion pictures than in the musical dramas of Wagner where music dominated.

A great part of the world's population is constantly bombarded with musical sounds from recordings and radio. Such performances are to be heard in all one's waking surroundings, the home, the market, the office, the factory, the playground, the sports field. These areas, however afford no outlet to the serious composer. In fact this function of music is largely psychological, affording an antidote for the multifarious sounds that surround humans at all times. The kind of music played has no intent to raise or lower public taste. A negative result is the fact that it induces the hearer to pay little or no direct attention and makes him, therefore, a less discriminating listener.

The Church, except in a very few isolated instances, is even more cut off from the contemporary composer than ever before. Some composers of stature have been commissioned by the Church. Most choir directors find contemporary religious music too difficult for amateur choirs to perform. While there have been many movements in Catholic and Protestant churches to raise the quality of the music used in the service, these have resulted only in the revival of much of the fine music of the past, especially the sacred repertoire of the Baroque and Renaissance, and even earlier periods.

While the opera still functions as an important means of reaching a large public, its activity varies greatly from country to country. Whereas central Europe has a tremendously active opera life, the United States is restricted to short seasons. In recent years, however, the number of cities that have developed opera companies in the United States has increased dramatically from two or three centers to almost every metropolitan area. The opera houses everywhere tend to function as museums for musical dramatic works rather than as places where the public is introduced to new and vital compositions. European opera houses generally tend to devote a portion of their repertoire of contemporary works while the American University workshops and opera studios provide an opportunity to contemporary composers especially in the field of chamber opera.

In the field of television there has not yet been an artistically satisfying union of music and media. European and public television in the United States, however, devote a large amount of time to the broadcasting of concert and operatic performances including contemporary works. These broadcasts are for the most part adaptations of the stage or concert platform for the television screen. One of the exceptions is the musical commercial, in which media and music are often skillfully combined. The television offers a completely new avenue of communication to the imaginative composer of the twentieth century which as yet has not been completely realized.

B. **Some Recent Developments**

In general the functions of music already evident in the early part of the twentieth century were continued in the era after the Second World War.

Special festivals and concert series organized for the purpose of presenting works of contemporary composers, especially of avant garde nature, have multiplied since the middle of the century. Such events are to be found in all countries. In addition there are a number of festivals devoted to music, both old and new, from nonwestern cultures. Many of these take place in universities and schools of music where programs are devoted to experimental and exotic music of the twentieth century. A number of foundations, both private and governmental, as well as individuals are giving support to the composition and performance of music of the twentieth century.

Since the middle of the century there has been a particular emphasis on the employment of composers as teachers in the musical institutes and universities in all countries. In many instances such positions are announced as *composers in residence* and parallel the situation in the Renaissance and Baroque periods when the composers were attached to both small and large courts. The functions of the composer and his music in these situations is twofold. He provides instruction through precept and example to those who wish to engage in the creative effort, and he provides musical fare whereby the general university community can experience the idiom of the contemporary composer.

Because many colleges and universities have the resources in both teaching and performance, they have become fertile ground for the experimental and avant garde composer. In fact some of the most elaborate resources for the electronic music in the United States are to be found in educational institutions. However, in Europe, the broadcasting studios have also been in the vanguard of this movement. Moreover, educational institutions can also supply audiences that are eager to experience new sounds and techniques of composing and performance.

The second half of the 20th century has seen the rise of the Broadway musical and ballet to a position of high importance. The latter is a development of a traditional classic form with greater freedom in movement and more emphasis on dramatic action. The techniques developed by Martha Graham, Isadora Duncan, Mary Wigman and Agnes DeMille have led to the composition of ballet music by many of the contemporary composers. The broadway musical is a descendant of the opera comique and the operetta but with a distinctive American flavor that has commanded attention in many world centers even in the European opera houses of long established tradition. Ballet has been effectively combined with this new form of musical theater.

III. CHARACTERISTICS OF STYLE

The break with the nineteenth century was felt as a compelling necessity by most of the twentieth century composers. Musical techniques employed to achieve the realistic, impressionistic, and nationalistic ends of the previous century had been pushed about as far as possible. The composer felt the necessity of finding new ways to say new things. Musically this meant that melody, harmony, rhythm, and tone quality must be reassessed and studied.

The first attempts at a new mode of composition in any age are likely to be of more academic interest than artistic. New techniques and devices must first be tried in the fires of experimental creativity until those less effective are weeded out and a kind of consensus is established among the creative forces as to what the truly new and viable musical innovations are which can serve to express them in their own milieu.

Two answers to the composers' search for new ways to say new things presented themselves: discover more tonal material than the twelve tones of the octave with which to build, or find new principles of construction with the old material. The first answer gives rise to attempts at splitting the octave into smaller intervals than the twelve half steps. This device, *microtonality,* has been attempted by a few composers using newly constructed instruments—quarter-tone piano and others—or by taking advantage of those kinds of instruments which can play, in their present form, intervals smaller than the semi-tone— the violin family, the trombone, or the human voice. Following this trend the advances in electronic tone production has developed instruments of very sophisticated nature, tonal synthesizers, which can be used to create tones of infinitely small pitch differences under the control of the operator.

The second answer, that of finding a new principle of construction using the traditional media such as the twelve-tone technique has involved most of the composers of the twentieth century. In the 50s and 60s there have been many attempts to combine both the above answers to their problem: using new pitch differences as well as new principles of construction. The emphasis on tonal color and rhythmic complexity has likewise often displaced pitch as the important element in formal construction.

Since the 1960s there has been an increased interest in a kind of new romanticism (neo-romanticism) among composers, both serious and popular. Perhaps the commitment to the new technology is weakening and the result is a resurgence of a more humanistic expression in music.

A. **Formal Organization**

1. *General Considerations*

   a) One of the most significant characteristics of twentieth century formal organization is the recognition of the variation principle as basic in musical composition.

   b) An important new device of formal organization is the so-called twelve-tone or dodecaphonic method of composition. This system, later called serial composition, used the twelve chromatic tones as independent entities without reference to a tonal center. The composition was based on a set pattern of the twelve tones called the tone row, repeated continuously throughout the work in many varied forms. The basic row is subjected to the various forms of contrapuntal

Family Group—Moore (1945–49). This work uses a style of organic free forms, but with enough objectivity to be representational. Some twentieth century composers rejected the avant-garde influence and retained a semblance of traditional harmony and identifiable melodic lines in much the same vein as the Moore sculpture. (Collection, The Museum of Modern Art, New York. A. Conger Goodyear Fund)

treatment traditionally used to secure variety in imitation: inversion, retrograde (cancrizans), retrograde inversion, augmentation, diminution. Moreover the tone row could be transposed to any of the twelve levels of the chromatic scale. In more advanced serial composition the *series* might consist of less than the entire twelve tones, and might even be a rhythmic or tonal pattern. The basic device of the serial technique is, of course, nothing more than a construction of a tonal pattern (of twelve or less notes) and the continuous variation of this construction.

c) There is a tendency toward brevity in all new musical composition. Thematic structures give way to motival elements. Long, spun out themes are displaced by short epigrammatic motives. All musical elements are tightly organized.

d) True repetition and contrast are used less frequently than before. Literal repetition is used for expressive purposes, not for formal organization. Repetition actually becomes variation.

e) The desire for brevity and economy of means tends to eliminate or at least shorten such formal structures as bridge passages, modulatory sections, dissolution of thematic material, and closing sections.

2. *Some Recent Developments*
   a) Complete or total serial composition is used to describe works in which all the elements, melody, harmony, rhythm, dynamics and tone color are treated in a serial fashion. The composition is no longer formally organized around a tone row but rather around the serial arrangement of all the musical elements.

   b) There has been a tendency toward chance music, often referred to as *aleatoric* or *indeterminate* music. There are various ways by which this can be achieved: (1) by the element of chance in composition but determined in performance, (2) by structured composition but the element of chance in performance, and (3) by the element of chance in both composition and performance.

This kind of composition can result in *non-music*. In such cases there is no notation of any kind, nor is there an observed performer. Each member of the audience is asked to *compose* the sound which comes to his attention during a given period of time. In such cases melody, rhythm, harmony, and tone-color cease to be in any way traditional or functional.

B. **Melody**

1. *General Considerations*

a) Melody is completely dominated by the instrumental idiom, whether for voice or instrument. The melodic line is often subjected to wide intervallic skips and a high degree of rhythmic complexity. In addition it is often placed in unusual vocal and instrumental range in order to make use of extreme tonal qualities.

b) Vocal melody is subjected to contours that are expressive of the text even to the extent of losing specific tonal designation as in the tecnique of *sprechstimme*. This term is literally translated as "speech voice" or "speech intonation." A similar technique is apparent in the presentation of popular music where the singer does not confine the textual rendition to a well defined melody, but exaggerates and stresses the actual pitches according to the intensity of emotional expression conveyed by the words. In the following example the vocalist is instructed to avoid the absolute pitches of the notes which are designated by the cross on the stems (ex. 36).

Example 36   Schoenberg

Den   Wein, den man mit   Au - gen trinkt,   giebt

   c) Melody loses symmetrical form of phrase
      and period. There is a tendency to form a
      melody from short motival fragments.
   d) The consecutive notes of a melodic line are
      often spread over several octaves and given
      to different instruments rather than con-
      tained within the range of a single instru-
      ment.
   e) The general tendency to write in a contra-
      puntal style lessens the importance of mel-
      ody as a dominating vehicle for the musical
      material. Even in works which use a solo
      voice or instrument, the solo part becomes
      one of the lines of the contrapuntal fabric
      rather than a dominating melodic line.
2. *Some Recent Developments.* Strictly speaking melody has disappeared from much of the music of
   the post Second World War period. Many of the
   extreme contemporary compositions are devoted
   to displays of tonal color and rhythmic complexities. Not only electronic music, but many works
   for traditional instruments are so overwhelm-
   ingly concerned with these two elements that
   melody is virtually non-existent.

C. Rhythm
   1. *General Considerations*
      a) Rhythms are characteristically irregular and
         asymmetrical. Much use is made of odd
         numbered metric patterns—five, seven,
         eleven (ex. 37).

Example 37   Stravinsk

b) Rhythmic irregularity also consists in the use of several different rhythms simultaneously (polyrhythms), and in the rapid succession of changing rhythms as for example 5/4 followed by 3/8, 2/4, 7/8, etc. (ex. 37).

c) Metric designations are often limited to the designation of only the unit of measure, quarter note, eighth note, half note, without designating the number of notes to a metric unit. In some more recent music, traditional metric units are no longer viable. Time is often measured in seconds or even left to the discretion of the performer.

d) Rhythm is emphasized to the point where a total composition or at least parts of a work are made up of rhythmically exploited sonorities which are lacking in melodic significance and harmonic purpose.

e) Free rhythms such as were found in medieval and Renaissance music are once more used. Bar lines are often omitted.

2. *Some Recent Developments*

a) The rhythmic complexities cultivated in the music of African, Oriental, and other non-western cultures has been highly influential in popular music as well as in art music. The rhythmic freedom of popular music has also had a significant influence on the art music of the twentieth century.

b) Music composed by means of electronic equipment, tone synthesizers, sound generators, tape recorders, and computers, makes possible intricate rhythmic patterns and complexities that defy human performance. Such music exists only in recorded form.

D. Harmony

1. *General Considerations*

a) Twentieth century harmony is recognized as being much more dissonant than that of previous eras. Those intervals which were considered dissonant in the harmonic practice of the eighteenth and nineteenth centuries are now used with great freedom.

b) In music which still adheres to the tradition of tonality these dissonant harmonies, while much more freely used, are still recognized as dissonants and are eventually subjected to resolution even if delayed for long periods in the course of a composition.

c) In twentieth century music which does not adhere to the tradition of tonality, music is often referred to as *atonal*. The distinction between dissonance and consonance is purely academic and ceases to exist in actuality. Harmony is recognized as a relationship of all the tones to one another rather than the relationship of all the tones to a single central one. Under such circumstances all relationships are possible and usable. There is no hierarchy of dissonance and consonance.

Example 38   Ive

d) Traditional harmony has extended its use in dissonance through several devices. One is the use of bitonality and eventually polytonality, the use of two or more tonal centers at the same time (ex. 38).

e) Another device is the traditional construction of harmony on nontraditional scale patterns. Such scale patterns are derived from medieval modes, folk scales, and those constructed arbitrarily on non-western scales.

f) A technique midway between *atonal* and tonally dissonant harmony is achieved by the use of non-harmonic tones. Such usage also leads to a greater or less degree of dissonance.

2. *Some Recent Developments.* Harmony in any way related to its traditional definition is comletely denied in some works, particularly those of electronic origin. The combination of different pitches is no longer based on the principle of function within a tonal system but rather on the function of tonal color. Hence tones of different pitches are combined in clusters or constellations, and not by any principle of tension set up by consonance and dissonance.

E. **Texture**

1. *General Considerations*

a) Contrapuntal texture is most often employed by twentieth century composers, especially the twelve tone composers.

b) With those composers who write in a neo-Romantic style the texture, both harmonic and contrapuntal, is inclined to be very thick and heavy. Full, rich, chordal structure derived from the tendency to achieve a modern style through the use of dissonance is achieved by contrapuntal and harmonic style.

c) Twelve-tone and serial composers exploit a thin, almost ephemeral, contrapuntal texture in which notated silences tend to play as important a part as the notated sounds.

d) Contrapuntal practice is not restricted to a counterpoint of individual melodic lines, but often extends in ensemble and orchestral works to a counterpoint of rhythms in which several rhythmic patterns are used simultaneously, to a counterpoint of tonal qualities in which various groupings of instruments and sound sources are pitted against one another, to a counterpoint of complete and somewhat independent compositions in which each of several individual groups engage in a simultaneous presentation of individual material.

2. *Some Recent Developments.* Sound blocks, clusters, or constellations replace voice leading. Such clusters can be transparent or thick and opaque in texture, depending on the pitches selected and the multiplicity of tones in the cluster.

F. Media and Tone Color

1. *General Considerations*

a) While compositions using large forces are still written, there is a marked tendency to use small ensembles in which unusual combinations are specified. A kind of heterophony of tonal color is achieved by the contrast of widely differing tonal colors in combination.

b) Wind instruments are used more often in solo and choir form.

c) In ensembles there is a tendency to combine wind instruments and string instruments in more nearly equal numbers.

d) The voice if often combined with instruments as an integral part of an ensemble, and is exploited to give a greater variety of tonal color.

2. *Some Recent Developments*

a) The revival of instruments which have long been obsolete or infrequently used in art music is common. Such instruments as the harpsichord, the guitar, the mandolin, and a great list of percussion instruments such as the xylophone and tuned drums are often used.

b) Electric devices and electrically constructed instruments have been added to the performing media. These instruments often act as substitutes for existing instruments, but some use has been made of them as new media of sound production.

Electronic instruments are capable of producing sounds of definite pitch rich in overtones, pure tones which are completely devoid of overtones, and *white* sounds. White sounds contain the entire spectrum of audible frequencies just as white light contains all colors of the spectrum. By being able to filter out selected overtones a variety of sound coloring is possible. Variation in speed of recording is another means of achieving new tonal colors. A tuba, for example, can be pitched at the level of a piccolo by accelerating the recording speed. Such new tonal colors are only achievable through electronic media.

c) The percussion instruments receive greater attention with their number and types greatly increased.

d) Traditional tonal qualities of the traditional instruments are distorted in the attempt to gain new color. This has been especially true in jazz and popular music.

e) Through amplification, traditional instruments and the voice, as well as new and electronic instruments can be brought to high levels of intensity some of which can even threaten the human aural capacity.

f) See Appendix A for description of instruments.

IV. PRACTICE AND PERFORMANCE

A. General Considerations

While notational and dynamic differences are often increasingly specific, there is the opposite tendency in some compositions to leave greater freedom to the performer by calling for purely improvisational passages. Many of the directions are found in the vernacular rather than in traditional Italian, and indicate the attempt to communicate even more clearly than heretofor.

Notation of much modern music is expressed in terms of graphs, charts, and symbols which are specifically defined for the particular composition.

The rise of jazz as a vehicle for the creative (improvisatory) expression of the performer is a marked and important phenomenon which had a strong influence on composers of aleatory music in the twentieth century. Such spontaneous creativity varies from the decoration of a cantus firmus taken from the popular song literature to completely original improvisatory performance.

In all musical performance including that of old or new music, emphasis on perfection of performance calls for superlative technical proficiency.

The criteria established by the high standard of instrumental and vocal performance also makes such technical considerations as purity of tone, intonation, and technical clarity of first rank in the evaluation of musical performance. While virtuosity is no longer a leading element in the musical enjoyment of performance it is a sine qua non of all performers, and as such is taken for granted.

The extremely high degree of specialization and competition has resulted in a separation between the act of composing and that of performance in most cases. Whereas in the past composers were often virtuoso performers, the expectation of technical perfection in performance, both live and in recording, make demands on the performer which usually excluded creative activity.

Pianists such as Ignace Paderewski, Artur Rubinstein, Vladimir Horowitz, Rudolph Serkin, Artur Schnabel, Sviatoslav Richter and many others have become noble performers of the music of all composers from Bach to the present time. A few pianists such as Sergei Rachmoninoff, Leonard Bernstein, Ferruccio Busoni and Sergei Prokofiev have gained reputations both as pianists and composers.

Fritz Kreisler, Jascha Heifitz, David Oistrakh, Joseph Szigeti, Nathan Milstein, Yehudi Menuhin and Issac Stern were violinists who also specialized in the performance of all styles of music from the past to the present.

The list of singers who have gained extraordinary reputations as performers in concert and opera is almost endless, partly because of the limited years available to them as performers. Consequently, it is fruitless to compile a list of the great singers of our time.

Orchestral conducting demanded the same virtuoso performance as other performers. Arturo Toscanni, Leopold Stowkoski, Sergei Koussevitzky, Wilhelm Furtwängler, Bruno Walter, Leonard Bernstein, Otto Klemperer, Eugene Ormandy, Herbert von Karajan and others have brought remarkable and definitive performances to millions via the concert hall, radio and recordings.

Because there are so many younger performers and conductors who are active at this time, it is futile to name them all. The following is a list, however, of those who in the early 80s have become almost household words through their concerts, recordings, television and radio appearances.

Violinists: Itzhak Perlmann, Pinchas Zukerman; pianists: Glenn Gould, André Watts, Vladimir Aschkenazy, cellists: Mstislav Rostroprovitch, Jan Starker; flutists: Jean Pierre Rampal, James Galway; conductors: Zubin Mehta, Seiji Ozawa, Sir George Solti, André Previn.

B. Some Recent Developments

Several phases of amateur performance have experienced widespread attention. One is the revival of interest in performance on early instruments such as the recorder and guitar. This interest has been widely stimulated through music instruction in the public schools. Another phase is the proliferation of amateur orchestral groups, some of which have achieved a high level of competency and artistry.

The tendency toward perfection and definitiveness leads to the revival of old instruments in the performance of the literature of past eras. Among those instruments which have been most successfully revived are the harpsichord, recorder, baroque organ, classic guitar, lute, and a variety of old string instruments, notably several forms of viols.

V. INSTRUMENTAL COMPOSITIONS

There is no form which is peculiar or unique to the twentieth century. As a result composers in the area of instrumental music return to the classic forms of the sonata and sonata-form as the central ideal of contemporary instrumental composition. The composite sonata with its sonata-form movement takes on many changes in the hands of modern composers. The old symmetry of phrase, period, and sections gives way to a balance which is based on calculated psychological principles. While most composers have retained the traditional terminology of the classic era it must be realized that new schemes of formal organization, melody, harmony, rhythm, texture, and tone quality have given them a new meaning and character.

A. Single Movement Forms

1. *Overture and symphonic poems.* The overture has continued as a single movement form quite apart from its original purpose as a prelude to a dramatic work. Most overtures in the twentieth century are really short symphonic poems, often of dramatic expressive quality. Modern dramatic musical works rarely employ an overture in the traditional sense so that there are few overtures of this kind in the modern repertory.

Ex: *Outdoor Overture,* Copland
Big Ben Overture, Toch
Threnody for the Victims of Hiroshima, Penderecki
Chronochromie, Messiaen

2. *Variation.* Because modern composers are generally concerned with the problems of construction, the variation form has regained its popularity. However, the traditional techniques of variation have given way to such devices as variations on a tone-row, on tonal coloring, and on rhythmic patterns.

Ex: *Variations for Orchestra, Op. 31,* Schoenberg
Variations for Piano, Op. 27, Webern
Variazione per Orchestra, Dallapiccola

3. *Short Forms: Dances, Poetic Pieces.* Many short works have been written whose forms are usually that of some dance, generally a modern or exotic one, or a simple two- or three-part song structure. Most of these works are written for piano though solo instruments combined with piano and small ensembles or even orchestral compositions are sometimes cast in these forms.

Ex: *Mikrokosmos,* Bartók (piano)
Three Pieces in the Shape of a Pear, Satie (piano)
Sarcasms, Prokofiev (piano)
Construction in Metal, Cage (percussion orchestra)
Eight Etudes and a Fantasy, Carter (woodwind quartet)

4. *Electronic Media.* Electronic composition includes single movement as well as composite forms. Harmony and melody in the traditional sense play no part as shaping forces in the formal structure of such works. Color, rhythm and dynamics are the elements of formal organization. The first electronic compositions were created through the manipulation of sounds of concrete objects or musical instruments. The invention of the electronic synthesizers made it possible to create completely unique sounds, entirely independent of pre-existing sources such as musical instruments, machines, voices, etc. In many works, traditional instruments and/or voices are combined with taped recordings of purely electronically produced sounds. All electronic music, whether completely independent or combined with instrumental or vocal performance exists only in recorded form. Computers have also been used to create musical compositions. By the use of computers and electronic instruments intricacies of rhythm and dynamics, as well as tonal qualities, can be achieved which are completely beyond the capabilities of the human performer. Television frequently employs electronically generated sound as background for dramatic performance, especially in the presentation of station signatures and sponsor's advertising. These sounds act as a subtle introduction to the listening public of a new sound media.

Ex: *Gesang der Jünglinge,* Stockhausen
Synchronisms No. 5, Davidovsky
Computer Piece No. 1, Ussachevsky
Prelude No. 4 for Piano and Electronic Tape, Subotnik

B. **Composite Forms**

1. *Sonata, chamber music, and symphony.* The composite sonata presents the modern composer with the principal vehicle for extended instrumental composition whether these are for solo, chamber ensemble (string quartet) or orchestral (symphony) media. In its most typical contemporary

style it is a constructivist piece in which brevity is emphasized. Such brevity is achieved by reducing the recapitulation section of the sonata-form, by use of fragmentary motives rather than extended themes, by avoiding repetition except in extremely varied form, by omitting transition and bridge passages between motival statements, and by reducing the instrumentation to its barest minimum. Often the whole sonata is found in a reduced number of movements if not in a single movement, with several related sections in differing tempos and moods. In some instances the juxtaposition of movements of the composite form and the mixing of the composite movements with sections of the sonata-form are used to achieve new formal constructions.

While the strict harmonic relationship of tonic and dominant which dictated the formal structure of the classic sonata is no longer valid, this principle is still suggested in the modern sonata. This relationship or tension can be realized in a multitude of ways outside the harmonic realm and the twentieth century composers have experimented and continue to experiment with such devices.

Those works labeled as sonatas embrace the many neo-classical instrumental works for piano as well as those for single melodic instrument with keyboard. The idiom and style vary from composer to composer. The technical difficulties posed for the performer also vary greatly from the works which come under the type of *gebrauchsmusik* to those which obviously are meant exclusively for concert performance. The former were written with the amateur and student musician in mind while the latter require proficiency of the highest grade.

Due to its essential classicism, chamber music affords the twentieth century composer one of the prime areas of musical expression. Outside the adoption of the general principles of contemporary music, composers of chamber music have gone far in using newly conceived combinations of instruments and voice in their works. The traditional string quartet is still frequently employed as well as several other classic combinations, but there has been a great amount of writing for groups of from two to fifteen performers in which not only the standard instruments of all families have been combined, but often rarely used instruments have been incorporated. Percussion instruments of all kinds, especially those with tuned bars, are frequently used. Instruments rarely used in recent times have been reinstated in the chamber ensemble. The inclusion of the voice in small ensembles has been especially characteristic of modern chamber music. The use of these instruments is more than mere exploitation of new and unusual media, for the most radical composers have used tone color itself as a means of formal organization.

The symphony continues to be the principal large form for instrumental composition. In the case of some writers, particularly those whose style still favors the Romantic, this form is likely to be of an extended character, with colorful orchestration, and often combining voices with the orchestra. At the other extreme are those symphonic writers who have collapsed the symphony to a mere shadow of its classical self. The serial composers have made the most use of this kind of treatment. A large number of composers lie somewhere between these extremes and use many devices to rejuvenate the classic symphonic form.

Ex: *Sonata for Violin and Piano,* Bartók
      Quintet for Brass, Carter
      Piano Sonata, Copland
      Sonata for Trombone and Piano, Hindemith
      Sonata for Cello Unaccompanied, Kodály
      String Quartet, No. 6, Bartók
      Duo for Violin and Violoncello, Ravel
      Piano Trio, Kirchner

Ode to Napoleon, Schoenberg (Chamber Music)
Songs of Anacreon, Dallapiccola (Chamber Music)
London Symphony, Vaughan Williams
Symphony in Three Movements, Stravinsky
Symphony for Small Orchestra, Op. 21, Webern

2. *Concerto.*   The frequent return in the twentieth century to ideas of early music is reflected in the revival of the concerto grosso as a prototype. Solo concertos are frequently written, but the orchestral concerto in which many of the instruments act as soloists or in which groups of instruments are pitted one against the other is very typical of the return to early forms within the idiom of the twentieth century. In the case of the solo concerto the composers handle their material in much the same way as in the symphony. The solo instrument is no longer exploited only for virtuoso effects although virtuosos technique is required for performance. The tendency to exhibit the instrument at the expense of the orchestral body is abandoned in favor of a kind of composition in which the soloist and orchestra exploit the musical material in *concert.* Cadenzas are employed only if they are appropriate means of developing the musical material.

Ex: *Piano Concerto,* Schoenberg
Violin Concerto, Berg
Violin Concerto, No. 2, Prokofiev
Concerto Grosso, No. 1, Bloch
Concerto for Piano and Woodwinds, Riegger
Concerto for Orchestra, Bartók
Violin Concerto, Penderecki

3. *Suite.*   The twentieth century suite is usually a selection of scenes or sections from a larger work such as a ballet, incidental music to a drama or motion picture, or a series of pieces connected rather loosely by thematic relationship, mood, or extra-musical idea. Only in some few instances is the suite based on the tradition of the dance suite. As a consequence it is often the product of the more romantically inclined composers due to its connection with extramusical purpose. The name

is used for compositions of this character ranging from orchestral to keyboard suites.

Ex: *Lyric Suite*, Berg (for string quartet)
Appalachian Spring Suite, Copland (for orchestra)
Lieutenant Kije, Prokofiev (for orchestra)
Suite No. 2 for Orchestra, Bartók
Suite, Op. 29, Schoenberg (for piano)

4. *Ballet.* The instrumental theatrical work known as the ballet continues into the twentieth century in a form that is much more concise than its predecessor of the nineteenth century, and in a form that is much more abstract than the set of closed dances which made up the so-called classic ballet. Most of the ballets of the twentieth century are one act works, with one or more scenes. The music rarely consists of set dances but is rather in the form of a highly rhythmical symphonic poem which is interpreted by the dancers in appropriate pantomime and dance gestures. The stylized figures of the dancers of the classic tradition give way to free gestures and movements which symbolize the dramatic libretto in collaboration with the musical symbolism of the orchestral score. The ballet has been one of the most successful vehicles in the presentation of modern music to a receptive public. In the United States it has been the most successful form of dramatic music. Ballet music constitutes one of the most frequently heard forms in orchestral concert programs since the music can be given in its entirety or in suites made up of selected scenes from the score.

Ex: *El Sombrero de tres picos*, Falla
Le Sacre du printemps, Stravinsky
The Creation of the Earth, Milhaud
The Age of Gold, Shostakovitch
The Labrynth, Henze

5. *Incidental music for film and drama.* A great quantity of music used to accompany dramatic presentations is written in the twentieth century. While the greatest portion of this music is merely

"background music," there is some that has achieved independent value, and appears in concert form. This is more generally the case with incidental music to the staged dramas than that for the motion picture. This music, however, when done by very competent composers is so much a part of the film itself that it cannot, and often should not be heard except as a part of the picture.

Ex: Motion picture music:
     Of Mice and Men, Copland
     Quiet City, Copland
     Major Barbara, Walton
Ex: Incidental music to drama:
     Divertissement, Ibert
     Oedipus, Honegger

VI. VOCAL COMPOSITIONS

In general it might be said that vocal forms used in the twentieth century are the traditional ones found in the preceding periods. Examples of every vocal form found in all the earlier periods since the Romanesque are adapted to the contemporary contrapuntal and harmonic idiom. The voice in solo and choral compositions is now treated more as an instrument than previously. The range is expanded, intervallic skips which are not technically difficult on an instrument are demanded of the voice, dynamic changes are instrumental in character, and instrumental tonal qualities are often demanded. The vocalist is confronted with technical demands on vocal productions that seem at times unsurmountable. In both solo and choral works the voice is often freed from verbal considerations. Shouts, screams, or grunts are used.

A. **Single Movement Forms**

1. *Art song.* The art song continues to be a popular vehicle for composers. Texts generally tend to be of a more complex nature both in structure and idea than those of the Romantic period, and avoid the sentimentality of the more typical Romantic art song. This is in keeping with the more angular melodic treatment that is given the voice

and the added emphasis on the accompaniment, whether this be the traditional piano or the chamber music ensemble of various kinds which is so often used. The term accompaniment, in fact, is inaccurate in designating the instrumental part of most twentieth century vocal compositions since the voice and whatever instruments used form a total ensemble rather than a vocal line with instrumental background. In many instances composers have turned to folk melodies and given them setting in modern idiom, or at least a setting that is not governed by the lush harmonic texture of Romantic music. Such works have often employed an instrumental chamber group instead of the piano.

A modern phenomenon of song writing has been the disintegration of the melodic line into a highly inflected declamatory part. The device known as *sprechstimme* (speech voice), has been used by a number of the twelve-tone writers as well as other composers in combination with small instrumental groups. In this case the vocal part is almost pure declamation without exact tonal designation, but with rhythmic notation and general inflection indicated.

Ex: *Songs,* Ives
Chansons madécasses, Ravel
Goethe Lieder, Dallapiccola
Marienleben, Hindemith
Pierrot Lunaire, Schoenberg

2. *Short choral works.* A great demand for choral compositions for secondary school and university use as well as for fine amateur and professional choirs has given rise to many shorter choral works usually unaccompanied but often using the piano in support of the voices. These works are usually one movement in length and are settings of significant poems or prose texts of historical or timely interest. The modern treatment of such texts tends to be one of contrapuntal texture with a highly developed independence of line and

very free rhythmic treatment. In many cases such treatment is also used in the settings of folk songs. A great wealth of choral material is available in this form ranging from the traditional to very extreme modern style.

Ex: *Peaceable Kingdom*, Randall Thompson
     Mörike Lieder, Distler
     Dirge for Two Veterans, Holst
     Lux Aeterna, Ligeti

B. **Composite Forms**

1. *Opera.* The opera tends to retain something of the symphonic character of the Wagnerian tradition; however, it has become much more compact and dramatically dynamic. The general tendency towards economy of material makes the dramatic presentation much more concise and intense. There is sometimes a return to closed forms of aria and chorus, with composer reverting to the simplicity of the Baroque opera in this respect. Entire texts of dramatic works are often used as operatic librettos without any adaptation for musical setting. In some cases the operas are written in large symphonic forms so that several scenes are treated as movements or sections of abstract music such as the sonata, variation form, etc. An extreme of the operatic world is the setting of the writings of avant garde literary figures of the twentieth century as, for example, the "stream of consciousness" writers. Such works achieve their dramatic expression through the use of such advanced styles as the twelve-tone method of composition as well as highly dissonant chromaticism. The other extreme is the reversion to the ballad opera of the seventeenth century with its simple closed forms such as the popular street and folk songs. The Broadway musical comes close to a revival of this kind. Harmonically and melodically it parallels the nineteenth century tradition. Rhythmically it has much of the liberty of twentieth century jazz, and the general mood of the works reflects a certain

freedom of expression that is so typically American that several examples of this kind of composition have established themselves in the repertoire of opera houses in many countries.

Despite the degree of extremes represented in the various types of musical dramatic works, an economy of treatment, realism, expressionism, dramatic intensity, a greater or lesser degree of dissonant harmony, and irregularity of rhythym characterize all the twentieth century musical dramas.

Ex: *Wozzeck,* Berg
The Rake's Progress, Stravinsky
Mathis the Painter, Hindemith
Moses and Aron, Schoenberg
The Three Penny Opera, Weill
Porgy and Bess, Gershwin
Peter Grimes, Britten

2. *Musical Theater.*   The twentieth century musical theater is a partial revival of the operetta, which was popular in the nineteenth century especially in Austria. It was usually romantic in nature with spoken lines, choreography, choruses and music that is related to popular song and jazz. The popularity of musical theater has been enhanced by many of its productions being transferred to the medium of motion pictures and television.

Ex: *West Side Story,* Bernstein
My Fair Lady, Loewe
Sound of Music, Rodgers
Consul, Menotti

3. *Oratorio: Choral works with orchestra.*   The oratorio in the twentieth century remains almost as dormant as it was in the latter half of the nineteenth century. Only occasionally is a contemporary composer moved to write a work of dramatic expression and length to be performed as a concert presentation. Those that are written generally employ the traditional plan of this form albeit in a style that is in keeping with the twentieth century. The settings of less dramatic forms

of texts for chorus, soloists and orchestra are much more common in the twentieth century than oratorio settings. Many composers have used poetic as well as prose texts in works of several movements. Sometimes these are only for chorus and orchestra; sometimes soloists are added. Composers have experimented with various types of instrumentation in such works since one of the attributes of contemporary ensemble music is the emphasis on tonal color. In most of these works the instrumental body is again more than a mere accompaniment and the vocalists are something less than soloists. Choral works of this kind tend to be cast in forms dictated by the texts which are usually of the finest literary quality.

Ex: *Symphony of Psalms,* Stravinsky
Songs of Prisoners, Dallapiccola
Psalmus Hungaricus, Kodály
Belshazzar's Feast, Walton
Carmina Burana, Orff
Passion According to St. Luke, Penderecki
Mass, Bernstein

4. *Liturgical music.* Actually there is little music written for purely liturgical purposes by the composers of the twentieth century. Some settings of the mass for the Roman Catholic Church have been done in an extreme style as the twelve-tone system, but these are rare and their performance as liturgical music is even rarer. Likewise some able composers have written music for the Protestant church and the Jewish synagogue. A considerable amount of contemporary liturgical music uses a style that might be called neo-Baroque, an adaptation of contrapuntal style to the dissonant idiom of the twentieth century.

Ex: *Mass,* Stravinsky
Sacred Service, "Avodath Hakodesh," Bloch
Christmas Cantata, Honegger
Choral-Passion, Distler
Messe de la Pentacôte, Messiaen

VII. IMPORTANT COMPOSERS

It is impossible to state with any authority that one or another of the composers of the twentieth century belongs categorically to either lists of composers found in this chapter. Some composers have already established themselves in what seems at the moment to be a permanent historical position because of the value of their works. Others have had or are having marked influence on the musical production of the twentieth century even though there may be doubt as to the intrinsic value of their compositions. This section, Important Composers, contains men in both these categories. The authors recognize that perhaps large numbers of those listed in the following section, Other Composers, may have written works that may prove to have more lasting value. The authors have, however, tried to avoid subjective evaluations as much as possible. Moreover, there is no claim as to the exhaustiveness of these lists. More United States composers are listed than composers from other countries, but this seems understandable in the light of the nature and purpose of the book.

The Second World War gives some indication of acting as a dividing point between early and late twentieth century music. Without the perspective afforded by time, however, it is virtually impossible to make a sharp division between composers and styles before and after 1950. The roots of every movement of the post-1950 period are plainly discernible in the first half of the century. For example, many of the characteristics of electronic music (new tonal color, epigrammatic themes, extreme pitch ranges, micro-tonal pitches, total serial construction) on which much emphasis has been placed since 1950 were already present in the works of Varése, Webern, Haba, Stravinsky, Cage, Partch, and many others.

Lack of perspective also makes the categorization of the individual styles of twentieth century composers an impossibility. It is obvious that some composers are predominantly given to one style, but the great majority, as often in the past, have composed in several styles, often with equal success. Consequently the authors have decided to avoid placing the important composers under stylistic headings, but rather have mentioned the important stylistic characteristics in the description of each composer.

1. *Leoš Janáček* (1854–1928) was one of the renowned Czech composers. While he lived the
greater portion of his life in the nineteenth century most of his significant works were composed very late, in fact in the last decade of his
life. His operas, *Kat'a Kabanova* (1921) and *From
the House of the Dead* (1928); the *Glagolitic Mass*
(1926), the *Sinfonietta* (1926) and the *Concertino for
Piano and Chamber Orchestra* (1925), are examples
of his late production. His musical expression is
terse and economical, based on motivic construction which was derived from a study of speech
inflection. While he wrote several chamber music
and orchestra works, it is his operas which first
brought him world-wide recognition and which
are finding special favor again some fifty years
after his death. Besides the works mentioned the
operas *Jenufa, Mr. Brouček's Excursion to the Moon,*
and *Mr. Brouček's Excursion Into the Fifteenth Century* are among his important works.

2. *Erik Satie* (1866–1925) was a French composer
whose importance lies more in the personal influence he had on his contemporaries than in his
few compositions. He was the counselor, before
the First World War, of the group of young composers in France who came to be known as *Les
Six*, a group which included Darius Milhaud, Arthur Honegger, Francis Poulenc, Georges Auric,
Germaine Tailleferre, and Louis Durey.

His style can be characterized as one of complete
simplicity. He used the simplest of harmonies,
melodies, polyphonic texture, and formal structures. There is no attempt to be profound. This
trend toward simplicity was the forerunner of the
break with Romanticism and impressionism and
the gradual turn toward neoclassicism. His utter
disregard for the sentimental and pretentious was
reflected in the titles which he attached to many
of his works, for example, *Cold Pieces, Airs to Make
One Flee, Three Pieces in the Shape of a Pear*. These
and other piano pieces such as *Gymnopédies* and
Gnosiennes are among the best known works of

Satie. Two important works among larger forms are the symphonic drama *Sophocles,* based on the dialogues of Plato scored for four sopranos and chamber orchestra, and the ballet, *Parade.*

3. *Ralph Vaughan Williams* (1872–1958) was an English composer who very consciously and ardently allied himself with the great folk song revival of England which centered about Cecil Sharp. For a number of years he participated actively in the search for, and study of, folk songs of the English people. While he seldom quoted folk songs in his works and rarely used actual folk melodies as thematic material, his whole output is infused within the idiom of the English folk song. He never develops a style that is at the same time national and twentieth century, but the idiom of English folk song scarcely allows such a combination. While his works are characterized by modal polyphonic treatment he is essentially a melodist and used chromaticism and dissonance very sparingly. He wrote in all the many areas of musical composition though his symphonic works and vocal compositions are the more regularly heard. Among the nine symphonies the *London Symphony, no. 2;* the *Pastoral, No. 3;* and the *Fourth Symphony* are the best known. *On Wenlock Edge* for tenor, string quartet and piano, and a number of sacred compositions as well as several operas are among his important works. These include the opersa *Riders to the Sea,* and *Hugh the Drover; Mass in g minor,* and a cantata, *The Pilgrim's Progress.*

4. *Arnold Schoenberg* (1874–1951) was an Austrian composer most widely known as the founder of the *method of composing with twelve-tones.* Schoenberg's earliest compositions were in the romantic tradition of Wagner. His preoccupation with sonorities that avoided the function of tonal harmony placed him, however, in the forefront of the radical composers often referred to as expressionists, before the end of the first decade of the

Palace at 4 A.M. Giacometti (1932–33). This is a fantasy in construction that gives a surrealistic expression to a variety of subconscious memories with the barest images. Twentieth century composers who adopted the twelve-tone technique, such as Schoenberg and Webern, achieved an extremely economical use of musical material in which every phase of musical expression is reduced to its minimum. (Collection, The Museum of Modern Art, New York)

century. Exploitation of a new relationship between tonal material was finally concluded with the publication in 1923 of the *Five Piano Pieces, Op. 23.*

In the *Suite for Piano, Op. 25,* Schoenberg writes the first composition to be built exclusively on the principle of twelve-tone composition. Schoenberg contended that his new system was not revolutionary but evolutionary, a natural outcome of the tradition of western European music. A considerable group of disciples who had already gathered about him in the early years of the century adopted his techniques and along with Schoenberg himself laid the foundations of the twelve-tone style.

Schoenberg's influence as a practicing teacher continued throughout his long life, from his early years in Vienna where he was ultimately engaged as a professor of composition at the Vienna

Academy, through a professorship at the Prussian Academy of Arts in Berlin, which had to be relinquished with the advent of the Nazi regime in 1933. From 1933 until his death he resided in the United States, where he was a member of university faculties until his seventieth year.

Schoenberg has been influential in the stylistic development of a large number of pupils and followers. Among the most important of these are Berg, Webern, Krenek, Dallapiccola, Skalkottas, Kirchner, and a score of others who have adopted principles of Schoenbergian technique if not the system exclusively. Even Igor Stravinsky in his seventies began to use techniques now called serial composition which stem from Schoenberg.

Among the most widely heard works of Schoenberg are those of his early romantic period, *Verklärte Nacht* (Transfigured Night) originally a string sextet, later transcribed for string orchestra; the *Gurre-Lieder*, for chorus, soloists, and orchestra; and a number of chamber music works such as the *String Quartets Nos. 1 and 2, Pierrot Lunaire,* and a large quantity of songs. The most outstanding of the works in the twelve-tone system are the *Piano Concerto, Violin Concerto, Op. 36, String Quartets Nos. 3 and 4,* as well as chamber music for unusual instrumental combinations. An incomplete opera, *Moses and Aaron,* first performed posthumously, has had great success.

5. *Charles Edward Ives* (1874–1954) was one of the most unusual of American composers. Trained as a musician he hesitated to subject his creative talents to the economic demands that would be made on these talents if he were to devote himself to the career of a composer. As a consequence he entered the business world and became a very successful insurance broker, leaving his composition free from all remunerative considerations. This double life led to a physical breakdown in 1918 that ended his compositional career. The result of his early decision was that almost all of his works were written in the years between 1896 and 1918.

In some respects he foreshadowed many of the practices of later twentieth century composers such as Schoenberg and Stravinsky. His use of polytonality, polyrhythms and the contrapuntal proceedings that are part of the serial composers' techniques, inversion, retrograde, augmentation, and diminution, are all characteristic of his music. While his works are always constructed on a tonal basis he achieved a considerable amount of dissonance, in some cases almost a feeling of atonality with these devices. Despite all the characteristics of modern music, Ives' musical ideas were deeply rooted in New England folk and religious music with themes from folk songs and New England hymnals. Strangely enough almost none of his compositions were performed until the 1940s. The *Third Symphony*, which received a Pulitzer Prize, was performed in 1947, almost forty years after it was written. The *Second Symphony* was given its first performance exactly fifty years after it was written. Their influence on American composers was not felt until a few years before Ives' death. His output was devoted mainly to orchestral, chamber, piano, and song literature. Among his most important compositions are the four symphonies, several symphonic poems, *Three Places in New England, Central Park in the Dark, The Unanswered Question,* a large number of songs among which *General Booth Enters Heaven* is thoroughly representative, and many piano pieces including the *Concord Sonata,* and some choral works.

6. *Maurice Ravel* (1875–1937) was a French composer whose mixture of impressionistic style with classic clarity would best label him as a post-impressionist. He was not a pupil of Debussy but stood in close relation to him in many aspects. He extended the practice of unresolved dissonances but rarely came to the point of atonality. In many respects he remained closer to the romanticists than to those who came to be considered the radical twentieth century composes. Ravel's love of the exotic in music was revealed not only in his use of rhythms and scale

construction derived from his Basque background but also in his predilection for expression in other exotic idioms. His settings of *Deux Melodies Hebraiques* (Two Hebrew Melodies), *Five Popular Greek Melodies*, and the *Songs of Madagascar* as well as his occupation with oriental themes in a number of his compositions such as the *Scheherazade* exhibit this love for the exotic. Likewise he was very much influenced by medieval as well as unusual folk tonal systems. His *Rapsodie Espagnole, Pavane for a Dead Infanta*, and *Tsigane* represent these interests. Even in those compositions in which he exhibited a decided neo-classic tendency the harmonic idiom, as well as the instrumentation, reflected Ravel's deep interest in old and unusual systems and tonal colors. Among such neo-classic works are *Le Tombeau de Couperin*, the *Mother Goose Suite, String Quartet in F major*, the *Two Piano Concertos*, and a number of piano works, an area in which Ravel was outstanding; *Gaspard de la nuit, Jeux d'eau* (Fountains), *Sonatine*. Ravel also wrote a few stage works among them the operas *L'Heure Espagnole, L'Enfant et les Sortilèges* (Dreams of a Naughty Boy), and the ballets *Daphnis and Chloe, La Valse,* and *Boléro*.

7. *Manuel de Falla* (1876–1946) was the most important Spanish composer since the Renaissance. While his style is essentially that of the French impressionists he combined impressionism with a very conscious Spanish nationalism as in *Nights in the Garden of Spain*. He was not unmindful, however, of twentieth century stylistic advances and he combined these with a musical expression that has a real authenticity of Spanish idiom. His love of Spain induced him to exile himself from his native land when it fell to the anti-Republicans, and he lived his last years in the Argentine. His most successful works have been ballets, among which are *El Amor Brujo* (Love the Magician), and *El Sombrero de Tres Picos* (The Three Cornered Hat). A *Concerto for Harpsichord, Flute, Oboe, Clarinet, Violin, and Cello* is representative of his interest in abstract forms as well.

8. *Ernest Bloch* (1880–1959) was a Swiss composer who lived a large portion of his productive life as composer, conductor, and teacher in the United States. Bloch was an intensely expressive writer, first in a neo-Romantic style and later in a somewhat more neo-Classic style. His influence as a teacher of twentieth century American composers was widespread, with such men as Roger Sessions, George Antheil, and Leon Kirchner, among others, as his students. His major works include a number of symphonic poems among which *Schelomo, Trois Poèmes Juifs* (Three Jewish Poems), and *America* are representative examples. His neo-classicism is expressed in the *Concerti Grossi Nos. 1 and 2.* He wrote a substantial amount of chamber music including five string quartets, some piano music with orchestra and solo works for various instruments. A single choral composition, the *Sacred Service* has been very successful. A single opera, *Macbeth,* has also gained recent attention.

9. *Béla Bartók* (1881–1945) was the most distinguished Hungarian composer of the twentieth century. While his harmonic idiom was not based on any preconceived theory, Bartók's music reflected the twentieth century character of freely combined tonal sonorities. His music is essentially tonal in structure but he made extensive use of nonharmonic tones. His harmonic as well as his rhythmic and melodic style was derived from an intense love and study of primitive folk music. The use of exotic scales derived from this source gave rise to melodic and harmonic practices which conformed generally to the twentieth century breakdown of the tonally centered tradition. Bartók also made extensive use of polytonality, a device which results in a kind of controlled dissonance.

Folk music for Bartók was not a means of romantic nationalistic expression, but rather a source of expressive material, universally applicable. His scholarly interest in folk music extended beyond his own national culture and included the music of all the Balkan peoples and even that of North Africa. His music not only reflects his interest in the rhythmic, melodic, and harmonic aspects of primitive folk music but he applied the impulse of the primitive to his use of instruments, in particular to the piano, which he treats as a truly percussion instrument.

In his earliest works Bartók was obviously influenced by the impressionism of Debussy. This influence never completely disappeared from his compositions and is to be found in many of the slow movements of later works. The most distinctive design employed by Bartók is the arch form, a symmetrical balance of movements within the composite form of the sonata.

His compositions, which succeeded in finding wide performance and acceptance only after his death in New York in 1945, have since become extremely popular. Among the most distinguished are the three *Piano Concertos;* the *Violin Concerto;* six *String Quartets;* the ballet, *The Miraculous Mandarin;* the opera, *The Castle of Duke Bluebeard;* the *Mikrokosmos,* a series of instructional pieces for piano in modern idiom; *Concerto for Orchestra,* and many songs.

10. *Igor Stravinsky* (1882–1971), a Russian by birth, lived most of his productive career in Paris and Hollywood. While his style has been one of the principal influences on other composers in the twentieth century, particularly the French and those men schooled in France, he has never been attached to any institution or academy and only occasionally has lectured on the general aesthetics of music. He has had no pupils as such. With the composition of his ballet, *Le Sacre du Printemps* (The Rite of Spring) 1913, Stravinsky adopted a dissonant harmonic technique which, however, was not based on any preconceived plan or theory. Earlier compositions already showed dissonant tendencies in the use of such devices as bitonality. Further adoption of polytonality and use of free dissonance, nonharmonic tones, etc., showed an expansion of the complex chromaticism of the nineteenth century, though never to the point of complete denial of tonal center. It was not until the middle 1950s that Stravinsky assayed an adoption of the serial technique with its atonal implications.

Stravinsky's style is characterized not only by its harmonic innovations but perhaps even more by its use of primitive and brutal rhythmic patterns, whose complexities are the result of the consecutive use of widely varying metric patterns and a kind of polyphony of widely differing rhythmic strata. The improvisatory freedom of jazz rhythms was often employed. In many instances long passages are almost exclusively rhythmic in nature.

Stravinsky also exploited tonal color to its utmost. This is true in both large and small instrumental combinations. Unusual scoring such as the elimination of all the violins, violas and clarinets in the orchestra of the *Symphony of Psalms,* or the accompaniment of four pianos and percussion in *Les Noces,* are typical examples.

Perhaps no other twentieth century composer exhibited so many exclusive uses of diverse styles as Stravinsky who was a prolific composer for over a period of fifty years. His rich output of compositions dating from 1908 when he was studying with Rimsky-Korsakov never abated, and the list of well-known and often heard works makes him the one twentieth century composer whose recognition was comparatively immediate and universal. This was probably due in part to the great number of stage works, principally ballets, which made the introduction of his music to the general public somewhat easier than if his compositions had been more predominantly in the form of abstract orchestral or chamber music.

Stravinsky could be classified at various times as a post-romantic, a primitivist, a neo-classicist, a neo-romantic, an abstractionist, an expressionist, a constructionist, though withal he maintained a certain personal idiom that marks all of his compositions.

Some of the important works under various headings are: ballets—*The Firebird, Petrouchka, Rite of Spring, Histoire du Soldat, Jeux de cartes* (Game of Cards); orchestra—several suites taken from the ballets, *Fireworks, Concertos for Piano and Wind Instruments, Symphony in C, Dumbarton Oaks;* chamber music—*Pribautki, Octet for Wind Instruments, Septet for Piano, Wind and String Instruments;* choral—*Symphony of Psalms, Mass, Canticum Sacrum;* piano—*Capriccio for Piano and Orchestra, Sonata for Two Pianos.*

11. *Alban Berg* (1885–1935) was an Austrian composer, pupil of Schoenberg, and recognized as one of the most expressive composers in the twelve-tone technique. As in the case of Schoenberg, his early compositions show a marked influence of Wagner and Mahler. In his masterpiece, the opera *Wozzeck,* Berg organizes the musical dramatic material into abstract forms such as a rhapsody, suite, theme and variations (passacaglia). The opera caused great protest when first performed in the 1920s but has since established itself as one of the great repertoire pieces of the twentieth century. Another opera, *Lulu,* only partially finished, and a number of songs as well as some orchestral and chamber music round out a short but productive life. Among the instrumental works the string quartet, *A Lyric Suite,* the *Violin Concerto,* and the *Chamber Concerto for Piano, Violin, and Thirteen Wind Instruments,* are frequently played.

12. *Anton Webern* (1885–1945) was another of the twentieth century Viennese group of Austrian composers who were pupils and disciples of Arnold Schoenberg. Webern adopted the twelve-tone method to his pointilistic technique, which resulted in an extremely economical use of musical material in which every phase of musical expression is reduced to its barest minimum. Thematic material is often replaced by motives that seem to be compressed. The polyphonic texture is varied by the device of placing the successive notes of the contrapuntal line at different octave levels, and by changing the tonal qualities of each note by using different instruments to perform the individual notes of any one line. The compositions are of extreme brevity, an entire symphony lasting only a few minutes. The performing media consists of very few instruments and these are used only sparingly.

Such techniques give rise to the application of the descriptive term *pointilistic* to the writing of Webern. Webern wrote a rather large number of individual works but their brevity reduces his total output to something less than three or four hours of performance, a remarkable fact when compared with the total output of other composers of the past or even the present.

Mid-century trends tend to indicate that Webern might stand out as one of the most important of twentieth century figures. His influence among the serial and electronic composers is especially significant. The most important works of Webern are *Symphony, Op. 21, String Quartet, Op. 28* and the *Cantatas, Op. 29 and 31.*

13. *Edgar Varèse* (1885–1965), a French composer who lived most of his productive life in America, was perhaps the greatest innovator of the twentieth century. His attitude toward music is one of an experimenter. His better known works exhibit an engagement with sounds for the sheer sake of tonal masses, a characteristic that finally led him to exploration in the use of electronic sounds. Although he started his musical career as a romanticist and impressionist all traces of these characteristics, as well as the compositions dating from these periods, disappeared. In his search for tonal depth he exploited the tone qualities of all kinds of unusual instruments and instrumental combinations, being particularly interested in percussion instruments or the percussive effects that can be generated by more conventional instruments. The works which have been most frequently performed are *Hyperprism*, scored for two wood winds, seven brass, and sixteen percussion instruments, *Ionisation* written for thirteen performers on thirty different percussion and friction instruments. *Octandre* a chamber work for eight performers, and *Density 21.5* for solo flute.

14. *Heitor Villa-Lobos* (1887–1959), one of the foremost South American composers, was a native of Brazil where he was eventually engaged as superintendent of musical and artistic education in Rio de Janeiro. Villa-Lobos' idiom is highly influenced by the folk music of Brazil and sometimes is actually based on folk song themes. He was very interested in fusing the peculiarities of Brazilian music with the tradition of western Europe. An example of this style is to be found in the *Bachianas Brasileiras*, a set of nine suites in which Brazilian folk music idiom was combined with Bachian counterpoint. A more typically original Brazilian form was the *Choros*. In a series of fourteen of these works, Villa-Lobos combines the many elements of Brazilian folk, popular, and Indian music into compositions which use quite unusual instrumental and vocal forces. The most popular among these two groups of compositions are the *Bachianas Brasileiras Nos. 1 and 5* and the *Choros Nos. 1 and 7*.

15. *Sergey Sergeyevitch Prokofiev* (1891–1953) was one of Russia's outstanding composers of the twentieth century. He himself listed the following as the four elements of his style: (1) classicism (neoclassicism), (2) innovation which at first was represented in an individual harmonic style, later as an expression of strong emotions, (3) the motoric element, and (4) lyricism. He regarded another element, the grotesque, as an outgrowth of the others. Much of his music, however, is flavored by a certain puckishness or humorous quality.

   Prokofiev was widely known as a concert pianist in his early years. He lived in Paris until 1933 when he returned to Russia. His connection with modern practices of western Europe often brought him some criticism, but he remained a highly revered composer and undoubtedly has influenced the younger composers of the Soviet.

His musical output was very extensive. The total number of his works which eventually found concert performance was, perhaps, second only to Stravinsky among the modern composers. His compositions extended into every field with the exception of sacred. Among the best known are his *Seven Symphonies;* the *Third Piano Concerto;* the *Two Violin Concertos;* the symphonic poem, *Peter and the Wolf;* the orchestral suite, *Lieutenant Kije;* ten *Piano Sonatas;* and a great many short piano works among them *Sarcasms.*

16. *Arthur Honegger* (1892–1955), a Swiss composer, was closely allied with the French trends of the twentieth century by his inclusion in the group known as *Les Six.* While his early descriptive tone poem, *Pacific 231,* was looked upon as representative of the new machine age Honneger turned from this type of realistic writings to pursue a neo-Classic style. His dramatic oratorios, *Joan of Arc at the Stake* and *King David,* are two of the great choral works of the twentieth century. Among a large number of orchestral composition his five *Symphonies* stand out as worthy of note. Honneger also wrote a large amount of chamber and piano music as well as vocal literature.

17. *Darius Milhaud* (1892–1974) was one of the leading French composers of the older twentieth century generation who pioneered the modern idiom in the early part of the century. He was a very prolific composer with works in every area of music. He was active as a teacher for many years during which he taught in the United States extensively. His many experiments included use of jazz, polytonality, and eventually electronic devices. He did not subscribe to any form of atonality, though his use of dissonance in combination with a lively melodic line gave his work a distinct and individual style. His ballets, *The Creation of the World* and *Le Boeuf sur le toit* (The Beef on the Roof), are representative of his concern with jazz idiom. Other works illustrate his preoccupation with the melodies of his native

Provence, such as the *Suite Provençale*. Concertos, sonatas, symphonies, and many pieces of chamber music are among the large list of compositions which date from the first decade of the century to the 1960s.

18. *Carl Orff* (1895–1982), whose stage works have won him international recognition is, perhaps, one of the most conservative of twentieth century composers. Despite this he represents a number of trends which are typical of this century. In contrast to the nineteenth century musicians who regarded harmony as the principal shaping force, Orff is typical of the twentieth century in placing rhythm in this role. His rhythmic force is drawn from word rhythms, especially from ancient and folk speech, folk dances, and folk songs. He treats these rhythms with a kind of repetitious primitiveness that makes for intense dramatic feeling. Structurally his music is very simple. He avoids contrapuntal practice for the most part, resorting to the simply harmonized melodic line, with rather rare instances of clashing dissonances resulting from the use of non-harmonic tones. Percussion instruments appear abundantly in all his orchestrations. His best known works are the dramatic cantatas *Carmina Burana* and *Catulli Carmina* along with several operas among which *Der Mond* (The Moon), *Die Kluge* (The Wise Woman), and *Antigonae* are the most popular. In addition to these works Orff has written a series of five books called *Music for Children* which have done much to revolutionize music education in the past ten years.

19. *Paul Hindemith* (1895–1963) was a composer, performer, conductor, teacher, and one of the dominant musical forces in the twentieth century. Hindemith employed several styles of composition. In his earlier works of the 1920s he was openly rebellious toward tradition of all sorts. His music reflected a free contrapuntal character which made much use of dissonance. Hindemith was also very occupied with the idea of general

music education at this time in his production of so-called *Gebrauchsmusik* (music for use). This music, vocal and instrumental, was intended to introduce the young and the amateur to the idiom of modern times through school and home performance. A neoclassic turn is evident in much of Hindemith's music of the 1930s. Further study of old music led Hindemith to a polyphonic treatment which, while modern in harmonic idiom, is reminiscent of the thirteenth to sixteenth century practices. Even the lack of bar lines and metric signs, a characteristic of music before 1600, was imitated.

Hindemith was a very prolific composer writing in every conceivable field of musical composition. While he wrote solo works for almost every instrument he was not so much interested in the exploitation of tonal color as most contemporaries. Constructive rather than emotional expression characterizes his works.

The following are his best known works: a song cycle, *Das Marienleben* (The Life of Mary); an opera, *Mathis der Maler* (Mathis the Painter); *Wir Bauen eine neue Stadt* (We Build a New City) for children's performance; *Ludis Tonalis* for piano; *In Praise of Music* for chorus and orchestra; *Symphonic Metamorphosis on Themes of Weber* and *The Four Temperaments* for piano and strings.

20. *Rober Sessions* (1896–   ) is one of the foremost American composers. A pupil of Ernest Bloch, his early works tend toward the Romantic. He soon turned, however, toward a very complex counterpoint which contained much dissonance. While he eventually came under the influence of Schoenberg and has written much music which verges on the twelve-tone system and its atonal results, he has never adopted this style of composition. Sessions defies any label such as neo-romantic, neo-classic or expressionistic though he

partakes of each of these in some degree. He has not been a prolific composer, and has made his greatest contribution in the area of orchestral, chamber, and piano music. Among the four symphonies the *First Symphony* represents his early neo-classic style while the *Third Symphony* shows an individual use of twelve-tone technique. Other important works are the *Piano Sonata No. 2, Second String Quartet, Idyll of Theocritus* for soprano and orchestra, and *The Black Maskers,* an early work for orchestra written as incidental music to a play.

21. *George Gershwin* (1898–1937) was America's first and most successful composer to incorporate the popular jazz rhythms of the 1920s in classical forms. His success as a composer of popular songs and musicals was already well established when he turned to other types of expression. In these his melodic gift and rhythmic genius gained him success as a serious composer. In addition to numerous Broadway hits such as *Of Thee I Sing, Let 'Em Eat Cake,* and *Girl Crazy,* his more serious and lasting works are *The Rhapsody in Blue, An American in Paris, Piano Concerto in F major,* and the opera, *Porgy and Bess.*

22. *Ernst Krenek* (1900–   ) was born in Vienna, but spent a large part of his creative life in the United States. His music has shown the influence of almost all the stylistic experiments of the early twentieth century. An early opera (1972), *Johnny spielt auf!* utilized jazz idioms and had great success both in Europe and America. After many experiments, Krenek finally embraced a modified twelve-tone style. A prolific composer, he has composed eleven operas, three ballets, incidental music for seven plays, a large number of choral works, five symphonies, four piano concertos, six piano sonatas, and eight string quartets. He is also the author of several books including *Music, Here and Now.*

23. *Aaron Copland* (1900–   ) was a pupil of Nadia Boulanger, and is, perhaps, the most widely known of American composers. He has adopted numerous style and techniques, jazz, neo-Classic constructivism, and modified twelve-tone. His most successful works have reflected the American scene through symphonic poems, ballets, and operas, as well as a large number of works for radio and motion picture some of which have had the rather unique distinction of being used as concert music. Copland has also written a large quantity of music of a more abstract nature, symphonies, chamber music and piano works. Among his best known compositions are the ballets, *Appalachian Spring, Billy the Kid, Rodeo;* the orchestral works, *El Salon Mexico, Outdoor Overture, Lincoln Portrait, Third Symphony;* and the piano works, *Passacaglia, Piano Variations,* and *Piano Sonata.*

24. *Luigi Dallapiccola* (1904–1975) was the foremost of the modern Italian composers. He combined the dodecaphonic technique with the Italian tradition of vocal line in a very expressive fashion. His masterful adaptation of the twelve-tone system to lyrical expression is best illustrated in his *Canti de Prigionia* (Songs of Captivity) a set of choral songs, and in his opera *Il Prigioniero* (The Prisoner). A number of chamber music works employing voice and instruments of various kinds are also noteworthy.

25. *Dmitri Shostakovitch* (1906–1975) was the leading composer of the younger Soviet group. His *First Symphony* written as a graduation piece when he was eighteen years of age brought him immediate fame. He was under severe official criticism for incorporating the techniques of western European modern music with its dissonant qualities into his music, as in the case of his opera *Lady Macbeth of Mtzensk.* Obediently he turned to the traditional forms and styles of the Classic and Romantic periods with tremendous success within the Soviet. With the exception of a small number of works of a few other composers, those of Shostakovitch are the only compositions by Soviet composers that are heard outside Russia today.

Six string quartets and a *Piano Quintet* are the best known of his chamber music. He wrote eleven symphonies of which the fifth has been the most successful. A large number of ballets and operas, of which only short excerpts have been heard outside Russia, and a great number of film compositions are numbered among his compositions.

26. *Olivier Messiaen* (1908–   ), a French composer, theoretician, and organist, who pioneered in the area of total *serialism,* an organization of sounds, durations, dynamics, and articulations. In his efforts to find new effects he makes use of exotic percussion instruments, generators, and bird calls of which he was particularly fond. His importance as a theoretician can be noted through the works of his students such as Boulez, Stockhausen, and Nono. Among his important compositions are *Oiseaux Éxotique, Réveil des Oiseaux, Catalogue d'Oiseaux.*

27. *Elliott Carter* (1908–   ) is an American composer whose music is essentially twentieth century in its contrapuntal texture and its occupation with rhythm and meter as form building elements. Carter's works are infused with modal counterpoint though he has made use of a personal type of twelve-tone technique. In his latest works he has devised a system of *Metric Modulation* whereby he has been able to modulate from one speed to another by changing the rhythmic values of the basic units. Carter is not a prolific composer but his works are of refined techniques. His *Variations for Orchestra, Eight Etudes and a Fantasy* for woodwind quartet, and *String Quartet, No. 2* are typical of his output.

28. *John Cage* (1912–   ) is an American composer whose radical tendencies in composition have expressed themselves in the derivation of new tonal colors in preparing the piano by placing on the strings of the instrument such objects as metal, erasers, and screws. He has also experimented in the area of chance or random composition. The latter is accomplished by chance selection of pitch, note values, dynamics, instrumentation, either from notated suggestions or from pure chance as in the case of one of Cage's own

works, *Imaginary Landscape,* in which twelve radios, dialed according to predetermined wave lengths, give forth whatever programs or lack of program that happen to be on the air at the moment. For the prepared piano Cage has written Sixteen Sonatas and Four Interludes.

29. *Benjamin Britten* (1913–1976) was a prominent British composer. While he wrote in many fields of musical composition it was through his operas and choral works that he achieved world-wide recognition. Britten's style was essentially vocal. He was clearly a classicist in his approach to musical composition and consequently was not interested in the Wagnerian idea of *endless melody,* but rather stressed the concept of closed forms in operatic writing. He was not an adherent to any set method or technique of composition, but was influenced by a number of widely varying composers in whose individual styles he found certain elements of interest. His operas include: *The Rape of Lucretia, Peter Grimes, Albert Herring, Billy Budd, The Little Sweep* or *Let's Make an Opera* and *Midsummer Night's Dream.* In the field of choral works, *The War Requiem* and those compositions which are essentially a cycle of vocal works, *A Ceremony of Carols, Spring Symphony* and *A Boy Was Born,* are among his most impressive. Not least illustrative of his love for the variation form is the very popular *The Young Person's Guide to the Orchestra.*

30. *Witold Lutoslawski* (1913–   ), a composer whose early concern with twelve-tone technique has given way to ultra-modern practices including electronic composition. He has been widely recognized as one of the most significant of the modern Polish composers. He has composed principally for orchestra and chamber music ensembles. Among his best known works are his First and Second Symphonies, *Paroles Tissees* for tenor and chamber orchestra, and *Trois Poèmes d'Henri Michaux* for twenty voice choir and orchestra.

31. *George Rochberg* (1918–   ) is an American composer who combines twelve tone influences with a logical harmonic style into a singularly personal idiom. His compositions cover a wide range of instrumental and vocal forms except for opera. He has also published a number of articles dealing with the problems of twelve tone composition. Rochberg teaches at the University of Pennsylvania. A number of his works employ quotations of other composers from the sixteenth to the twentieth century, such as Schütz, Bach, Mahler, Ives, Boulez and Varèse. Among his works are four symphonies, a Violin Concerto and three string quartets.

32. *Leon Kirchner* (1919–   ) is an American composer, teacher, and brilliant pianist who came under the influence of Schoenberg in his first musical studies. Later he studied with Ernest Bloch and finally with Roger Sessions. All of these men influenced him greatly, but he never adopted a system from any one of them. His music fluctuates between a very highly chromatic idiom and an atonal one. Most characteristic is its motoric drive whether the medium be the orchestra, the piano or the string quartet. Kirchner's music is imbued with an intensity of expression that is almost exhausting in its demands on the listener. His importance in the mid-century musical scene of America is evidenced by the large number of awards and commissions he has received. His *Concerto for Piano and Orchestra, Sinfonia,* and *String Quartet No. 1* are representative of his finest style.

33. *Iannis Xenakis* (1922–   ). Born in Greece, Xenakis now lives in the United States. He was a student of Messiaen and was also associated with the architect, Le Corbusier. His music is structured on the principles of mathematical probability in terms of traditional instruments and traditional notation. The result is music which is often indeterminant in performance. His important works include *Archosippsis, Strategy,* and *Metastasis* for orchestra; and *Eonta* for piano and brass.

34. *Gyorgi Ligeti* (1923–   ) was born in Hungary but presently lives in Germany where he is professor of composition at the Hamburg Academy of Music. His activities have taken him into almost all European countries as well as America. He has been associated with the Studio for Electronic Music in Cologne and is one of the leaders of the International Courses for New Music in Darmstadt. His works are characterized by an emphasis on tonal colors and masses of sound to achieve which he employs all varieties of noise makers as well as electronic generated sounds. His compositions, however, have exploited all musical media from the organ and string quartet to the symphony orchestra as well as small and large vocal ensembles. Among his works are *Volumina* for organ, *Requiem* for solo voices, chorus and orchestra, *Poème Symphonique* for 100 metronomes all running at different speeds and *Lux Aeterna* for 16 solo voices.

35. *Luciano Berio* (1925–   ), composer of the avant garde, developed an early interest in electronic experimentation. He has frequently combined performances with electronic tapes. His most significant works show a deep concern with music combined with gesture and dramatic action. *Circles,* a setting of poems by E. E. Cummings for voice and percussion instruments, is designed for visual and spatial realization. Berio's further involvement with music and dramatic action as well as the relation between words and music is illustrated in his opera, *Passaggio,* and the composition *Visages,* a taped composition using both electronic and vocal sounds.

36. *Pierre Boulez* (1925–   ) is one of the more controversial of the younger twentieth century men who has developed a very comlex style of serial composition and has more recently turned to electronic music. The best known work of Boulez is *Le Marteau sans Maitre* (The Hammer Without a Master) written for contralto and a group of six instruments. The unusual instrumentation of flute in G, viola, guitar, vibraphone, and *percussion* is indicative of Boulez' concern with tone color, particularly with that of the percussion type instruments. Boulez has been one of

the most active participants in the festivals of contemporary music.

37. *Hans Werner Henze* (1926–   ) is a composer active in all fields of composition. His early works evidenced a complete mastery of the twelve-tone technique which he later utilized in a manner that appealed more readily to the larger audience. He has been particularly successful in operatic composition. Such works as *Der Junge Lord, Der Prinz von Homburg,* and *König Hirsch* have had great success.

38. *Karlheinz Stockhausen* (1928–   ) is a German composer who has given most of his attention to the field of electronic music, although he started his career as a disciple of Webern using the conventional instruments. *Kontra-Punkte* for ten solo instruments is a representative work of this period. Another phase is the *Piano Piece XI* which is a work constructed on the basis of random selection and improvisatory treatment of nineteen notated fragments. The best known of his electronic compositions is *Gesang der Jünglinge* (Song of the Youths) which is written for human voice and electronic sound generator. The notation of such music being in graphs and geometric figures precludes any performances other than by those few persons capable of reading such notation. The electronic equipment employed by Stockhausen, and those associated with him at the Northwest German Radio Studio in Cologne, in no way attempts to imitate the sound qualities of conventional instruments. The sounds produced by the signal generators and the electronic synthesizers are exploited for their intrinsic value as *new* sounds.

39. *George Crumb* (1929–   ) is an American composer who combined study at American Universities with study in Berlin. His compositions reflect a certain tendency to relate traditional formalities with very extreme demands on technical resources. Exceptional combination of electronic instruments and conventional instruments as well as electrically amplified instruments result in extraordinary tonal effects. This interest in unusual sound qualities is demanding of

his vocal forces in the singing of microtonal intervals, the use of shrieks, hisses, whisperings and unusual oral sounds. Works such as *Night of the Four Moons* for alto flute, banjo, electric cello and percussion; *Songs, Drones and Refrains of Death* for baritone, electric guitar, electric double bass, electric piano and percussion and *Lux Aeterna for Five Masked Musicians* for soprano, bass flute, sitar and two percussion players are representative of Crumb's interest in such sound effects. Crumb is on the faculty of the University of Pennsylvania.

40. *Krzysztof Penderecki* (1933–   ), whose compositions cover all fields of instrumental and vocal production, is perhaps the most widely known of the young Polish composers. He has developed a style that is quite original and independent of any of the fixed systems of the twentieth century. A certain amount of freedom of improvisation is often left to the performer, only governed by specific time limits. He has achieved novel tonal effects in the use of traditional instruments as in his *String Quartet* and the *Threnody to the Victims of Hiroshima*. The *Passion According to St. Luke* is one of the most impressive choral works of the twentieth century.

41. *R. Murray Schaefer* (1933–   ) is a Canadian composer interested in exploring physical sounds. Compositions range from chamber music of unusual instrumentation to operatic and symphonic pieces employing electronic music as well as aleatoric devices. Among his many compositions are *North/Light* for orchestra, Two String Quartets, and *Apocolypse* for 500 performers.

42. *Peter Maxwell Davies* (1934–   ) is an English composer whose works are characterized by controlled improvisation and by an abundance of various styles and idioms from Renaissance polyphony to extreme serialism. Some of his important works are the *Saint Michael Sonata, Eight Songs for a Mad King* and the *Second Fantasia on Taverner's "In Nomine."*

VIII. OTHER COMPOSERS

A. Argentina
1. *Alberto Ginastera* (1916–1983)
2. *Mauricio Kagel* (1931–   )

B. Austria
1. *J. M. Hauer* (1883–1959)
2. *E. Wellesz* (1885–1974)
3. *Ernst Toch* (1887–1964)
4. *Paul Pisk* (1893–   )
5. *Johann N. David* (1895–1977)
6. *Hans E. Apostel* (1901–1972)
7. *Hans Jelinek* (1901–1969)
8. *Karl Schiske* (1916–1969)
9. *Gottfried von Einem* (1918–   )
10. *Dieter Kaufmann* (1941–   )
11. *Klaus Ager* (1946–   )

C. Belgium
1. *Marcel Poot* (1901–   )
2. *Henri Pousseur* (1929–   )

D. Bulgaria
Dimiter Christoff (1933–   )

E. Canada
Claude Champaigne (1891–1965)
Sir Ernest Campbell MacMillan (1893–1973)
Harry Somers (1925–   )
Serge Garant (1929–   )

F. Chile
1. *Domingo Santa Cruz* (1899–   )

G. Czechoslovakia
1. *Bohuslav Martinů* (1890–1959)
2. *Alois Habá* (1893–1975)
3. *Vaclav Dobiáš* (1909–1978)
4. *Jan Cikker* (1911–   )
5. *Karel Husa* (1921–   )
6. *Jindřich Feld* (1925–   )
7. *Oldřich Flossman,* (1925–   )
8. *Zdenek Lukáš* (1928–   )

H. Denmark
1. *Carl Nielsen* (1865–1931)
2. *Vagn Holmboe* (1909–   )
3. *Niels Viggo Bentzon* (1919–   )

I. England

1. *Frederick Delius* (1862–1934)
2. *Gustav Theodore Holst* (1874–1934)
3. *John Ireland* (1879–1962)
4. *Sir Arnold Bax* (1883–1953)
5. *Sir Arthur Bliss* (1891–1975)
6. *Sir William Walton* (1902–   )
7. *Constant Lambert* (1905–1951)
8. *Michael Tippett* (1905–   )
9. *Peter Racine Fricker* (1920–   )
10. *Harrison Birtwistle* (1934–   )
11. *Oliver Knussen* (1952–   )
12. *Dominic Muldowney* (1952–   )
13. *Robert Saxton* (1953–   )

J. Finland

1. *Joonas Kokonen* (1920–   )
2. *Einojuhani Rautavaara* (1928–   )

K. France

1. *Charles Koechlin* (1867–1950)
2. *Albert Roussel* (1869–1937)
3. *Florent Schmitt* (1870–1958)
4. *Nadia Boulanger* (1887–1979)
5. *Louis Durey* (1888–1979)
6. *Jacques Ibert* (1890–1962)
7. *Germaine Tailleferre* (1892–   )
8. *Georges Auric* (1899–1983)
9. *Francis Poulenc* (1899–1963)
10. *Jean Martinon* (1910–1976)
11. *Jean Françaix* (1912–   )

L. Germany

1. *Hans Pfitzner* (1869–1949)
2. *Max Reger* (1873–1916)
3. *Hans Eisler* (1898–1962)
4. *Kurt Weill* (1900–1950)
5. *Werner Egk* (1901–1983)
6. *Boris Blacher* (1903–1975)
7. *Gunther Bialas* (1907–   )
8. *Wolfgang Fortner* (1907–1979)
9. *Hugo Distler* (1908–1942)
10. *Bernd Alois Zimmerman* (1918–1970)
11. *Hans Christian Dadelsen* (1948–   )
12. *Detlev Müller-Siemens* (1957–   )
13. *Wolfgan von Schweinitz* (1953–   )
14. *Hans-Jürgen von Bose* (1953–   )

M. Greece
1. *Nikos Skalkottas* (1904–1949)
2. *Yannis Papaioannau* (1910–   )
3. *Dimitris Terzaki* (1930–   )

N. Hungary
1. *Ernst von Dohnanyi* (1877–1961)
2. *Zoltán Kodály* (1882–1967)

O. Italy
1. *Ferruccio Benvenuto Busoni* (1866–1924)
2. *Ottorino Respighi* (1879–1936)
3. *Ildebrando Pizzetti* (1880–1968)
4. *Gian Francesco Malipiero* (1882–1973)
5. *Alfredo Casella* (1883–1947)
6. *Riccardo Zandonai* (1883–1944)
7. *Mario Castelnuovo-Tedesco* (1895–1968)
8. *Goffredo Petrassi* (1904–   )
9. *Mario Peragallo* (1910–   )
10. *Bruno Maderna* (1920–1973)
11. *Luigi Nono* (1924–   )
12. *Sylvano Bussotti* (1931–   )

P. Japan
1. *Yoritsune Matsudaira* (1907–   )
2. *Ysushi Akutagawa* (1925–   )
3. *Toshiro Mayuzumi* (1929–   )
4. *Toru Takemitsu* (1930–   )
5. *Yori-Aki Matsudaira* (1931–   )

Q. Yugoslavia
1. *Milko Keleman* (1924–   )

R. Mexico
1. *Julian Carrillo* (1875–1965)
2. *Carlo Chavez* (1899–1978)
3. *Silvestre Revueltas* (1899–1940)
4. *Blas Galindo* (1910–   )

S. Netherlands
1. *Daniel Ruyneman* (1886–1963)
2. *Willem Pijper* (1894–1947)
3. *Henk Badings* (1907–   )
4. *Hans Henkemans* (1913–   )
5. *Luctor Ponse* (1914–   )
6. *Ton de Leeuw* (1926–   )
7. *Peter Schat* (1935–   )

T. Norway

1. *Fartein Valen* (1887–1952)
2. *Klaus Egge* (1906–1979)
3. *Gunnar Sonstevold* (1912–   )
4. *Finn Mortensen* (1922–   )
5. *Arne Nordheim* (1931–   )

U. Poland

1. *Karol Szymanowski* (1882–1937)
2. *Grazyna Bacewicz* (1913–1969)
3. *Kazimierz Serocki* (1922–   )
4. *Tadeusz Baird* (1928–   )
5. *Boguslaw Schaeffer* (1929–   )
6. *Henryk Gorecki* (1933–   )

V. Russia

1. *Nikolai Miaskovsky* (1881–1950)
2. *Aram Khatchaturian* (1903–1978)
3. *Dmitri Kabelevsky* (1904–   )
4. *Tikhon Khrennikov* (1913–   )
5. *Edison Denisov* (1929–   )
6. *Andrei Volkonsky* (1933–   )
7. *Leonid Grabovsky* (1935–   )
8. *Valentin Silvestrov* (1937–   )

W. Spain

1. *Joaquin Turina* (1882–1949)
2. *Frederico Mompou* (1893–   )
3. *Carlos Surinach* (1915–   )

X. Switzerland

1. *Othmar Schoeck* (1886–1957)
2. *Frank Martin* (1890–1974)
3. *Willy Burkhard* (1900–1955)
4. *Rolf Liebermann* (1910–   )

Y. Sweden

1. *Lars-Erik Larsson* (1908–   )
2. *Karl-Birger Blomdahl* (1916–1968)
3. *Ingvar Lindholm* (1921–   )
4. *Bo Nilsson* (1937–   )
5. *Jan W. Morthenson* (1940–   )
6. *Sven-David Sandstrom* (1942–   )
7. *Michael Edlun* (1950–   )
8. *Ragnar Grippe* (1951–   )

Z. United States of America

1. *Charles Martin Loeffler* (1861–1935)
2. *Carl Ruggles* (1876–1971)
3. *John Powell* (1882–1963)
4. *Charles Tomlinson Griffes* (1884–1920)
5. *Louis Gruenberg* (1884–1964)
6. *Walingford Riegger* (1885–1961)
7. *Marion Bauer* (1887–1955)
8. *Douglas Moore* (1893–1969)
9. *Bernard Rogers* (1893–1968)
10. *Walter Piston* (1894–1976)
11. *Leo Sowerby* (1895–1968)
12. *William Grant Still* (1895–1978)
13. *Bernard Wagenaar* (1894–1971)
14. *Howard Hanson* (1896–1981)
15. *Virgil Thomson* (1896–   )
16. *Henry Cowell* (1897–1965)
17. *Quincy Porter* (1897–1966)
18. *Roy Harris* (1898–1979)
19. *Randall Thompson* (1899–1984)
20. *George Antheil* (1900–1959)
21. *Otto Luening* (1900–   )
22. *Harry Partch* (1901–1974)
23. *Vittorio Giannini* (1903–1966)
24. *Marc Blitzstein* (1905–1964)
25. *Norman Lockwood* (1906–   )
26. *Samuel Barber* (1910–1981)
27. *William Schuman* (1910–   )
28. *Alan Hovhaness* (1911–   )
29. *Gian Carlo Menotti* (1911–   )
30. *Vladimir Ussachevsky* (1911–   )
31. *Ingolf Dahl* (1912–1971)
32. *Hugo Weisgall* (1912–   )
33. *Henry Brant* (1913–   )
34. *Norman Dello Joio* (1913–   )
35. *Irving Fine* (1914–1962)
36. *Roger Goeb* (1914–   )
37. *David Diamond* (1915–   )
38. *Vincent Persichetti* (1915–   )
39. *Milton Babbitt* (1916–   )
40. *Lou Harrison* (1917–   )
41. *Ulysses Kay* (1917–   )
42. *Leonard Bernstein* (1918–   )
43. *William Bergsma* (1921–   )
44. *Andrew Imbrie* (1921–   )
45. *George Walker* (1922–   )

46. *Lukas Foss* (1922–   )
47. *Peter Mennin* (1923–1983)
48. *Mell Powell* (1923–   )
49. *William Kraft* (1923–   )
50. *Gunther Schuller* (1925–   )
51. *Aurelio de la Vega* (1925–   )
52. *Seymour Shifrin* (1926–1979)
53. *Earle Brown* (1926–   )
54. *Barney Childs* (1926–   )
55. *Donald Erb* (1927–   )
56. *Pauline Oliveras* (1932–   )
57. *Morton Subotnik* (1933–   )
58. *Charles Wuorinen* (1938–   )

IX. IMPORTANT WRITERS ON MUSIC

The rise of musicological research in the European and American universities has resulted in the publication of a tremendous volume of books dealing with all phases of music by eminent scholars. Many of these works, however, deal not with the twentieth century but with the historical past. The following list has been limited to those books by twentieth century authors who have contributed to the understanding of the music of this century. Lists of scholarly works dealing with research in the historical past are readily available and the most important of these in the English language have been listed in the Introduction.

1. *Guido Adler* (1855–1941), Austrian musicologist, was the leader in the development of the science of musical research. Among his many publications, his editing of the monumental collection, *Denkmäler der Tonkunst in Oesterreich* (Monuments of Austrian Composition), which comprises eighty-three volumes from its inception in 1894 to its completion in 1938, served as a scientific research model for the many subsequent collections and anthologies of music history.

2. *Heinrich Schenker* (1863–1935) was an Austrian theorist whose system of analysis has been very influential in the theory of composition. While Schenker himself was concerned principally with eighteenth and nineteenth century composition, his disciples such as

Felix Salzer have extended his theories to twentieth century styles. His works, all published in German, cover a period from 1906 to 1935. *Structural Hearing* by Salzer is one of a number of English publications dealing with Schenker's theories.

3. *Ferruccio Benvenuto Busoni* (1866–1924), an Italian composer and piano virtuoso, was a champion of the new music at the turn of the twentieth century. His book, *Entwurf einer neuen Aesthetik der Tonkunst*, Trieste 1907 (*Sketch of a new aesthetic of composition* translated by Dr. Th. Baker, New York, 1911) was a general encouragement for the "modern" composer of that time. Another important work in English translation is *The Essence of Music and Other Papers*, London 1957, translated by Rosamond Ley.

4. *Arnold Schoenberg* (1874–1951) was known as a teacher and theorist as well as a composer. His most important work, *Harmonielehre*, appeared in English as *Theory of Harmony*, (New York 1948). In this work as well as in subsequent English volumes Schoenberg discusses his theory and aesthetics of music. *Style and Idea* (New York 1950) and *Structural Functions of Harmony* (New York 1954) are two volumes among a large number of articles and monographs that Schoenberg published during his long life.

5. *Igor Stavinsky* (1882–1971), while not a teacher nor given to discussions concerning his music, did deliver a series of lectures at Harvard which were subsequently published under the title of *Poetics of Music* (Cambridge 1947). He discusses his own musical aesthetics as well as the musical aesthetics of a number of other composers both past and present. A later series of volumes under the title of *Conversations with Igor Stravinsky* were written in collaboration with Robert Craft and discuss all matter of musical questions particularly those concerning modern music.

6. *Rudolf Reti* (1885–1957) a Serbian by birth, lived most of his life in the United States and wrote several books the most important of which was published after his death, *Tonality-Atonality-Pantonality* (New York 1958).

7. *Ernst Toch* (1887–1964) was a Viennese by birth but lived in the United States since 1935. He was active as a teacher during much of his carrer in Europe and America. A German work, *Melodielehre* (Berlin 1923), is one of the few dealing with this subject. An English book, *The Shaping Forces in Music* (New York 1946) deals with general theory and aesthetics of music both past and present.

8. *Joseph Yasser* (1893–   ) of Polish birth fled Russia in the 1920s and has lived in the United States since that time. His most important work among many others is *A Theory of Evolving Tonality*. In this work he offers an hypothesis not only for the origin of the pentatonic and heptatonic scales but for a future scale which he envisages as being implied in the work of the twelve-tone composers.

9. *Paul Hindemith* (1895–1963) always interested himself in the teaching of music. His compositions in the 1920s which he called *Gebrauchsmusik* or *music for use* were evidence of this interest at an early age. From 1940 to 1949 he held the post of professor of the theory of music at Yale University in the United States. Among a large number of books that he wrote, two stand out as particularly pertinent to twentieth century theory and composition, *The Craft of Musical Composition* (New York revised, 1945) and *A Composer's World: Horizons and Limitations,* (Cambridge 1952) state the individual theory of Hindemith's composing technique as well as his aesthetic concepts concerning music of the twentieth century.

10. *Joseph Schillinger* (1895–1943) was born in Russia and was active in the United States for the last fifteen years of his life. He taught composition according to a rigid system of mathematics. His most important work, *The Schillinger System of Musical Composition,* New York 1946, in two volumes, presents his theories of composition by musical patterns.

11. *Roger Sessions* (1896–   ) has been actively engaged in university teaching for the greater part of his life. His very keen and analytical mind has prompted him to write several books which are the result of his long years of experience as composer and teacher. The *Musical Experience of Composer, Performer, Listener*

(Princeton 1950) and *Reflections on the Music Life in the United States* are two important works dealing with current problems in music.

12. *Howard Hanson* (1896–1981) was a composer, conductor, and teacher. His influence on the musical life of the United States has been very great. He has written a great deal in furtherance of the modern composer. His book *The Harmonic Materials of Modern Music* (New York 1960), gives a mid-century view of the musical theory of the twentieth century.

13. *Ernst Krenek* (1900–   ) has been active as a teacher and writer as well as a composer, and writes of the contemporary scene with a large amount of personal knowledge and involvement in his book *Music Here and Now* (New York 1939).

14. *Aaron Copland* (1900–   ) is known as a writer and teacher as well as a composer. Three books dealing with music in general but of great importance to the understanding of modern music have come from his pen. *What to Listen for in Music* (New York 1939), *Our New Music* (New York 1941), and *Music and Imagination* (Cambridge 1952) constitute a valuable addition to the writings on contemporary music.

15. *Theodor Wiesengrund Adorno* (1903–1969) was a German philosopher, musicologist and composer. Adorno championed the new composers of the twentieth century, particularly those of the Schoenberg school, and wrote profusely concerning the relation of music and society. Among his many works are two books, *Einleitung in der Musiksoziologie*, Frankfurt 1949 and the *Philosophie der Neuen Musik*, Tübingen 1949. The latter, his most important contribution, an excursion into dialectic, shows how the antagonism of the social condition along with the ruling consciousness hinders the greatest composers from finding self-expression in complete works.

16. *Felix Salzer* (1904–   ), an Austrian born musical theorist has been active in America since 1940. His two volume work, *Structural Hearing, Tonal Coherence in Music*, New York 1952 (an unabridged and corrected edition by Dover Publications, New York, appeared in 1962) is based on Heinrich Schenker's conception of tonality and musical coherence.

17. *Leonard B. Meyers* (1918–   ) is an American musicologist and aesthetician. A student of the humanities and musical composition, he has written many articles on aesthetic questions as well as several books. Among the latter are *Emotion and Meaning in Music* (Chicago, 1956) and *Music, the Arts and Ideas* (Chicago, 1967). He also collaborated with Grosvenor Cooper on a volume, *The Rhythmic Structure of Music*, (Chicago, 1960).

Supplementary Readings

Austin	pp.	178–537
Borroff	pp.	567–715
Cannon-Johnson-Waite	pp.	419–454
Crocker	pp.	483–526
Grout	pp.	682–752
Hansen	pp.	3–421
Lang	pp.	990–1030
Machlis	pp.	3–635
Oxford, vol. 10	pp.	1–700
Schirmer	ch.	40
Wold-Cykler	ch.	14

Further References

Cage, John. *Silence.* Middletown, Conn.: Wesleyan University Press, 1961.

Cope, David. *New Directions in Music.* Dubuque: Wm. C. Brown Company Publishers, 1984.

Forte, Allen. *Contemporary Tone Structure.* New York: Columbia University Press, 1955.

Kislan, Richard. *Musical: A look at the American Musical.* Englewood Cliffs: Prentice-Hall, 1980.

Leibowitz, Rene. *Schoenberg and His School.* New York: Philosophical Library, 1949.

Martin, William R. and Drossin, Julius. *Music of the 20th Century.* Englewood Cliffs: Prentice-Hall, 1980.

Meyer, Leonard B. *Music, The Arts and Ideas.* Chicago: University of Chicago Press, 1967.

Modern Music Quarterly (1923–1946). Published by the League of Composers, New York.

Perspectives of New Music (a bi-annual journal). Princeton University Press for the Fromm Music Foundation, 1962.

Pleasants, Henry. *The Agony of Modern Music.* New York: Simon and Schuster, 1955.

Reihe, Die. (An intermittently appearing journal dealing exclusively with serial and electronic music). Bryn Mawr: Presser, 1955.

Salzman, Eric. *Twentieth-Century Music: An Introduction.* Englewood Cliffs: Prentice-Hall, 2nd. ed., 1974.

Schwartz, Elliott and Childs, Barney, eds. *Contemporary Composers on Contemporary Music.* New York: Holt, Rinehart and Winston, 1967.

Strange, Allen. *Electronic Music.* Dubuque: Wm. C. Brown Company Publishers, 1983.

Stuckenschmidt, H. H. *Twentieth Century Music.* Translated by Richard Deveson. New York: McGraw Hill, 1969.

American Dream—Indiana (1961). An example of Pop art, the American Dream is a comment on the dream of getting rich quickly and the passion for entertainment, especially among the youth. Popular music of the 1950s and 60s, such as free jazz and rock, echoed the same desire for exciting entertainment among the young. (Collection, The Museum of Modern Art, New York. Larry Aldrich Foundation Fund)

9

Popular Music of the
Twentieth Century

I. SOCIOCULTURAL INFLUENCES ON POPULAR MUSIC

The first eight chapters of the *Outline History of Music* have dealt with the usual historical account of the development of the art music of the western world. Besides the countless musical examples which constitute the evidence of such a history, there has always been a comparably vast amount of what, for want of a better term, can be called *popular* music. Any attempt to define popular music in a strict sense will fail since the border between popular and art music is often indistinguishable. The term popular will be used in general to denote that music which is "immediate" in its reception and appreciation, while art music demands some degree of intellectual understanding. Obviously popular music can run the gamut from simple, immediate responsive feeling to complex intellectualization, while art music can vary from logical response to highly complex structure, to simple and immediate emotional understanding. Under no circumstance is the difference between art and popular to be construed as equivalent to good or bad. At best popular and art designations are only attempts at describing differences that are commonly felt but elusive to definitive description.

Popular music was almost entirely a non-notated music up to the nineteenth century, its record is very fragmentary, since it depends almost entirely on its inclusion in the art music of recognized composers. Illustrations and accounts of folk song and folk dance give evidence of the existence of popular music from the earliest times, but it was not until the nineteenth century that any real attempt was made to collect and notate such music.

The record of popular music is sparse, indeed, until the end of the nineteenth century, by which time not only popular folk music was being collected and published, but songs and dances were being written and published for the general public. While unnamed composers continued to invent folk music such as the black and white spirituals, as well as early ragtime dances, protection of composers through copyright laws, along with enlarged production of sheet music, began to flood the market with quantities of popular tunes. The twentieth century ushered in the real widespread dissemination of popular music when mass printing was superceded by electronic communication and reproductive media.

The social and political upheavals resulting from World Wars I and II, and the technological developments spread popular culture in all its forms, including music, to all corners of the globe. A tremendous increase in the role of popular music in the post 1950s can be attributed to the following: (1) dissemination of popular music by means of the electronic media, (2) the attractive possibility of business profit generated by the laws of copyright and patent of published music, (3) recorded tapes and records, (4) television, radio and motion picture, (5) the enormous audience supplied by revolting youth with their antagonism toward the music of their elders. All of this has resulted in an outburst of popular music production such as the world has never seen before. This inundation of the airways, and the recording media have had their influence on all phases of musical life.

Without attempting to reconstruct the many details of its development, a short account of the popular music of the twentieth century seems justifiable because of its enormously widespread acceptance and sociological significance, as well as its musical implications. In a sense we are in the midst of a phenomenon which has occurred many times in past history. Unfortunately our historical records of past performances are very scant. It appears that the spread of twentieth century popular music is of a size and speed that has never before been experienced. Today we are able, moreover, to record this phenomenon by means that never before existed. It is as if we were watching and recording by motion picture, television and audio media the eruption of a volcano. Volcanoes have existed in the past, but we have no knowledge of their behavior except through the geological record they have left us. For us today an eruption itelf seems "all important." Actually the geological record that is left behind is of prime importance.

Similarly, the present wave of popular music may seem "all important" to us. We must realize, however, that its very popularity calls for continuous change, and that ultimately interest will be in that which establishes some element of historical and permanent value just as the volcano's value lies in its geological contribution. Nevertheless it is of interest to note *how* such value is created by popular music.

II. FUNCTION OF MUSIC

Many of the functions of popular music are those in which it has served since time immemorial: dance, love, war, entertainment, etc. Some functions, however, are now either greatly intensified or are definitely peculiar to the present day. The first widespread surge of popular music in the twentieth century was that of music for dance. As the waltz and polka craze in the nineteenth century swept all of the western world, so the foxtrot, the samba, the charleston and many others had their period of ascendency in the twentieth century. Now, however, the rage was world wide.

In the post World War II period the interest in popular music turned from its dance function to that of entertainment as a concert experience, and was closely tied to youth's revolt. This was represented in protest songs and ultimately in the emphasis on an escape from reality through both instrumental and vocal performance. These employed such factors as extremely loud dynamics, reliance on lighting effects that tended toward the psychodelic, and dependence on use of drugs both by performers and audience to further the escape.

Worship of performers of popular music became an important element in the success of individual musicians and groups in their wide popularity, in concert, and in recorded activities. Star worship of Frank Sinatra, Elvis Presley, The Beatles, The Grateful Dead, and many others by youth, has rivaled the worship accorded military and political heroes of the past in sheer numbers and universitality. Such adulation has often resulted in a form of mass hysteria.

The use of sound track in motion pictures has provided both art and popular music the possibility of reaching a world wide audience. The universal use of radio, tape, and cassette recordings has made possible the almost constant use of music in all places of work and business. Miniature radio and tape recorders have made music, and especially popular music, a constant accompaniment of life everywhere.

III-IV. CHARACTERISTICS OF STYLE– PRACTICE AND PERFORMANCE

While popular music of the twentieth century is generally associated with the term "jazz", it also encompasses a great variety of "peoples music" from folk, gospel, country western to the various styles of rock music.

It is generally accepted that jazz originated in the late nineteenth and early twentieth century in New Orleans. There was a mixture of African black, together with the French and Spanish influence, stemming from the Creole and French portions of what had been the Louisianna Purchase. All of these people loved their own music and wanted to keep alive the sounds of their origins. This strange amalgamation of cultural differences resulted in an exotic romanticism of popular music from a variety of diverse cultural backgrounds.

A. New Orleans Jazz

Early New Orleans jazz was characterized by a type of free counterpoint played by three instruments, clarinet, trombone and trumpet, with the trumpet as the dominant or "lead" instrument. All of this was supported by a rhythmic section of drums, string bass, and piano or banjo. The music was more or less improvisatory with the trumpet being accompanied by the other instruments in their own variations of the basic melody.

New Orleans jazz combined two basic styles, ragtime and the blues. Ragtime was characterized by a feeling of strong syncopation, making the weak beat strong, or a strong beat weak over a regular rhythmic beat of the percussion. The blues, as it was called, was an outgrowth of the so-called sorrow songs of the blacks.

The blues utlized a regular twelve bar pattern with a free interpolation of both words and music. Performers suggested their own personal woes by the flatting of the interval of the third and seventh.

B. Dixieland

While the early New Orleans jazz was largely the province of the blacks and creoles, white bands came on the scene with what is generally known as Dixieland jazz. It was through this movement that jazz went north to Chicago and New York. This development of Dixieland made its big name about the time of World War I in Chicago. It was here that the first recordings were made of Dixieland jazz. Stimulated by the Dixieland style young white high school and college students developed what was known as the Chicago style of jazz. This was usually called the two-beat jazz with a quick step beat emphasizing the first and third beat.

C. Swing Jazz

Swing jazz came on the scene in the early thirties using a four-beat style with the emphasis on all four beats of a measure. Swing led to the era of the big bands. Benny Goodman, Count Basie and Louis Armstrong were among the most prominent. Included in the big bands were also a number of soloists, Gene Krupa, Fats Waller and others. The orchestra and soloists combined to make an impression of big sounds merged with a lighter texture of solo against an orchestral background in much the same manner as the concerto grosso of the seventeenth century.

D. Bebop

By the end of the thirties swing had become a big business in popular music. As so often happens, there was a revolution which turned away from the established style. This new style called "bebop" emerged from Kansas City and then on to New York. Its distinguishing musical characteristics was the use of the flatted fifth. This interval prevailed not only in the harmonic structure, but also in the melodic line. This was also known as the "blue-note" which had appeared much earlier in the sorrow songs of the blacks. The general concept of the music of bebop was that of a nervous, racing style with melodic fragments—not a sustained melodic line. It has been described as a musical short-hand with everything that is logical and obvious excluded.

E. Cool Jazz

During the fifties jazz entered a period of calm and melodiousness, sometimes referred to as "cool jazz". While there was still a good deal of improvisation, it emphasized long linear melodies. It was a relaxed and dreamy kind of jazz with a certain amount of advanced harmony and rhythmic writing. The rich full tones of the big band era gave way to the lighter subdued sounds. Dotted eighths and sixteenth note passages were replaced by legato ones with an evenness of eighth notes. The rhythm lagged behind the beat rather than pushing ahead as in the bebop styles.

F. Free Jazz

In the sixties there came what was called "free jazz". One of the innovations was that of atonality, a characteristic which emerged in concert music at least fifty years previous. There was also a kind of disintegration of rhythm in beat, meter and symmetry. Free jazz also incorporated non-Western music, that is music from other cultures such as India, Africa and the Far East. There was also an intensity of sound that bordered on ecstatic, frenetical and even religious orgies. At times free jazz almost approached the realm of noise, with trumpets sounding like steel drums, pianos like crackling wire and trombones like the sliding sounds of conveyer belts.

G. Rock

Rock can be characterized as having an amplified hard beat. There are massive amounts of sound brought to a very high level of decibels. Electric guitars, electric pianos and the synthesizer helped to establish "hard rock" as a kind of musical hysteria during the sixties.

A part of the rock hysteria included physical gyration of the performers.

H. Country and Western

Country and western music became very popular from the fifties on. It consisted of an unsophisticated vocal style of ballads and folk songs which were usually narrations about life, love and sorrow. It is simple with no musical innovations. Country and western supported the vocal line with violin, string bass and guitar. Nashville, Tennessee became the mecca of the country western style of folk music.

I. Blue Grass

This is a type of country western music that springs from the rural areas of the south, especially Kentucky. Blue grass depends on the banjo, guitar and the violin, played in the old-time fiddler fashion. Melodies are derived from Kentucky, Carolinas, etc., with influences of the folk music of the British Isles.

The jazz styles of the seventies seem to be softened rock sounds of the sixties. There seems to be a fusion of rock sound, folk, soul, country western and early jazz. It appears that the popular music of the seventies reflects the diverse tastes of a wide listening audience. In reality there does not seem to be a distinctive style that is exclusively the product, or trade mark, of jazz in the seventies.

V-VI. VOCAL-INSTRUMENTAL COMPOSITIONS

Popular music shows no real division between vocal and instrumental compositions. In general, instrumental performances of popular music are adaptations of vocal works. In many instances vocal performance is combined with instrumental rendition. Any vocal song or tune may become an instrumental work and might also be performed in any dance or purely instrumental style.

Popular music by its very nature is not given to large forms. Its basic form is the three part song form with varied presentations. With some few exceptions such as the longer compositions of Stan Kenton, Duke Ellington, and Dave Brubeck as

Drowning Girl—Lichtenstein (1963). In an era when comics were an integral part of our culture for people of all ages, Lichtenstein exalted such heroes as Steve Canyon and others in this form of Pop art. The same kind of adulation came to such popular singers as Elvis Presley and the Beatles. (Collection, The Museum of Modern Art, New York. Philip Johnson Fund and gift of Mr. and Mrs. Bagley Wright)

well as the theatrical rock musicals such as *Hair* and *Jesus Christ Super Star*, which verge on the desire to present popular music in the formal aspect of art music, there are no extended forms of composition. The song is the basic single movement form and the composite form is really nothing more than either a series of varied presentations of the single basic unit or a mingling of two or more different units.

VII-VIII. IMPORTANT COMPOSERS, ARRANGERS, AND PERFORMERS

Because the majority of those included in popular music were composers, arrangers, and performers, it seems practical to list them in terms of the styles of popular music with which they were involved. Because of the large number of composers, arrangers, and performers in each of the following styles of "peoples music" the authors make no attempt to include them all. Only those who seem to be most influential in their own idiom have been listed. A number of these spanned a wide variety of styles and will be mentioned under each.

New Orleans Jazz:

> W. C. Handy, Jelly Roll Morton, Sidney Bechet, Scott Joplin

Dixieland:

> Papa Laine, Louis Armstrong, Bix Beiderbecke, Fletcher Henderson, Duke Ellington, "Fatha" Hines.

Swing:

> Duke Ellington, Wayne King, Guy Lombardo, Woody Herman, Harry James, Tommy Dorsey, Benny Goodman, Gene Krupa, Charlie Barnet, Count Basie, Artie Shaw, Glenn Miller, Cole Porter, George Gershwin.

Bebop:

> Dizzy Gillespie, Thelonious Monk, Lennie Tristano, Charlie Parker, Billy Eckstein, Art Tatum, Errol Garner.

Cool Jazz:

> Woody Herman, Lennie Tristano, Miles Davis, Dave Brubeck.

Free Jazz:

> John Coltrane, Ornette Coleman, Gunther Schuller, Dave Brubeck, Yusek Kateef, Stan Kenton.

Rock:

> Beatles, Jefferson-Airplane, Rolling-Stones, Blood- Sweat and Tears, Grateful-Dead, Stevie Wonder, Elvis Presley, Bill Haley, Little Richard, Elton John, Michael Jackson.

Country and Western:

> Glenn Campbell, Johnny Cash, Charley Pride, Loretta Lynn, Roger Miller, Bobbie Gentry.

Bluegrass:

Earl Scrugges, Lester Flatt, William "Bill" Monroe, Osborne Brothers, Olivia Newton-John.

Further References

Berendt, Joachim. *The Jazz Book*. Westport, Ct.: Lawrence Hill, Rev. ed., 1975.

Byrnside, Ronald. *Sound and Sense*. Dubuque: Wm. C. Brown Company Publishers, 1984.

Ewen, David. *All the Years of American Popular Music*. Englewood Cliffs: Prentice-Hall, Inc., 1977.

Feather, Leonard. *The Encyclopedia of Jazz in the 60's*. New York: Horizons, 1967.

Feather, Leonard and Gitler, Ira. *The Encyclopedia of Jazz in the 70's*. New York: Horizon, 1976.

Hodier, Andre. *Jazz: Its Evolution and Essence*. New York: Grove Press, 1956.

Roxon, Lillian. *Rock Encyclopedia*. New York: Grosset and Dunlap, 1971.

Schuller, Gunther. *Early Jazz: Its Roots and Musical Development*. New York: Oxford University Press, 1968.

Smithsonian Collection of Jazz, Smithsonian Institute, Washington, D.C.

Tanner and Gerow. *A Study of Jazz*. Dubuque: Wm. C. Brown Company Publishers, 1984.

Appendix
Instruments

I. STRINGS

A. Bowed Strings

1. *Rebec:* a one-stringed instrument was introduced into Europe from Arabia in the eighth or ninth centuries. It has a rather long neck with a small round or pear-shaped body and played with a loosely haired bow. It has a very nasal tone quality. The rebec was the ancestor of the bowed string instruments.

2. *Viols:* a large group of bowed string instruments was in use from the Gothic through the Renaissance and Baroque periods. The viols differ from the violin family in that (a) they had deeper ribs, (b) the shoulders sloped from the neck, (c) the number of strings was generally six but might be more or less, (d) frets were placed on the fingerboard, (e) the bridge was quite flat enabling the playing of chords, (f) the viol bow stick was convex and held palm up, (g) the instruments were held on or between the legs of the performer. The viol tone quality was somewhat nasal. Viols were made in various sizes: bass, tenor, alto and discant (soprano). The revival of viol playing in the twentieth century has been generally concerned with the tenor instrument which was the model used for solo performance in the works of Baroque composers.

3. *Violins:* the modern bowed string instruments date from the early Baroque. The most important members of the family are the violin (soprano), the viola (alto), the violoncello (tenor) and the contrabass or bass viol. The latter taken over from the viol family and often built in that form. The most famous makers were Italians, dating from the seventeenth and eighteenth centuries. Among them were Gaspar da Salo, Amati, Stradivari and Guarneri who made Cremona famous as the center for violin construction.

The violin, viola and cello are all four-stringed instruments tuned in fifths. The bass viol retains the tuning in fourths of the viol family. The bow used in playing the violin family instruments differs from the earlier bow in being convex and held with the palm down except for the bass viol where both the violin and viol style bows are still used. The violin and viola are held on the shoulder, the cello and string bass in a vertical position resting on the floor. The tone of the violin family is of a rich sweet quality rivaling that of the human voice.

B. **Plucked String Instruments**

1. *Harp:* one of the oldest known instruments was used among the early civilizations at least 3000 years B.C. It appears in various forms among all folk people. The modern instrument (double harp) was invented by Erard in 1810 and is capable, by use of pedals, of a complete chromatic scale of six octaves. While already called for by composers of the 16th century, the harp as a solo and orchestral instrument makes its real appearance in the 19th century.

2. *Psaltery:* a very ancient instrument was worldwide in one form or another. It has a flat soundboard over which a number of strings are stretched. The strings are plucked by both hands of the performer.

3. *Lute and Guitar:* plucked string instruments are held in the lap. They have fretted fingerboards of varying lengths and a various number of strings. Strings are fingered with the left hand and plucked by the right. The lute family is characterized by a pear-shaped body with both short and long fingerboards. The guitar is a flat instrument, the body of which is somewhat in the shape of the violin.

The lute was the most important instrument of the Renaissance period. Players of virtuoso capacity encouraged a large literature to be written. The introduction of keyboard instruments resulted in the decline and eventual disappearance of the lute. The guitar because of easier performance became very popular in the seventeenth century and has remained so to the present day. The lute has been revived in the twentieth century due to the interest in Renaissance and Baroque music.

4. *Harpsichord:* a large variety of instruments in which the strings are plucked by a set of plectrums attached to key levers. The key levers are arranged like the keys of the modern piano and when depressed the plectrums pluck the strings resulting in a sound very much like that of the lute or harp. Harpsichords were built in various shapes and sizes and given various names such as clavicembalo, cembalo, clavecin, virginal and spinet. It is well to remember that the harpsichord mechanism was *not* the forerunner of the piano action. It could be regarded more reasonably as a mechanized lute or harp.

C. **Struck Strings**

1. *Dulcimer:* this is variety of psaltery whose strings are struck by small hammers held in the hand rather than plucked. In this manner it becomes the forerunner of the piano.

2. *Clavichord:* a small keyboard string instrument is usually in the form of a rectangular box in which

metal wedges attached to keys strike the individual strings. The placement of the wedges determine the length of the vibrating strings and, therefore, their individual pitches. The tone is very soft and the instrument was often used in the household for teaching and practice purposes. The clavichord might be thought of as a mechanized dulcimer.

3. *Pianoforte:* this popular instrument, invented by Cristofori in 1709, is a string instrument in which the strings are sounded by the striking of a set of felted hammers attached to keys. Improvements in the mechanical construction of the piano have been concerned with the various intricacies of the key and hammer action, the construction of the sounding board and the frame of the instrument upon which the strings are stretched. The full name of the pianoforte was an indication that this instrument could play both loud and soft, and indeed could sustain a tone without having to keep the keys depressed. Unlike earlier keyboard instruments, this could be accomplished because of its action and the use of sostenuto and damper pedals.

II. WIND INSTRUMENTS

A. Wood Winds

1. *Flute:* one of the oldest and most wide spread of all instruments is the flute in all variety of shapes and sizes. Both the whistle or recorder type as well as the transverse type were known in earliest times and used simultaneously throughout music history. The transverse type consists of a tube of wood or metal closed at one end and with a side hole across which the player blows. A number of finger holes enable the performer to play the entire chromatic scale. Modern flutes are made of metal and are fitted with a refined mechanism that enables rapid technical performance and accuracy of pitch. Besides the more common

soprano flute there is the very high pitched piccolo, the alto and bass flutes.

The recorder type flute is fitted with a mouthpiece into which the performer blows. It is made of wood and was preferably used until about 1750 when the transverse flute displaced it. In the twentieth century the recorder was revived with great enthusiasm by the interest in Baroque and earlier music. Because of limited range, recorders are made in various sizes to cover the vocal range of soprano, alto, tenor and bass.

2. *Obsolete and folk flutes:* the Occarina is a globular flute usually made of clay with an embouchere hole and finger holes. The syrinx or pan pipes is a set of individual closed pipes, bound together, which can be sounded by blowing over the open ends.

B. **Organ**

Wind instrument consisting of many individual pipes which are activated by wind from a wind chamber. By the use of keys connected to the wind chest the performer can select the various pitched pipes. Through the various shapes, the addition of a metal reed, and the combination of pipes, tone qualities characteristic of the organ itself and of various orchestral instruments are available. Organs vary in size from the small portative (movable) organ of the Renaissance, consisting of a single set of pipes, to the large 19th century instruments with several thousands pipes and several keyboards. Other instruments using the principle of the wind organ are the regal, bagpipe, accordion and harmonium.

C. **Reeds**

1. *Single Reeds*

   a) *Clarinet:* a cylindrical pipe of wood has a bell-shaped opening at the lower end and a beak-like mouthpiece at the upper end, to which is attached a single reed of cane. The breath of the player activates this reed and, with the aid of holes and keys, can play a wide range of pitches as well as distinctly varied tone colors in the several registers of the instrument. The modern clarinet dates from the early eighteenth century. The fingering mechanism was greatly improved in the nineteenth century. The clarinet is found in several sizes: E flat (very high), B flat (most common) and A are soprano instruments, E flat alto, B flat bass and B flat contrabass.

b) *Saxophone:* a family of single reed instruments consists of a conical metal pipe. Soprano (B flat), Alto (E flat), Tenor (B flat), Baritone (E flat) and Bass (B flat) constitute the usual members of the family. They were invented by Adolphe Sax in the middle of the nineteenth century. The alto and tenor saxophones are especially used in jazz and symphonic bands. A wide variety of tonal qualities is possible with all types of saxophones.

2. *Double Reeds*

a) *Oboe:* a conical pipe made of wood and fitted with a double reed at the upper end. The tone quality is reedy and nasal. The modern instrument, which made its appearance in the middle of the seventeenth century, is highly mechanized. The reed is held directly by the lips of the performer who, thereby, has considerable control over the tone quality.

b) *English Horn:* an alto oboe, longer than the oboe, is fitted with a pear-shaped bell at its lower end, and the reed is attached to a bent tube. The bell accounts for a rather muffled, soft tone quality.

c) *Oboe da caccia and oboe d'amore:* alto oboes whose place has been taken by the English horn, occasionally is used in the performance of Baroque music.

d) *Heckelphone:* a baritone oboe invented by Heckel in 1904. Like the English horn, it has a pear-shaped bell and is much larger than the oboe. It has been used very little.

e) *Sarusophone:* in this family of double reed brass instruments only the larger ones are infrequently used. The contrabass saruso-phone is used by a number of French com-posers in preference to the contrabassoon.

f) *Shawm:* a family of double reed instruments, forerunners of the oboe, were in use up to the seventeenth century. The tone was very strident and the instruments were particu-larly used for outdoor music. Its mechani-zation was minimal.

g) *Bassoon:* the bass instrument of the modern double reeds has not changed materially from its earlier predecessors in shape or fin-gering. Its long wooden pipe is doubled upon itself enabling the player to finger the instrument with comparative ease despite its great length. It has a large range of tones and serves as a very agile bass instrument. The contrabassoon can reach the lowest pitched notes of the orchestral pallet.

h) *Dulzian:* the forerunner of the bassoon came in a number of sizes. Its main difference from the bassoon was the fact that it was made of a single block of wood.

i) *Encapsuled double reeds:* double reed instru-ments are of various sizes and shapes in which the double reed was covered by a wooden cap into which the performer blew. The resulting wind pressure activated the reed. The range of these instruments was very limited, since they could not be over-blown. The crumhorn, rauschpfeif and kor-tholz were different shapes of this type of instrument.

D. **Wind Instruments with Cupped and Funnel-Shaped Mouthpieces.** (Brass Instruments)

These instruments, originally made of wood or animal horns, were later made of various metals. Fitted with a cupped mouthpiece, the performer set the column of air into vibration with his lips stretched over the mouthpiece. The single column of air could only sound the natural overtones of the basic pitch of the pipe. Early instruments solved this problem in two ways. One was by boring holes in the pipe which could be covered or opened as in a flute, and the other was by the use of a slide mechanism in the metal trumpets and trombones. The introduction of valves in the nineteenth century enabled all the brass instruments to play the entire chromatic scale.

1. *Trumpet:* a high pitched metal tube with cupped mouthpiece comes in various pitches: B flat, A, E flat and C. By the addition of three valves, either piston or rotary, the modern trumpet with its brilliant tone has become a very versatile instrument. The cornet is a variant of the trumpet. Its shorter length and longer concial section give it a less brilliant tone than that of the trumpet.

2. *Trombone:* a lower pitched brass instrument most generally fitted with a slide mechanism, which enables the performer to shorten or lengthen the tubing and thereby play the entire chromatic scale, has maintained its basic present form since the fifteenth century. The early trombones were known as sackbuts and had a smaller and less brassy tone quality due to the smaller bore of the tube and mouthpiece. Two sizes of modern trombones are usually in use today, the tenor and bass. Some use is also made of a valve trombone in the brass bands.

3. *Tuba:* the largest and deepest sounding of the brass family. Conically bored it is played with a cup-shaped mouthpiece. Tubas are made in many pitches. The most common of them are the tenor tubas (barytons), bass and double bass.

4. *Zink or Cornetto:* wooden tube has a cup-shaped mouthpiece and fitted with finger holes. These Renaissance and Baroque instruments were made in various sizes: soprano, alto, tenor and bass. The latter was shaped like a letter "S" and called a serpent. The serpent maintained itself into the nineteenth century until displaced by the modern valved tuba.

5. *Horn* (French Horn): a conical metal tube wound into a spiral is played with a funnel-shaped mouth-piece. Because of its narrow bore, its playable natural tones enabled it to be one of the most versatile brass instruments even before the invention of valves. Its tone is rich and suited to solo work. It blends with other brasses and with the wood winds.

III. PERCUSSION

A. **Indefinite Pitch**

1. *Drums, tabor, and tambourin:* these instruments are to be found among all peoples in all shapes, sizes and in all periods of history. Those of indefinite pitch vary from very high (snare drum) to very low (bass drum). All consist of a wooden or metal frame over which a membrane is stretched and are played by striking with wooden or metal sticks or by the hand of the player.

2. *Cymbals, Gong, Castanets, Triangle, Tam tam, etc:* along with numerous other sound generators these are all instruments of a single fixed pitch or sound quality made of metal or wood. Some are struck with hammers or rods as in the case of the Gong and Triangle. Others are self sounding like the castanets or cymbals.

B. Definite Pitch

1. *Timpani.* (Kettledrums): the name given to the drum whose head is stretched over a large metal kettle-like form and can be tuned to a limited range. They are the most important orchestral percussion instruments.

2. *Glockenspiel, Bells, Xylophone, Marimba, Celeste, etc:* tuned bars of metal or wood forming several chromatic octaves are played with various types of hammers: wood, metal or rubber. The celeste is played by means of a keyboard.

Glossary

A Cappella—A term used to designate choral music without accompaniment.

Aleatoric Music—A type of composition based on the element of chance in both the selection of sounds and their performance.

Ballet de Cour (Ballet of the Court)—A dramatic presentation in dance at the seventeenth French Royal Court.

Basso Continuo—The bass part in music of the Baroque period performed by the harpsichord or organ together with a viol, bassoon, or cello.

Binary Form—A form consisting of two sections: A-B.

Cadence—A melodic or harmonic ending of a phrase or movement. Authentic, plagal and deceptive are terms used to describe the degree of repose.

Chord—A combination usually of three or more tones sounded simultaneously.

Chromatic Alteration—Altering a tone of the diatonic scale by means of accidentals.

Clavecin—The French term for harpsichord.

Coloratura—Virtuoso type ornamentation and embellishment on a melodic line.

Consonance—In traditional harmony an interval or chord which produces an effect of repose or agreeableness.

Contrary Motion—The movement of two voices in opposite directions.

Contratenor—The third voice in addition to the tenor and discant in fourteenth and fifteenth century vocal compositions. It is sometimes called the male alto voice.

Counterpoint—The combination of two or more distinctive melodic lines into a single musical fabric. It is often used synonomously with polyphony.

DIATONIC—The natural scale made up of five whole tones and two semi-tones. The term is also used to describe melodic motion in the natural scale without alterations.

DISSONANCE—In traditional harmony, an interval or chord which produces an effect of harmonic tension.

DOMINANT—The fifth degree of the diatonic scale or, in harmonic practice, a chord built upon the fifth degree.

DOUBLE-STOP—The simultaneous playing on two strings of a bowed instrument.

DRONE BASS—A sustained bass note that is retained throughout a section or a whole piece. The note is usually the tonic, but it sometimes alternates between the tonic and dominant.

DYNAMICS—Signs, abbreviations and words used to indicate degrees of loudness and volume of sound.

EPISODE—A secondary passage or section which digresses from the main theme. Episodic form is sometimes referred to as a Rondo form.

EQUAL TEMPERAMENT—A system of tuning in which the octave is divided into twelve equal semitones (see Apel's *Dictionary of Music*).

FALSETTO—A style of singing by the male voice in which a very high head tone is produced.

FIGURATION—Stereotyped chordal patterns used in the realization of a figured bass.

HARMONY—A simultaneous sounding of two or more tones; the theory and practice of chord construction and progressions.

HOMOPHONY—Music in which one melodic voice is supported by a chordal accompaniment.

INTERVAL—The difference and distance in pitch between two tones played either successively or simultaneously. Measurement is made by counting the steps of the diatonic scale upwards from the lowest to the highest note (see Apel's *Dictionary of Music*).

INTONATION—The degree of accuracy of pitch.

INVERSION—(1) An interval is inverted by transferring its lowest tone to the octave above, or by transferring its highest tone to the octave below. (2) A chord is inverted by placing any other than its root or fundamental tone in the bass. (3) A melody is inverted by changing each descending interval to the same ascending interval.

LIED—The German term for *Art Song*.

LITURGY—The official order of service in the Roman Catholic church. The word also applied to authorized services in most Christian churches.

MELISMA—A flowing, ornamented melody sung on one syllable.

METER—The measurement of time in music by means of accented and unaccented beats.

MODULATION—The process of moving from one tonal center to another in the course of a single composition.

MONOCHORD—An instrument consisting of a single string stretched over a resonating body.

MONOPHONY—A single melodic line without accompaniment.

MONO-THEMATIC—A composition based on only one melody or theme.

MOTIVE—A short melodic or rhythmic figure that is repeated to give design to a melodic or rhythmic phrase.

MUTATION—The transition used by a voice in moving from one hexachord to another in medieval music.

ORNAMENTATION—Added notes to a melody such as trills, turns.

OSTINATO—A short melodic figure that is repeated in one voice, usually the bass, throughout a section, movement, or composition. This is also known as ground bass.

PARALLEL MOTION—Two or more voices moving in the same direction at the same interval.

PERIOD—A group of measures that makes a natural division of the melody, usually two phrases, analogous to a sentence in speech or writing.

PHRASE—A segment of melody that has a natural pause or ending. It is analogous to a phrase in speech or writing.

PITCH—The quality of a tone determined by the number of vibrations per second.

PIZZICATO—To pluck the string of a bowed instrument.

POLYPHONY—A musical texture made of two or more simultaneous melodies sounded by independent voices or instruments.

POLYRHYTHMS (cross rhythms)—The use of different rhythmic patterns simultaneously.

POLYTHEMATIC—A composition based on more than one melody or theme of equal importance.

RANGE—The distance between the highest and lowest pitch of a melody, voice or instrument.

REFRAIN—One or two melodic phrases repeated at the end of each stanza.

RITORNELLO—(1) An instrumental interlude before or after an aria or scene; (2) the tutti section of a concerto grosso; (3) the last two lines of the stanza in the fourteenth century madrigal.

SCALE—A series of adjacent tones arranged according to whole and half tones, or any other regular increment of pitch.

SEQUENCE—The repetition of melodic motive in the same part above or below the original.

SONG CYCLE—A series of art songs connected by a central poetic idea.

STROPHIC—A song of which all stanzas are sung to the same music.

SYNCOPATION—A rhythmic device that displaces the accent from a strong beat to a weak beat or a weak portion of the beat.

TABLATURE—Name for the various early system of notation in which symbols, letters, or figures were used instead of notes on the staff.

TEMPO—The rate of speed by which the music moves. Tempo marks are words and abbreviations used to indicate various degrees of speed; for example, *rubato* indicates a flexible tempo.

TERNARY FORM—A form consisting of three sections: A-B-A.

TETRACHORD—A scale-series of four tones, the highest and lowest of which form the interval of a perfect fourth.

TEXTURE—The density of melodic and harmonic elements designated by such terms as homophonic, polyphonic, chordal (see Apel's *Dictionary of Music*).

THEME—A distinctive melody, or musical idea, that serves as a basis for musical composition.

THROUGH-COMPOSED—The opposite of strophic; a song that has different music for each stanza.

TIMBRE—Quality (color) of a tone as produced on a specific instrument or voice; also referred to as *tone-color.*

TONALITY—The result of harmonic organization around a central tone, called the tonic or keynote.

TONIC—The first note of the scale, also called the keynote.

TRANSCRIPTION—A composition originally written for one media that has been arranged for another voice, instrument, or combination of voices or instruments.

TREMOLO—(1) The rapid repetition of a single note a number of times; (2) the rapid alternation between two different notes.

TRIAD—A chord consisting of three tones.

TRI-TONE—The interval made up of three whole tones, also called the augmented fourth.

TUNING (temperament)—A system of determining the intervals of the octave. Various methods are known as: Pythagorean, Just intonation, Mean-tone, Equal tempered.

TUTTI—Marking in a score that indicates entrance of all instruments or voices after a solo passage.

VIBRATO—A minute fluctuation of pitch both below and above the tone for the purpose of tonal coloring.

VIRTUOSO—A performer with a superior technical facility.

For more complete information on musical terminology the student is urged to consult Apel's *Harvard Dictionary of Music.*

Index